MW00368204

TERROR AND CIVILIZATION

TERROR AND CIVILIZATION

CHRISTIANITY, POLITICS, AND THE WESTERN PSYCHE

BY
SHADIA B. DRURY

TERROR AND CIVILIZATION
© Shadia B. Drury, 2004

All rights reserved. No part of this book may be used or reproduced
in any manner whatsoever without written permission except in
the case of brief quotations embodied in critical articles or reviews.

First published 2004 by
PALGRAVE MACMILLAN™
175 Fifth Avenue, New York, N.Y. 10010 and
Houndmills, Basingstoke, Hampshire, England RG21 6XS
Companies and representatives throughout the world

PALGRAVE MACMILLAN is the global academic imprint of the
Palgrave Macmillan division of St. Martin's Press, LLC and of Palgrave
Macmillan Ltd. Macmillan® is a registered trademark in the United
States, United Kingdom and other countries. Palgrave is a registered
trademark in the European Union and other countries.

ISBN 1–4039–6404–1 hardback

Library of Congress Cataloging-in-Publication Data
Drury, Shadia B., 1950–
    Terror and civilization: Christianity, politics, and the Western
psyche/by Shadia B. Drury.
        p. cm.
    Includes bibliographical references and index.
    ISBN 1–4039–6404–1
        1. Political violence—Religious aspects—Christianity—History.
2. Terror—Religious aspects—Christianity—History. I. Title.

BT736.15.D78 2004
261.7—dc21   2003050572

A catalogue record for this book is available from the British Library.

Design by Newgen Imaging Systems (P) Ltd., Chennai, India.

First edition: January, 2004
10 9 8 7 6 5 4 3 2 1

Printed in the United States of America.

Transferred to Digital Printing 2005

For My Sister
Wafaa

Contents

ACKNOWLEDGMENTS

First and foremost, I am indebted to other critics of Christianity—especially Edward Westermarck, Walter Kaufmann, Bertrand Russell, William Empson, and Richard Robinson. I do not always share the views of these critics (my disagreements with them are outlined in the notes and bibliography), but their forthrightness and their courage has been an inspiration to me. Earlier versions of "Treachery with a Clear Conscience" and "Augustinian Chic" in Part II, were published in *Humanitas*, Vol. XII, No. 2 (1999), pp. 27–45, under the title "Augustinian Radical Transcendence: Source of Political Excess." They were originally presented at the Annual Voegelin Society Meetings of 1994 in New York City. I would like to thank Professor Ellis Sandoz for inviting me to the Voegelin Society on various occasions. Most of all, I would like to thank Professor Ken Reshaur of the University of Manitoba for his advice on the chapter on Voegelin, as well as his encouragement and support over many years. Parts of the chapter on Freud were presented at the Canadian Political Science Association in Toronto, June 2002. "Terrorism: From Samson to Atta," in Part V, is forthcoming in *Arab Studies Quarterly*.

I am grateful to Arthur Wolf for introducing me to the work of Edward Westermarck, and for the conversation we had about Freud when he visited the anthropology Department in Calgary. He made me feel that I was not alone in an intellectual wilderness. I would like to give special thanks to my colleagues, Carol Prager, Jack MacIntosh, and Terence Penelhum for reading the manuscript and making many helpful suggestions and comments.

I am indebted to the intellectual atmosphere in Calgary. I was fortunate to have been a member of the ethics group at the University of Calgary, where debate and disagreement are combined with mutual respect—Mark Magotti, Brenda Baker, John Baker, Elizabeth Brake, Trudy Govier, Noa Latham, Dennis McKerlie, Rob Epperson, and Bob Ware are models of scholarly excellence and integrity. I have learned a lot from them. I have also enjoyed my participation in the Apeiron

Society for the Practice of Philosophy, which gave me the opportunity to present early drafts of my work for discussion. Petra von Morstein (president of the society) and Peter Fitzgerald Moore (secretary of the society) have been very successful in creating an atmosphere of open discussion even about the most sensitive topics. I am particularly indebted to Janet Sisson, a philosopher and an active participant in the Apeiron Society, for her encouragement and moral support. I also owe a debt to Roman Struc whose literary insights never fail to remind me that feeling is the thing, and that reason has serious limitations. I would also like to thank historian Marty Staum for his friendship and for giving me the best references. I am also thankful to my colleagues in Political Science for their interest in my work and their many conversations— especially Katrin Froese, Len Wilson, Ron Keith, and Allison Dube. I was fortunate to have Dave McFaul as a research assistant—he was definitely the most informed assistant I ever had. I was touched by his devotion to the tradition of Social Gospel. I am indebted to the University of Calgary's Killam Resident Fellowship Award for the release time to complete this book.

Outside Calgary, the continued support of John Yolton, Jack Gunnell, Gordon Schochet, and Morton Schoolman have meant a great deal to me. The friendship and support of Margaret Ogrodnick and Ken Reshaur has made my retreat in Manitoba a most enjoyable one. Last but not least, the support of my family has been invaluable. I am delighted with the recent interest that my sister Wafaa has taken in my work. Her help with the chapter on terrorism made it so much fun to write. I also owe a great deal to my mother, who has kept an open mind throughout our many discussions of the Bible. She is proof that faith in Christ's love and salvation is compatible with tolerance and open-mindedness. My greatest debt is to Dennis Drury, without whose love and support my life would lack all luster.

PREFACE

The relation between terror and civilization has been seriously misconstrued in the history of the West. Two contradictory theories have flourished side by side—the naïve and the cynical. Interestingly, both have their roots in biblical religion. The naïve view is simple-minded. It assumes that terror and civilization are deadly enemies that stand in stark opposition to one another. This view is profoundly dualistic. It divides the world into good and evil, God and Satan, the defenders of civilization, and the enemies of civilization.

Side by side with this naïve and dualistic view is a deeply cynical, but more sophisticated view, which has also informed the Western understanding of the relation between terror and civilization. The Christian assumption that human nature has been profoundly corrupted by the mythical Fall has led to the view that repression, terror, and tyranny are necessary to civilize a fallen and thoroughly wicked humanity. Far from being opposites, terror and civilization are intimately linked. The assumption is that terror—spiritual, political, and psychological—is the secret of the success of civilization. Supposedly, fear of violence and death—fear of the executioner, the pedagogue, and the strap—keeps violence in check. In other words, civilization succeeds because it fights brutality with even greater brutality. But, as society becomes stronger, it manages to turn man's savage instincts inward against the self. In this way, its grip on the instincts becomes more complete. As a result, it is able to relax and dispense with its more gruesome punishments—drawing and quartering, boiling in oil, and the like. Power seems to be less terrible. But one should not be fooled by appearances. Terror has not disappeared; it has merely been internalized and transfigured into a spiritual and psychological terror. The result is the creation of an inner state of siege—a garrison in a conquered city. This is the more sophisticated view.

In this book, I will challenge both the naïve and the sophisticated view of the relation between terror and civilization. But in doing so, I will not deny that terror and civilization are intimately linked.

My claim is that the connection between terror and civilization has been seriously misconstrued. It is not for love of evil or love of self that human beings commit murder and mayhem. The worst atrocities have their source in the zealous pursuit of a sublime ideal that is believed to be so majestic, so magnificent, and so grand, that it is worthy of every sacrifice, every hardship, and every abomination. Christianity and Islam are examples of these exalted ideals. Only a grand ideal can combine treachery with a clear conscience. In other words, what is intended to civilize us can also make us monstrous.

Defenders of Christianity (and of Islam) believe that the evils done in the name of these religions are the work of opportunists, rogues, and scoundrels using religion to conceal their iniquity. These apologetic arguments have been used to excuse the Crusades, the persecution of heretics, the burning of witches, the killing of gynecologists, the persecution of homosexuals, the attack on the World Trade Center, and compulsory celibacy. Supposedly, neither Christianity nor Islam is to blame. But it is time to reconsider this view. It is time to critically examine the assumptions of these Biblical religions and their sacred texts. It is time to ask if these sacred texts do not lend themselves to the political extremism, violence, and intolerance perpetrated in their name.

I am not denying that Christianity and Islam have inspired people to do good work in private and public life. It seems to me that these religions have also inspired people to behave in ways that are more cruel and immoderate than they would have otherwise. It is not simply the case that wickedness hides behind the goodness of religion. Some of the evil deeds that are committed cannot be made sense of in the absence of religious beliefs and assumptions. In contrast to the cynicism about human nature that is characteristic of Christianity, I believe that people genuinely seek the good. But religious beliefs and superstitions often cloud and distort the already difficult search for the good and the right.

In examining how religious beliefs inspire pernicious and malevolent conduct we should begin with Christianity because it is our own, and because the Republicans who are in power in the United States are eager to re-empower the Churches. After 300 years of secular liberal revolutions in the West, re-empowering the Churches would be a serious mistake. The reason is not just that there are bad people running the Churches; the reason for resisting efforts to re-empower the Churches is that people who believe much of what Jesus believed are not likely to behave well in positions of power—unless they are willing to keep their religion out of politics as Jesus did. Any suggestion that the Churches should be re-endowed with political power has its source in historical amnesia. In my view, the political crimes committed in the name of Christianity were not historically contingent accidents; they were a logical consequence of Christian beliefs.

The resurgence of militant Islam has led some Christians to imagine that Christianity is a civilized religion of love and peace in comparison to the violent barbarism of Islam. It is time for the West to stop fooling itself into thinking that Christianity is superior to Islam. It is neither more moderate nor less zealous. My aim is to show that the freedom and prosperity of the West have been achieved in spite of Christianity and not because of it. It is because we have dethroned Christianity that our societies are more free and prosperous than the Islamic societies.

Instead of feeling smug and superior, Christians should be determined to save their religion by keeping it scrupulously out of politics. It seems to me that the Christian Right is perversely blind to the dangers of religion in politics. But anyone born in the Middle East (as I was) cannot ignore the disastrous effects of the mixture of religion (especially Biblical religion) and politics. In the Middle East, everyone is brought up to believe that their religion is just fine; all the problems of the world have their source in other people's religion. This is a terrible mistake. The world in general and the Middle East in particular, would be much improved if everyone were more cognizant of the flaws of their own people and religion. This explains my admiration for the likes of journalist Rick Salutin, historian David Noble, film critic and novelist Maurice Yacowar, theorist and playwright Chana Cox, and political scientist Richard Falk. We need more Arab writers critical of the Arab world and its religion. Of course, they risk having a *fatwa* on their heads. And that may explain why they are not as visible as they might be.

In Part I, "Metaphysics of Terror," I give a critical account of the religion of Jesus. Unlike other critics, I do not focus my critique on the Church; instead, I focus on the religion of Jesus as represented in the sacred texts and their canonized interpreters. Both the critics of Christianity and its defenders have focused their criticisms on Saint Paul and the Church. They blame Saint Paul for darkening the message of sweetness and light imparted by Jesus. They blame the Church for perverting the original teachings of the Gospels. In contrast, I argue that from its earliest and supposedly most idealistic beginnings, Christianity betrays a bleak austerity behind the apparently genial personality of Jesus. I focus on the major elements—faith, salvation, sin, death, and damnation. I explain why the religion of Jesus is zealous, immoderate, and unwise. And this is why Jesus cannot be totally absolved of the savage history of the Church.

In Part II, "Politics of Terror," I make the case against Christianity in politics. My argument is intended as a response to those who believe that Christianity has a salutary effect on politics—from Saint Augustine to George W. Bush. It has often been observed that Christianity oscillates between political resignation and militancy. On one hand, it assumes a passive and resigned attitude to political affairs. Overwhelmed by the enormity of human depravity, it resigns itself to the horrors of the world and awaits supernatural redemption. But as soon as Christianity gained political ascendancy in Rome, resignation gave way to militancy. But in my view, the two postures—resignation and militancy—are equally disastrous from a political point of view because they are equally antithetical to political moderation, sobriety, or restraint. It stands to reason that those who believe that they are in possession of the one and only truth necessary for salvation are unlikely to be generous, pluralistic, or just. In short, Christianity cannot be vested with political power without courting disaster. The political success of Christianity, then and now, invites the worst tyrannies—tyrannies that seek dominion not only over the actions of the body but over the thoughts, dreams, and longings of the mind.

In contrast to many of his followers, Jesus was apolitical. He did not aspire to political power; nor did he offer a political philosophy. He provided moral and spiritual guidance for the private lives of individuals. And even if we reject his religious doctrines, we must admit that his moral teaching is not without allure. Part III, "Ethic of Love," is a critical examination of the moral teaching of Jesus. I argue that the Jesus ethic is not simply a prudential ethic, as critics contend—if it were, it might be more palatable. I think it is more austere, but more fascinating than critics recognize. In contrast to Nietzsche, I do not think that Christianity has trumped fate or eclipsed tragedy. Whatever its shortcomings, the morality of Jesus is rich in tragic gloom. And far from coming into conflict with the metaphysics of terror, it is intimately connected with it, for reasons that I will explain.

In Part IV, I examine the "Psychology of Terror." It is my contention that the ethic of love has unwittingly fostered a conception of conscience as an inner state of siege. I argue that both psychoanalysis and postmodernism are the heirs of Christianity. In other words, our self-styled liberators are trapped within the Christian horizon. So much so, that it is no exaggeration to say that Freud has provided Christianity with scientific, historical, and psychological justification. He shares the Christian preoccupation with sin, sex, guilt, and expiation. Nor are Nietzsche and his postmodern troops free of the yoke of Christianity.

Like Freud, they assume that there is a profound conflict between human nature and civilization, and that the latter depends for its success on psychic terror. This understanding of the relation of terror and civilization is what I aim to challenge. I believe this worldview has deep Biblical roots, which have the effect of deprecating morality, inviting a Promethean revolt, and romanticizing evil.

In Part V, "Terror, Ideals, and Civilization," I reject both the naïve and the cynical approaches to the relation of terror and civilization. I argue that terror is neither the opposite of civilization nor the secret of its success. The relationship between terror and civilization is much more complex. I believe that ideals and their zealous pursuit, are at the heart of both the sweetness of civilization and its terrors. Christianity and Islam are examples. What makes the conflict between Islam and the West so deadly is not the radical difference between the antagonists but their similarity—both live in the shadow of Biblical religion, which accounts for the radical and polarizing nature of the conflict. Transcending the Biblical horizon is therefore the first step in the quest for political moderation and sobriety.

PART I
METAPHYSICS OF TERROR

In an age of test-tube babies, cloning, and stem cell research, many Christians believe that we are living in a "culture of death." Frankenstein has become a reality. Monsters are being created in laboratories by mixing the genes of humans with animals. Embryos are being manufactured only to be "harvested" for the purposes of "research." Not surprisingly, some feel that even though Hitler lost the war, his culture of death has triumphed.[1] Human life has become a commodity and a plaything to satisfy the insatiable scientific desire for conquest—the desire to be God.

In these frightful circumstances, Christianity has enjoyed a revival. Many believers imagine that Christianity alone can rescue us from the crude scientism to which we have fallen prey. They imagine that a return to the biblical idea that man is made in the image of God will bring back a reverence for human life. And in the absence of faith, they are willing to use the power of the state to enforce conformity to Christian morality and beliefs. In my view, this is a desperate tactic.

In an age that is disenchanted with science and technology but is hungry for authority, we long for the towering moral authority of the Church. Without realizing it, we long for a romanticized version of the Middle Ages. We long for a world in which the Church represented a transcendent moral order to which the state was subject. We long for a day when the Church provided a moral compass that sets limits on the power and iniquity of the state. We long for a time when submitting to the authority of the Church was proof that the state is legitimate—that it is more than the incarnation of force and fraud. We dream of a Church that can curb the immorality of society. We imagine a Church that can play the role of an international umpire, upholding justice and settling disputes between secular powers.

After the catastrophic turn of the French Revolution, reactionaries and Romantics longed for the age of faith and chivalry. They were convinced that reason and modernity led directly and logically to the guillotine. But we must resist this inclination to demonize reason and romanticize the Middle Ages. The latter was indeed an age of faith and chivalry but it was also a barbarous age, and the power of the Church was integral to that barbarity.

It behooves us not to forget this in a rush to re-empower the Church. We should also not forget that the Church is a master of dissembling. Despite her wretched history, she has always managed to present herself as the "bride of Christ." This ingenious symbol has been instrumental in concealing her crimes. It has allowed her to pretend that she has never wielded any secular, political, or coercive power. It has allowed her to promote the illusion that she is the representative of God on earth—a representative with *no will of her own*.

Christianity has a remarkable capacity for self-renewal and self-purification. Despite a history of terror—Crusades, Inquisitions, and witch burnings—it has displayed unusual resilience. It has managed to remain pure and untouched by the iniquities of its highest officials. Unlike other ideals, it seems untarnished by their crimes. No one says of Christianity what everyone says of Marxism—it is finished, forget it; it has been tried. On the contrary, there is reason to believe that the twenty-first century is on the cusp of a religious revival, if not also on the verge of religious wars.

1. The Apologetic Argument

The resilience of Christianity is ultimately a mystery. But at the heart of the matter is the capacity of the Christian ideal to separate itself from its historical incarnations. There continues to be faith in a pure, perfect, and pristine Christianity that transcends history. Christianity has been brilliantly adept at separating the ideal from its historically flawed manifestations. Appeal to this pure and pristine ideal of Christianity has been the cornerstone of the arguments of Christian apologists. In this chapter, I will make the case against the apologetic argument.

In my view, this argument contains a small truth but it also has serious limitations; and it has been more successful than it deserves to be. The apologetic argument appeals to a pure Christianity that transcends the dark history of the Church. Supposedly, Christian principles are flawless because they are inspired by Jesus Christ. But the Church is made up of mortal men who are not perfect.

The most recent example of Christian apologetics is the highly acclaimed book *Papal Sin*, by Garry Wills. In his book, Wills documents the moral decrepitude and intellectual bankruptcy of the Catholic Church in our time.[2] He thinks that the pope and the hierarchy of the

Church are monstrous, and that they have perverted an original, moderate, tolerant, and pluralistic Christianity. Like all apologists, his argument depends on faith in a pure and pristine Christianity that is forever distinct and separate from its own profoundly flawed manifestations. At the very minimum, Jesus is the cornerstone of this pure and perfect Christianity. But in some cases, Saint Paul, Saint Augustine, and other Church Fathers are included. Wills is one of the many admirers of Saint Augustine and considers him a champion of an unspoiled Christianity.[3]

The success of the apologetic argument has its source in the fact that it contains a partial truth. The argument rightly points to the tension between any original ideal and its founders on one hand, and the process of institutionalization on the other. There is definitely a certain conflict between the teachings of Jesus on one hand and those of Pope John Paul II on the other. The institutionalization of the ideal has no doubt led to a serious corruption of the original. But as I will argue, the original cannot be totally divorced or absolved from its decadent manifestations.

The tension between the original ideal and its institutional representations notwithstanding, the apologetic argument is nevertheless seriously flawed. Is it possible to believe that Christianity is not to blame for the horrors inflicted in its name? Is it possible to believe that all these evils wrought in the name of Christianity were the work of bad men whose wickedness was not inspired by Christianity itself? Consider the Catholic priesthood. Could its infamy have nothing to do with the policies, practices, and beliefs of the Church? What are we to make of all those priests who have abused the children entrusted to their care? Are we to believe that all this depravity has nothing to do with the sexual obsessions of Christianity and the Catholic enforcement of celibacy? Is the original Christianity as pristine as the Christian apologists would have us believe? Is Christianity altogether removed from the evils that are carried out in its name and under its banner?

In what follows, I will make the case against the apologetic argument. I will argue that Christianity is seriously flawed and that these flaws become particularly apparent whenever the Church manages to acquire political power. If the Church were to be empowered once again, the results are certain to be just as disastrous as they were in Rome, in the Middle Ages, in Calvin's reign of terror in Geneva, in the Puritan rule of England and dominance of New England. My argument is intended as a response to those who believe that the revival of Christianity in our time would have a salutary effect on the world in general and on politics in particular. In making this argument, I will refrain from laying the blame exclusively on the Church, which allegedly contains many bad

Christians. In this chapter, I will confine myself to Jesus. If there is a pure and pristine Christianity, it must rest with Jesus as presented in the Gospels.[4] Unlike the critics as well as the apologists of Christianity, I believe that Jesus cannot be totally absolved of the savage history of the Church. In what follows, I will show that Jesus's theology is singular, harsh, intolerant, and uncompromising; and this is why it lends itself to the abominations done in his name.

2. Was Jesus Moderate?

Jesus is a paradoxical figure who is far more interesting than the orthodox view would lead one to believe. According to the orthodox view, he is the paragon of love, humility, and meekness. Nor is this view of him confined to the Church and its apologists. The most visceral critics of Christianity also accept this view of Jesus. Critics exempt Jesus from their censure of his religion. Even the self-anointed antichrist, Friedrich Nietzsche (1844–1900), blames Saint Paul and the Church for the decrepitude of Christianity; he directs most of his assault on priestly rule.[5] He rants about the hypocrisy of priests, as if hypocrisy was the peculiar innovation of Christianity. But he is not critical of Jesus—he thinks that the only real Christian died on the cross.[6]

In his own quiet way, Edward Westermarck is a much more astute critic of Christianity than Nietzsche. But even Westermarck exempts Jesus from his criticism.[7] Like Nietzsche and other critics, he attributes the decrepitude of Christianity to Saint Paul and the fathers of the Church. In this way, the critics of Christianity join the apologists in suggesting that there is a pure and pristine Christianity that is represented by Jesus, at the very least.

There are three things that can be said in favor of Jesus that cannot be said of the Church. First, Jesus was apolitical—he did not aspire to worldly power or dominion. Second, Jesus did not use human depravity as an excuse for political tyranny and oppression. Third, Jesus did not harbor an irrational aversion to women. Nevertheless, he cannot be totally absolved of the evils done in his name. Nor can his doctrines be politically triumphant without courting disaster. If we wish to understand why Christianity has deleterious consequences for politics, we need to look at the religion of Jesus.

My childhood education was a mixture of Orthodox and Catholic— two traditions that do not encourage reading the Bible. In reading the New Testament as a scholar, I found to my surprise that Jesus was not as admirable a figure as I have always believed. Nor was his doctrine as sweet, mild, or genial as I had assumed. I found the flaws of his character to be closely connected to the defects of his doctrine.

Jesus is generally considered the incarnation of love, forgiveness, humility, and innocent suffering. This is indeed how he is depicted in the Gospels. But the Gospels also present another side of Jesus's personality that has been overlooked. All his goodness not withstanding, he is also autocratic and vindictive.

The Gospel of John provides what I think is by far the most autocratic portrait of Jesus.[8] It is noteworthy to recall that Martin Luther considered the Gospel of John as supreme among Gospels and by far superior to the so-called synoptic gospels of Matthew, Mark, and Luke.[9] The latter tell stories about Jesus and his miracles, but the Gospel of John gets to the heart of Jesus's beliefs about himself and his mission. But unwittingly, that Gospel paints a picture of a man who has all the qualities of a zealot—immoderate, intransigent, uncompromising, and autocratic. There are no ifs or buts in his speech; there is only one right way and it is his way. But one need not rely exclusively on the Gospel of John. The synoptic Gospels corroborate most of what is found in John.

The legendary humility of Jesus does not conceal his overbearing arrogance. "I am the light of the world," he says. "I am the way, the truth, and the life: no man cometh unto the Father but by me" (John 14:6). He also says: "I am the living bread . . . if any man eat of this bread he shall live forever . . . Whoso eateth my flesh, and drinketh my blood, hath eternal life" (John 6:51–54). Setting aside the cannibalistic imagery, which was partly responsible for the persecution of early Christians in Rome, this is a harsh doctrine. It is a very singular and self-righteous doctrine. It suggests that there is only one path to God, only one route to righteousness, only one right way, and only one right faith—faith in Jesus. Even the disciples find it a little much: "this is an hard saying; who can hear it?" (John 6:59). No doubt they were disturbed by the image of drinking blood and eating flesh—even as a metaphor.

Jesus may appear humble when he tells his fellow Jews that he has no purposes of his own; he is merely the agent of God who is his Father in heaven. But he adds, "I and my Father are one" (John 10:30). In other words, he is God. It is not surprising that the Jews throw stones at him. And when he asks them what he has done to deserve their abuse, they reply that it is nothing he has done, it is his blasphemy: because "thou, being a man, makest thyself God" (John 10:33). A reader has to already believe that Jesus is God in order to excuse his conduct.

The Pharisees complain that his self-proclaimed greatness make them suspect that he is a phony: "Thou barest record of thyself; thy record is not true" (John 8:12–13). But Jesus just brushes them off saying he knows who he is. Besides, God bears witness on his behalf, and they are not fit to judge him, for "ye are from beneath; I am from above: ye are of this world; I am not of this world" (John 8:16–23).

Jesus's autocratic spirit led him to encourage a zealous devotion to himself and his creed. He demanded an allegiance that assumed neglect of all other obligations, including duties to those who are nearest and dearest.[10] He asked people to leave their families for his name's sake and promised them extra rewards in this world as well as the next for doing so: they will "receive an hundred fold, and shall inherit everlasting life" (Matthew 19:29; Mark 10:29; Luke 18:29–30). He relied on the selfish desire for personal salvation (even to the neglect of one's familial duties) to inspired devotion to himself and his creed. Jesus set a bad example in his callous treatment of his mother and brothers when they came to see him at the synagogue; he failed to acknowledge them saying "Who is my mother, or my brethren?" And he pointed to his disciples saying that they were his real family (Mark 3:31–35; Luke 8:19–21). And when one of his admirers said I will follow you but "suffer me first to go and bury my father," Jesus replied, "follow me; and let the dead bury their dead" (Matthew 8:21–22). Jesus was hardly a champion of family values.

The exemplary forgiving spirit of Jesus as portrayed in the Gospels does not conceal a malevolent and vindictive side. The latter was generally directed at his fellow Jews and skeptics but it was also directed at nature and animals. The story of the fig tree is one example. Jesus was hungry and noticed a fig tree at a distance, but when he came up to it, he found that it had no figs. In his disappointment, he said to the tree "Let no fruit grow on thee hence-forward for ever. And presently the fig tree withered away" (Mathew 21:18–19). No doubt the author of the gospel is using this story as a manifestation of Jesus's power. But it is also a manifestation of someone whose temper is not under control and whose power is therefore badly used. Cursing the fig tree was totally uncalled for; it was probably not the season for figs.

Jesus did not always use his supernatural powers in a benign fashion. In one strange incident, Jesus banishes the devils in a man but allows them to enter into two thousand swine that are grazing on the hillside. As a result, the swine become crazed and race madly down the hill and plunge into the sea and to their death. This nasty little miracle made the people who owned the swine (and who probably depended on the swine for their livelihood) somewhat angry (Mark 5:11–17). It was certainly within his power to banish the devils altogether, as he does in many other instances. But in this case, he displays a gratuitous malevolence toward hapless animals.

Christian apocrypha provide a similar picture of Jesus as an impish child. In the "Infancy Gospels," Jesus is portrayed as having dangerous supernatural powers at his disposal, but no self-control or natural goodness. He is vicious, vindictive, and arbitrary. He kills, blinds, and maims those who displease him. Sometimes the stricken are restored if they grovel and beg his forgiveness. In one instance, he sees some children playing and he runs out to join them, but they run away and hide in a house. Jesus goes to the house and asks to play with the children, but is told by the adults that there are no children in the house. He agrees, there are no children, only goats. To the horror of their parents, the children were turned into goats. The mothers prostrated themselves before the little Jesus and beseech him to restore their children and to use his power for good. In this case, he relents and the children are restored and they all run off and play with the little Jesus.[11] Not surprisingly, the towns-people were terror-stricken, and Joseph was blamed for his son's conduct; but the poor man was beside himself and could do nothing to restrain his son's supernatural powers. Besides, his son did not listen to him and no tutor was able to rein him in. These Gospels also show Jesus maturing and getting his temper under control, and using his supernatural powers for good ends. The canonical Gospels reflect his benevolence but they also reveal glimpses of his youthful antics and his bad temper.

Jesus was particularly nasty to his fellow Jews. The latter were not convinced that Jesus was the messiah they have been waiting for because the redemption he offers is not the sort of thing the Jews had in mind. The messiah they are waiting for is someone like King David who could lead Israel to greatness, make her a blessing to the world, and inaugurate a reign of justice and prosperity.

To convince the Jews that he is the Christ that was prophesied in the Old Testament, Jesus must change the very nature of their expectations. He must persuade them that the kingdom of God is not of this world (John 18:36). This is nothing short of changing the nature of their faith. He must convince them that they have totally misunderstood the promises that God has made; what they are expecting is all wrong; for hundreds of years they have been mistaken in thinking that there can be any redemption in this world. At that time, some of the Jews were starting to think in terms of a life after death. By the time of Jesus, some Jews, such as the Pharisees, believed in the resurrection of the body but the Sadducees rejected the idea. On the whole, the idea did not play a large role in the history of Judaism before the time of Jesus.[12] The idea was largely the fruit of pessimism or hopelessness that Israel could ever be restored to her former glory.

Needless to say, the Jews were not impressed by his kingdom or by his self-proclaimed greatness. They were rightly skeptical. Jesus did not take well to either rejection or skepticism. When confronted with doubt about his extravagant claims, he became belligerent and threatening: "if ye believe not that I am he, ye shall die in your sins" (John 8:24). And: "Ye serpents, ye generation of vipers, how can ye escape the damnation of hell?" (Matthew 23:33).

The death of Jesus was tragic in the classic sense of the term. He suffered a horrible fate that was not deserved. But like every tragic hero, he was not without his faults; and his flaws contributed to the tragedy. His blasphemous remarks, his wild threats, his self-righteousness, and his moral denunciation of others especially of skeptics, made his fellow Jews hate him so much that they preferred to let a common criminal like Barabas go free than to withstand more of his censorious preaching. The Jews would have done better to refute or ignore him. By crucifying him, they made this eccentric zealot the focus of a world religion of monumental consequences.

Two of the less flattering aspects of the character of Jesus are reflected in his creed. His singular and autocratic character is reflected in the doctrine of sin as unbelief; his vindictive side is reflected in the doctrine of hell and damnation. I will examine each of these doctrines in turn.

3. Sin as Unbelief

The singular and autocratic character of Jesus is reflected in his moral condemnation of those who do not believe in him. At first blush it seems as if *doing* the will of God and following his commandments is the criterion for being saved or damned (Matt 25:30–46). But this reading misses the mark; it overlooks what is unique about the new religion. In the Gospel of John, Jesus identifies righteousness with *believing* in him and considers wickedness to be the reverse: "for if ye believe not that I am he, ye shall die in your sins" (John 8:24). In Matthew, Jesus says: "whosoever shall deny me before men, him will I also deny before my Father which is in heaven" (Matthew 10:33).[13] Not to believe in Jesus, not to believe that he is the only way to God, is a sin that merits damnation.

Believing in Jesus is the *only* route to salvation: "I am the way, the truth, and the life: no man cometh to the Father but by me" (John 14:6).

And: "everyone which seeth the Son, and believeth on him, may have everlasting life: and I will raise him up at the last day" (John 6:40). And: "he that believeth in me, though he were dead, yet shall live: And whosoever liveth and believeth in me shall never die" (John 11:25–26). In contrast, "he that believeth not is condemned already, because he hath not believed in the name of the only begotten son of God" (John 3:18). Saint Paul echoes Jesus when he declares "faith is counted as righteousness" (Romans 4:5). These views are in marked contrast to Jeremiah's plea, "O Jerusalem, wash thine heart from wickedness, that thou mayest be saved" (Jeremiah 5:14). The new religion ranks the right thoughts and beliefs so highly that they overshadow good conduct and eclipse right action.

If faith is the key to salvation, then skepticism and unbelief is sin, death, and damnation. It should therefore not surprise us to find Saint Augustine and Saint Thomas Aquinas claiming categorically that there is "neither true chastity, nor any other virtue" among unbelievers, because nothing qualifies as a true virtue if it is not directed to the true God as its end. Virtues are distinguished "by their end" and not by the act itself. So, it is not *what* you do but who you are and what you believe. If you are not a believer, your virtues are worthless and your good deeds are contemptible.[14]

Aquinas is true to Jesus when he declares, "unbelief is the greatest of sins."[15] We may live an exemplary life, but if we do not believe in Jesus, we are damned. The importance of faith for salvation is integral to Jesus's doctrine as expressed in the Gospels; it is not the invention of Luther and other "heretical" Protestants.

Despite his inclination to forgiveness, Jesus makes it clear that blasphemy against the Holy Ghost is the unforgivable sin in this world as well as in the next (Matthew 12:31–32). But he distinguishes the Holy Ghost from the Son of Man. Aquinas explains the distinction by saying that Father, Son, and Holy Ghost are three aspects or attributes of God that are not separate but distinct. The Father represents the power of God, the Son represents the Wisdom of God, and the Holy Ghost represents the goodness of God. Therefore, to blaspheme against the Holy Ghost is to blaspheme against the goodness of God. Those who say nasty things about Jesus, insofar as he is a man, might be forgiven. In the Gospels, we hear some say that he is a winebibber and a glutton. But to say that his power has its source in the devil is to speak ill of Jesus in his divinity, which is the same as disparaging the goodness of God or blaspheming against the Holy Ghost.[16] But why is blaspheming against the Holy Ghost more terrible than any other sin? Is it more terrible than torturing little animals for sport? Is it more terrible than cold-blooded murder? Obviously, Jesus thinks it is.

Aquinas explains, "in comparison with blasphemy, every sin is slight," because blasphemy is unbelief expressed in words.[17] Aquinas argues that blasphemy is even worse than perjury because it involves saying or thinking something false about God. And that is the most serious sin of all because it follows from unbelief. In other words, if I bear false witness in a court of law with the intention of harming someone or having someone unjustly put to death, my sin is "slight" in comparison to blasphemy. It is more grievous to have wrong beliefs about God than to commit perjury, no matter how malicious the intent and how dreadful the consequences. Therefore, to question, doubt, or disparage the justice and goodness of God, as I am doing here, is blasphemy. Critical thinking is monstrous wickedness that is unforgivable in this world and in the next.[18]

Christians have followed Jesus in defining wickedness as not believing what Christians believe. This assumption has been the source of untold wickedness in the history of the Church. It explains the profound intolerance that has led Christians to persecute others, not for doing harm but simply for being unbelievers or for harboring what Christian authorities think are false beliefs. The Inquisition and the burning of heretics was a classic case in point. It was about punishing people for their beliefs, not their actions. The assumption is that unbelief is itself a sin; this assumption is at the heart of the darkest chapters in the history of human tyranny in general and of the Church in particular. Even in recent times, the Church defends its history of persecution. It maintains that sympathy for heretics and calls for tolerance are symptoms of the decay of faith engendered by modernity.[19] It regards the real disease to be modernity and its inclination to tolerance. Accordingly, Pope Pius X (1903–14) established in every diocese "a board of censors" and a "vigilance committee" whose functions were "to find out and report on writings and persons tainted with the heresy of Modernism."[20]

Far from being an aberration that is not representative of Christianity, the persecution of heretics follows logically from the connection of faith and salvation as presented by Jesus in the Gospels. Since the correct beliefs are necessary for salvation, those who harbor wrong beliefs are not only compromising their own salvation, they are also a threat to the salvation of others. Heretics are a menace to the community at large because others may come to share their wrong beliefs and be damned. Because heresy was deemed contagious and deadly, heretics had to be exterminated to prevent the entire community from being infected. Even the moderate Aquinas, who maintained that a Christian commonwealth should allow Jews and (sometimes) pagans to practice their religions unmolested,[21] could not entertain any mercy for heretics:

> they deserve not only to be separated from the Church by excommunication, but also to be severed from the world by death. For it is a much graver matter to corrupt faith, which quickens the soul, than to forge money, which supports temporal life.[22]

The assumption is that correct faith is as essential to the life of the soul as money is to the life of the body. Of course, the Church must have mercy on those who stray and should only condemn them after the first or second admonition in the hope of saving their souls. But if they continue to be stubborn and there is no hope of converting them, the Church should start worrying about the salvation of others by excommunicating them and delivering them to the "secular tribunal to be exterminated thereby from the world by death."[23] Aquinas quotes Saint Jerome approvingly saying that the heretic is like a little leaven, and that it is better to

> cut off the decayed flesh, expel the mangy sheep from the fold, lest the whole house, the whole dough, the whole body, the whole flock burn, perish, rot, die. Arius was but one spark in Alexandria, but as that spark was not at once put out, the whole earth was laid waste by its flame.[24]

Heretics threaten the well-being of the whole community, not because of anything they do but simply because their beliefs may triumph over the orthodox views, and in so doing, destroy all hope for salvation. The right beliefs are *de rigueur*. And Aquinas is surely right in maintaining that his position is "not contrary to Our Lord's command."[25]

Arius (256–336) believed that Jesus, the Son of God, was not "Consubstantial" with the Father (i.e. not made of the same substance); the Son was created out of nothing and not "begotten." This sounds like a technical quibble but it was a matter of logic. Arius did not deny that Jesus was the Son of God nor did he deny his virgin birth. But he denied that Jesus and God were identical—he denied that Jesus was God. Arius was just being logical—Jesus cannot be both identical with and different from God; he cannot be both God and the Son of God.[26] The Arian quest for logic hurled the Church into an upheaval that lasted for more than a century. Hundreds of years later, Aquinas would refer to Arius when he wanted to invoke the demonic, just as we would cite Hitler. Yet Arius was not guilty of murder or massacre but only of "wrong" beliefs.

When faith has primacy over action, when salvation depends first and foremost on having the "right beliefs" (no matter how illogical), then any departure from the accepted dogmas threatens eternal life. The result is a preoccupation with doctrines and dogmas. Not surprisingly, ecumenical councils (starting with the first ecumenical council at Nicaea in 325) become a necessity.[27] Their function is to declare the Church's authoritative interpretation and to define and denounce heresy, so that the faithful will know what they must believe in order to have a chance at salvation. Those who dissent from the authoritative views are a menace to the community, and must be treated accordingly. Because so much is supposedly at stake, the Church claimed infallibility and demanded absolute power of life and death over anyone suspected of harboring dissenting opinions. These evils are the inevitable consequences of a theology that gives primacy to faith, as Jesus did. The totalitarian regimes of the twentieth century were equally preoccupied with the control of thought. But in comparison to their more successful antecedent (i.e. the Church), they were mere amateurs.

Nor were Protestants more tolerant. In his commentary on Saint Paul's Epistle to the Romans, Martin Luther takes what Christ says seriously. If sin is unbelief, then righteousness must be faith. And from these assumptions, Luther develops his doctrine of salvation by faith alone. He insists that belief alone is the key to righteousness. If you believe, then it does not matter what else you do: "We who are Christians are all kings and priests and so are lords of all, and may firmly believe that *whatever we have done* is pleasing and acceptable in the sight of God."[28] The Jews have been hated and persecuted for claiming to be God's chosen people, even though it is not clear what they were chosen for, other than suffering. But Christians make Jewish arrogance look like humility.

Luther does not invent the primacy of faith—he has it on good authority. He rightly points out, "Christ therefore singled out unbelief and called it sin. In John 16, He says, The Spirit will convict the world of sin because they do not believe in me" (John 16:8 f.).[29] Luther goes so far as to claim, "what is done in the absence of faith on one hand, or in consequence of unbelief on the other, is naught but falsity, self-deception and sin."[30] Luther makes this clear again and again throughout his work. The question is not what works are done, but "who it is that does them."[31] And, "if a man were not first a believer and a Christian, all his works would amount to nothing at all and would be truly wicked and damnable sins."[32] And again: "as the man is, whether believer or unbeliever, so also is his work—good if it was done in faith; and wicked, if it was done in unbelief."[33] And "nothing makes a man good except faith, nor evil, except unbelief."[34]

Luther considers nothing more perverse than the good deeds of those who have no faith in Christ. He calls this inclination to good a "perverseness of nature," which can become an "incurable evil," especially when the influence of custom "confirm(s) this perverseness of nature, as wicked magistrates" are inclined to do.[35] The result is that countless men are led astray and destroyed "beyond all hope of restoration."[36] And all this is the result of the perverse inclination to do good!

All this means that it does not matter how much good you do; if you do not believe in Christ, all your good works are either worthless (Aquinas) or damnable (Luther). But in either case, only the good works of Christians count in the eyes of God.

Even though Luther pushes the identity of faith and righteousness to great lengths, neither the doctrine nor his interpretation of it is his own invention. Saint Paul understood the words of Jesus in the same way: "he that doubteth is damned if he eat, because he eateth not of faith: for whatsoever is not of faith is sin" (Romans 14:23). So, everything that comes out of faith (no matter what it is) is righteousness and everything that comes out of unbelief (no matter what it is) is sin. In England, the notorious Ranters were a sect that took this doctrine seriously. They were antinomians—that is to say, they believed that the moral law is not binding on Christians. Because they were believers and were the elect of God, they were convinced that nothing they could do was sinful. As a result, they indulged in every abomination, and were particularly infamous for their sexual licentiousness.[37]

Luther was aware of the fact that his position invites this sort of radicalism. His reading of the Gospels implies that as long as we believe in Christ, we can spend our life indulging all our lust and not trouble ourselves about righteousness. But Luther rejected this conclusion. He shrank from the radical implications of his doctrine by saying that a man can't "take his ease" since he must "discipline his body by fastings, watchings, labours, and other reasonable discipline" to make sure that the "flesh is subject to the spirit" and will not "revolt against faith."[38] But this is a feeble answer. The Ranters were celebrating their freedom from the Law. There was absolutely no revolting against the faith; they were totally confident in their faith.

On behalf of Luther it is necessary to point out that he did not regard good conduct as irrelevant. Even though it could not earn you a place in heaven, it was an important sign of faith, election, and salvation. It follows that if you have any doubt that Christ is your savior or if you have any doubt about your election, and wish to assuage your anxiety over salvation, and convince yourself and others that you are not damned, then it would be a good idea to spend time doing good works. This was Calvin's solution. But on the other hand, if your faith is strong and unwavering and if you are extremely confident about your salvation (as the Ranters were), then you might as well relax and enjoy yourself.[39] But surely, such confidence is either foolhardy or unusual. It is foolhardy because faith is itself a gift of grace that can disappear as mysteriously as it appeared. This led Pascal to remark that even the martyrs had reason to fear. So we are back to Calvin's "solution" and its inherent difficulties, to which I will return later. It is sufficient to say here that even if Luther can escape antinomianism, he cannot escape the difficulties of Calvinism. However, these difficulties are not the creation of Luther, Calvin, or Pascal. They are inherent in the Gospels, as we shall see.[40]

Confidence in one's faith is not only foolhardy because faith is a gift of grace, it is unusual because the articles of faith are so taxing on one's credulity that only the most unthinking could escape the torments of doubt. No one has documented the spiritual anguish of doubt more vividly than John Bunyan in his autobiography, *Grace Abounding to the Chief of Sinners*.[41] Bunyan regarded doubts about his faith—doubts about the existence and goodness of God—as sins that had no equal. He thought that he was guilty of the unpardonable sin, the sin against the Holy Ghost, the sin of unbelief, the sin for which there is no remedy. Even while preaching, he was "violently assaulted with thoughts of blasphemy."[42] He was sure that Satan was behind these dreadful thoughts. Bunyan presents his spiritual saga as a life and death struggle with the devil. But to my mind, the struggle is against his intelligence and rationality. It is no accident that the devil has the best lines and makes the best points. Nor is it an accident that the devil is well versed in the Gospels, as Bunyan was. The devil is Bunyan's intelligence—his critical mind, his logical conclusions, and his extensive knowledge of the Gospels. It is not the devil but his intellect that Bunyan longs to silence.

But the devil would not be silenced; he continued his merciless assault: "How can you tell that the Turks had not as good scriptures to prove their Mahomet the Savior, as we have to prove our Jesus is; . . . Everyone doth think his own religion rightest, both Jews and Moors, and Pagans; and how if our faith, and Christ, and Scriptures, should be a think-so too?"[43] Bunyan's reaction was to pray to God to silence the Tempter. But the Tempter will not be silenced. Instead, he assaulted him with the constant reminder that these thoughts are unforgivable and that Bunyan is damned and will burn in hell for all eternity, because he was guilty of the one and only unforgivable sin. Nothing could change that. Christ is the bridge between man and God; to reject Christ is to give up the single source of salvation, the single route back to God, and the only opportunity for forgiveness.[44] He was doomed; he was the son of perdition. Bunyan scoured the Gospels for words of comfort, but to no avail. The Scriptures were unambiguous. He was particularly haunted by Mark 3:28–29:

> All sins shall be forgiven unto the sons of men, ... But he that shall blaspheme against the Holy Ghost hath never forgiveness, but is in danger of eternal damnation.

Bunyan was convinced that he was guilty of the greatest sin of all—the sin against the Holy Ghost. When he compared his sin with King David and King Manasseh, Bunyan felt himself to be (by far) the greater sinner. David's desire for Bathsheba led him to conceal his adultery with murder. He used his power as King to send Bathsheba's husband off to the front lines of battle and to his death (II Samuel 11:2 f.). King Manasseh of Judah worshiped idols, burned his own son, and shed much innocent blood (II Kings 21). Yet Bunyan was certain that his sin was much greater than all the sins of David and Manasseh put together. His reasoning was as follows. The sins of David and Manasseh were forgivable because they were sins against the Law; Jesus was the remedy for sins against the Law; he came to provide forgiveness for such sins; but there was no forgiveness for the sin against grace—the sin of repudiating Jesus as the manifestation of God's love and grace. The conclusion is that not believing in Jesus is worse than murder, adultery, the worship of idols, the practice of human sacrifice, and the shedding of innocent blood. For all the sins in the world there is a remedy, but not for the sin of unbelief. Bunyan found spiritual comfort only when he learned to abhor himself, silence his intelligence, and not trust his heart.[45] That was the only remedy for the tribulations implied by the assumption that not believing in Christ is the greatest sin.

The Catholic Church rejected the primacy of faith in favor of a more palatable doctrine according to which both faith and works are equally necessary for salvation. But it never denied the identity of sin and unbelief. And this meant that it could not escape the evils inherent in this doctrine.

Even when it escapes antinomian excesses, the view that unbelief is sinful undermines moral conduct by shifting the focus from actions to thoughts and beliefs as the locus of wickedness. This has the effect of legitimating the repression of dissenting views; it justifies the persecution of heretics and unbelievers; it explains the Church's ability to combine iniquity with self-righteousness; and it accounts for the spiritual afflictions of believers who take the words of Jesus as seriously as Bunyan did.

4. Hell and Damnation

The doctrine of hell and damnation is probably the darkest and most vindictive aspect of Christianity and its founder. The Jews were familiar with God's wrath—floods, famines, barren matriarchs, slavery in Egypt, military defeat, captivity in Babylon—these were the usual signs of His displeasure. At the time of Jesus, some Jews were starting to believe in the possible immortality of the soul.[46] But Jesus took the idea to new heights. He introduced a new brand of terror that was not meant to operate on the body in this world but on the body and soul in a world beyond the here and now.

Jesus prophesied that the world as they knew it will come to an end, and all the dead will rise, and "the angels shall come forth and sever the wicked from among the just" (Matthew 13:49). He told them that those who believe in him will have everlasting life, while those who do not believe in him will be cast into "outer darkness," they shall be "cast into the furnace of fire," there shall be "wailing and gnashing of teeth" and their torment will last for all eternity (Matthew 10:28; Matthew 13:50; Matthew 14:49–50; Matthew 25:30–46; Mark 3:29; Luke 12:5; John 5:28–29; John 6:30; John 6:51). All this talk of hell and damnation is repeated in *every* Gospel. This new brand of terror became the hallmark of the new religion. Jesus provides many terrifying details about the end of the world:

> When the Son of man shall come in all his glory, and all the holy angels with him, then shall he sit upon the throne of his glory: . . . Then shall the King say unto them on his right hand, Come, ye blessed of my Father, inherit the kingdom prepared for you from the foundation of the world: . . . Then shall he say also unto them on the left hand, Depart from me, ye cursed, into everlasting fire, prepare for the devil and his angels: . . . And these shall go away into everlasting punishment: but the righteous into eternal life. (Matthew 25:31–46)

Again and again the Gospels repeat Jesus's anticipation of the impending end of the world when he will sit on the right hand of God and his "enemies" will be his "footstools" (Mathew 22:44; Luke 20:43).

Belief in heaven and hell has an unmistakably vindictive appeal.[47] Jesus promises to help the elect avenge themselves against their enemies: "And shall not God avenge his own elect, which cry day and night unto him, though he bear long with them? I tell you that he will avenge them speedily" (Luke 18:7–8). And as to those who reject him: "those my enemies, which would not that I should reign over them, bring hither, and slay them before me" (Luke: 19:27). Vindictiveness toward one's enemies is an undeniable feature of the final judgment. Jesus makes it clear that his "enemies" are to be understood broadly: "All those who are not with me are against me" (Luke 11:23). The current president of the United States loves to echo this statement. It amounts to a dualistic vision of the world in which all claims to neutrality are suspect. We are on the side of the good and the right and our enemies are workers of iniquity allied with the devil and must be destroyed.[48]

Whatever happened to love and forgiveness? In the Sermon on the Mount, Jesus says, "resist not evil," and "love your enemies" (Matthew 5:39–44). At first blush, this sounds like the quintessential Christian doctrine of forgiveness; it sounds like the very antithesis of vindictiveness. But on closer examination, we find ourselves being reassured that we need not worry about punishing tyrants and bullies because the end of the world is at hand and God will take care of the wicked. In other words, we are being asked to sacrifice our instinct for vengeance, not in favor of love and forgiveness but in exchange for a much greater and more effective vengefulness—the vengefulness of God, who will punish the transgressors for all eternity. Saint Paul reveals the extent to which vengeance parades as love when he says: "Bless them which persecute you: bless and curse not. . . . if thine enemy hunger, feed him; if he thirst, give him drink: for in so doing thou shalt heap coals of fire on his head" (Romans 12:14–20).[49]

In the Gospel of John, Jesus says: "My kingdom is not of this world" (John 18:36). This may lead some to surmise that it is a purely spiritual kingdom. But that is a mistake. Jesus speaks of the soul as well as the body being resurrected and tormented. He says "And if thy right eye offend thee, pluck it out, and cast it from thee: for it is profitable for thee that one of thy members should perish, and not that *thy whole body* should be cast into hell" (Matthew 5:29, my italics). And he makes the same point about the right hand (Matthew 5:30).

Jesus makes it clear that hell is not just a spiritual condition but also a state of physical torment; and to experience the torments of burning alive in a fire, we must have bodies. But if we had the sorts of bodies that we have now, then the torments of hell would last only a short time or until our bodies were consumed by the fire. If the torments are to last for all eternity, we must have bodies that are different from the bodies we have now—bodies that can feel pain but will not be consumed by fire. We need bodies that do not have the luxury of death, which ends suffering. Jesus describes hell as a place where "their worm dieth not, and the fire is not quenched" (Mark 9:43–48).

There have always been decent Christians who were embarrassed by Jesus's words and were inclined to reinterpret them radically. The most ingenious and the most charitable interpretation of hell was provided by Origen of Alexandria (185-254).[50] He suggested that we should think of heaven as a type of pedagogy on God's part. God is like a father who "conceals his tenderness with threatening words" that are necessary for the edification and improvement of the child.[51] In other words, "the wrath of God is not so much wrath as a necessary part of his plan of salvation."[52]

Origen interpreted the story of the prodigal son as an allegory for the relation between man and God. Just as the son turns away from his father and squanders his inheritance, so man has turned away from God and squandered the blessings that God bestowed upon him. But just as the son eventually returns to the father, so man will return to God. And like the father, God will rejoice upon his return.[53] Having left by his own free will, he found himself "cast into outer darkness," which Origen understands as the experience of the soul in the absence of God. And after living out there, he becomes "thirsty for the light" and cries out to God to help him.[54] Jesus is the help that God sends, to cleanse us from our sins and prepare our way home to God. The sinner will return to God, just as the son returned to his father, with a deeper and greater appreciation of the Father than he ever had before—that is, before knowing the misery of estrangement from his father.[55] Christ comes to save us from our misery and to show us the way back to God. This work of salvation will be complete when all of humanity is reconciled to God.[56] So understood, damnation is the punishment inherent in sin itself; it is the agony of being alienated from God. And in the fullness of time, all humanity and all the fallen angels, and even the devil himself will put an end to this agony and return to God.

Augustine denounced this brilliant interpretation of hell as surpassing "all errors in its perversity."[57] Christianity without hell was unthinkable. The Church sided with Augustine, on the grounds that Holy Writ is very clear on the eternity of the torments of hell.[58] The Fifth Ecumenical Council (553) condemned Origen as a heretic and denounced a list of his doctrines. In particular, the Church denounced his pedagogical view of hell as a state of spiritual torment that lasts only as long as necessary for the improvement and rehabilitation of man, and that even the Devil and the other fallen angels will eventually be reconciled with God. So much charity and goodwill was intolerable. I think that the Church was right: Holy writ is very clear on such matters. Origen's interpretations are ingenious but too charitable to be true to the text. The fact is that the Church has never been a friend of truth, not even when it comes to Holy Writ; she is always willing to introduce innovations whenever it suits her. But clearly the innovations of Origen did not suit her. What good is Christianity without the eternal torments of hell?

A religion that relies so heavily on spiritual terror is not likely to fare very well in a skeptical age. It is therefore not surprising that in recent years, the Church has had a change of heart. It is fashionable today, even in the Vatican, to side with Origen and claim that the furnace of fire is just a metaphor for the spiritual torments of those who are deprived of the presence of God.[59] Of course that is not what Jesus said. If that is what he meant, then his threats would be empty. No one would have anything to fear whatsoever. On the contrary, those who are not impressed with either Jesus or his God would have every reason to rejoice, since they have absolutely no desire to be united with such a dreadful God, if they can help it. To be separated from such a God would be no torment at all. But that is not the impact of Jesus's words. He was not offering a spiritual gift that his listeners could take or leave. He was revealing the truth about the one and only God—a God who has the power to torment for all eternity.[60]

In days gone by, Church fathers such as Augustine and Aquinas had the courage to defend the hellish doctrine of Jesus without flinching. Augustine believed that fire burns the body while the worm that "dieth not" gnaws at the soul.[61] He insisted that the body plays a critical role in the next life. Augustine claimed that both the blessed and the damned will be "united with their bodies," which will endure eternal torment on one hand and everlasting bliss on the other.[62] Augustine goes to great lengths to argue against those who think that the idea of burning eternally is impossible. He uses examples from nature to show that burning without being consumed is possible—apparently, the asbestos of Arcadia once kindled cannot be put out. If this is possible in this mundane world, it must be possible in the world to come. Like asbestos, the bodies of the damned will burn eternally without being consumed but they will suffer like natural bodies.[63] Augustine's arguments were not directed only against skeptics but also against Christians who, like Origen, thought of hell in purely spiritual terms.[64]

The same is true of Saint Thomas Aquinas. Like Augustine, he argued vehemently against those who suggested that the kingdom of God is a purely spiritual kingdom without a material or bodily dimension. He believed that the resurrection involves a reunion of body and soul.

He claimed that the wicked will be punished "not only in soul but also in the body."[65] He insisted that the fire of hell is corporeal and that it will burn the resurrected bodies of the damned to all eternity.[66] He was somewhat concerned about the fact that fire also gives off light, but Jesus associates hell with "outer darkness." So, following Basil, Aquinas surmised that the heat of the fire will burn and torment the damned, but somehow ("by God's might" of course), the "brightness of the fire will be separated from its power of burning, so that its brightness will conduce to the joy of the blessed, and the heat of the flame to the torment of the damned."[67]

There is a small problem with this tidy solution that Aquinas fails to notice. On one hand, the damned must be deprived of light because darkness is their lot; on the other hand, Aquinas insists that the damned must witness the joys of the blessed so that they can be tormented by envy and regret as well as by fire.[68] But they cannot witness the joys of the blessed if they are totally enveloped in darkness. This is the sort of scholastic puzzle that Aquinas generally excels at, but he fails to solve this one. In any case, the upshot of the matter is that there will be no mercy for the damned because an eternal punishment is what God's justice requires. But why? Supposedly, as Aquinas explains, a punishment is appropriate when it is proportional to the one against whom the offense has been committed—namely God, who is eternal.[69]

This is not a particularly good argument because it makes all mortal sins of equal gravity because they are all sins against God. Since original sin (the inherited sin of Adam and Eve) is a mortal sin, infants who die at birth (before baptism) merit eternal damnation.[70] It follows that a homicidal maniac and a newborn infant merit the same punishment. But Aquinas shrinks from his own logic. Instead, he maintains that such infants will indeed go to hell, but God will ensure that they will not feel the burning of the fire.[71] In this case, Aquinas's decency triumphs over the logic of his Christianity.

It may be argued that hell is an idea that cannot withstand too much rational scrutiny. However, it should not be examined too closely since it is a useful fiction that lends support to morality, and without which humanity cannot be motivated to virtue.[72] But this argument is flawed.

In the first place, no one is improved by the torments of hell since they are already dead when this exquisite punishment is inflicted. In fact, everyone is already dead by the time this punishment is fulfilled. Therefore, no one can be deterred by witnessing this terrifying punishment. Nevertheless, it can be argued that the torments of hell act as a deterrent on the gullible through the imagination. And since the greatest bulk of humanity combine extreme gullibility with a vivid imagination, the fiction of hell is very useful indeed. But there is not much evidence for this view.

Imagine the effect of listening to the fire and brimstone sermons of New England preachers during the religious revival of the eighteenth century known as the Great Awakening. Here is a sample from the famous Jonathan Edwards (1703–58):

> The bow of God's wrath is bent, and the arrow made ready on the string, and justice bends the arrow at your heart, and trains the bow, and it is nothing but the mere pleasure of God, and that of an angry God . . . that keeps the arrow one moment from being made drunk with your blood. . . . all you that were never born again, and made new creatures, and raised from being dead in sin, to a state of new, and before altogether unexperienced light and life, are in the hands of an angry God. . . . it is nothing but his mere pleasure that keeps you from being this moment swallowed up in everlasting destruction. . . .
>
> The God that holds you over the pit of hell, much as one holds a spider, or some loathsome insect over the fire, abhors you, and is dreadfully provoked: his wrath towards you burns like fire; he looks upon you as worthy of nothing else, but to be cast into the fire; . . . you are ten thousand times more abominable in his eyes, than the most hateful venomous serpent is in ours. . . .
>
> O sinner! Consider the fearful danger you are in: it is a great furnace of wrath, a wide and bottomless pit . . . You hang by a slender thread, with the flames of divine wrath flashing about it, and ready every moment to singe it, and burn it asunder; and . . . nothing of your own, nothing that you ever have done, nothing you can do, to induce God to spare you one moment.[73]

A seasoned churchgoer is likely to shrug off the matter saying, "I'm not wicked, so why should I worry?" But Edwards has already anticipated and preempted this response:

> Doth it seem to thee not real that thou shalt suffer such a dreadful destruction, because it seems to thee that thou dost not deserve it? And because thou dost not see anything so horrid in thyself, as to answer such a dreadful punishment? The reason is that thou lovest thy wickedness; thy wickedness seems good to thee; it appears lovely to thee; thou dost not see any hatefulness in it, or to be sure, any such hatefulness as to answer such misery.
>
> But know, thou stupid, blind, hardened wretch, that God doth not see, as thou seest with thy polluted eyes: thy sins in his sight are infinitely abominable.[74]

You are a wretched sinner, and God is entitled to drop you in the fire at any moment, and you have absolutely no basis of complaint. It is only out of sheer magnanimity that God has not dropped you like a spider into the fire. It seems to me quite unlikely that so much self-contempt and a sense of worthlessness would inspire anyone to be noble, kind, and good. If one's depravity is so total that it is not even visible to one's polluted eyes, is there any point in trying to improve? The situation is so hopeless that we are likely to give way to despair and despondency. A four-year-old girl who heard one of Edward's sermons locked herself up in a closet and cried inconsolably. But even among adults, such sermons were inclined to lead to states of extreme emotional strain and even severe physical convulsions.

John Bunyan reports being terror-stricken as a young lad and suffering from dreadful nightmares, filled with devils, hellish fiends, and tormentors pulling him down into the pit of hell and binding him with the chains of eternal darkness.[75] And even as a grown man, he continued to suffer from terror, and tremble under a heavy load of guilt. Never does he report being inspired to do good. On the contrary, in his more lucid moments, the devil whispers in his ear, saying: you are a fool to suffer for nothing; you are not among the elect; God is not likely to choose a worthless fellow like yourself; you have absolutely no virtues that would merit election; it all depends on God's arbitrary mercy, so you might as well stop trying.[76] And anyone who is guilty, as Bunyan thought he was, of the unpardonable sin, the sin against the Holy Ghost, the sin of doubting the goodness of God, is sure to rot in hell. Bunyan found the condition of being a man so intolerable that he longed to be a dog or a toad, or any other creature that is not destined for an eternal life of torment.[77]

It is no wonder that Bunyan was overwhelmed by a deluge of blasphemies against God, Christ, and Scriptures.[78] And what Christian has not been assaulted, as Bunyan was assaulted, by an irresistible urge to blaspheme in the face of such terrifying circumstances? Finding his soul so engulfed in darkness, Bunyan was tempted by the logic of the devil. If you are destined to be damned, then you might as well be damned for many sins as for a few.[79] Bunyan refused to listen to the devil and chose to struggle against him. Indeed, Bunyan's whole spiritual saga is an effort to silence the logic of the Tempter.[80] More defiant characters are likely to rebel, not only against God but also against goodness itself. As I will argue in Part IV, the most likely response to so much self-contempt is defiance, revolt, and the romanticization of evil.

Even if one is determined to do battle with the devil, the terror of damnation and the impending threat of doom make even good men like Bunyan cold, heartless, and indifferent. Bunyan reports being surprised to find people who were

> distressed and cast down when they met with outward losses, as of
> husband, wife, child, etc. Lord, thought I, what a do is here about such
> little things as these?[81]

He could not fathom how one could care about such trifles (as the death
of loved ones) when one's soul is damning. This obscene self-absorption
is not a frame of mind that is conducive to moral decency, let alone noble
conduct. And when Bunyan reports being "overrun in [his] soul with a
senseless heartless frame of spirit" he is not referring to his dreadful insen-
sitivity to others but merely to his inability to experience the grace and
goodness of God, which is a necessary condition of his personal salvation.[82]

Perhaps the most likely reaction to the prospect of damnation is the
one described by Augustine in his autobiography. He prayed to God to
make him chaste, but not yet.[83] What's the rush? One may as well enjoy
sin now and worry about salvation later. After all, there is plenty of time
for repentance and forgiveness. Even Jesus was partial to the penitent
sinner: "I am not sent but unto the lost sheep of the house of Israel"
(Matthew 15:24). The same partiality to the penitent sinner is the
theme of the parable of the prodigal son. The father orders an elaborate
celebration to welcome home the prodigal son who has returned after
squandering his inheritance. But there is no rejoicing over the son who
has been righteous and loyal all along. Jesus compares God to the father
in the story when he says, "there is joy in the presence of the angels of
God over one sinner that repenteth" (Luke 15:10). All this rejoicing over
repentant sinners undermines the efficacy of hell as a deterrent to crime.
It is difficult not to conclude that the moral of the story is that it is
better to sin and repent than not to sin at all.

In conclusion, it seems that the slightest degree of reflection reveals
that the doctrine of hell and damnation neither improves nor deters
sinners. On the contrary, the dread of hell results in a spiritual torpor,
helplessness, and passivity that is more conducive to moral laxity and
self-absorption than to the capacity for noble actions and the concern
for others. Besides, the centrality of hell and damnation seriously undermines Christianity's claim to being the religion of love. What kind of
love is motivated by fear of punishment or expectations for reward?
What kind of love is granted under the threat of death? Of what worth
is a love that is not freely given? What is goodness if it does not emanate
spontaneously from a pure heart? I am not suggesting that love must be
totally selfless to be of the first order. On the contrary, the best love is

one that gives pleasure to the lover as well as the beloved. If Jesus really wanted us to love God with all our heart, and to love our neighbor as ourselves, he should have resisted the temptation of turning his creed into a metaphysics of terror. In the final analysis, hell is a fiction that serves only to magnify the wanton cruelty of the Christian God. And sadly, heaven makes matters even worse.

5. Is Heaven for Sadists?

The Islamic terrorists who flew the planes into the towers of the World Trade Center in New York on September 11, 2001, believed that they would be rewarded (for their martyrdom in defense of the faith) by going straight to heaven. However misguided these terrorists were, it is nevertheless quite understandable why Muslims might go to such lengths to get to heaven. In comparison to the Christian conception of heaven, the Islamic heaven is lusty and appetizing. The elect will enter "gardens of perpetuity," and they will be dressed in silk, with bracelets of gold and pearl.[84] There will be springs gushing forth and there will be fruits, palms, and pomegranates. And there will be virgins: "goodly beautiful ones" who are untouched by either "man or jinni."[85]

In contrast to the overtly hedonistic quality of the Islamic conception of heaven, the Christian vision is not that sensual. There are no springs, palms, or pomegranates. And some believed that there will be no women in heaven; only men will be saved.[86] But Jesus made it clear that there will be women in heaven but not sex. He implies that we will have bodies in heaven.

Jesus spoke about heaven in the context of a discussion with the Sadducees. The latter asked Jesus about a woman who was married to seven different brothers consecutively. Under Levirate Law, if a married man dies before having offspring his brother is required to marry the widow. The first born that she bears counts as the dead brother's offspring, so that "his name be not put out of Israel."[87] In the example provided by the Sadducees, the first brother marries the woman and dies before having any offspring. The next one marries her to fulfill his duty but dies before having any offspring, and the next one marries her, and so on. So, all seven brothers were married to the same woman. What the Sadducees wanted to know is: whose wife will she be in heaven? (Matthew 22:23–30; Luke 20:27). To my mind, there is something suspicious about that woman, and it is a wonder that she ever gets to heaven—but no matter, the Sadducees were just trying to make a point. In response, Jesus explains that in heaven we will all be like angels and not marry.[88]

As described by Christian writers from Saint Augustine to John Milton, heaven is a reconciliation of a proportion of humanity with God. It is the willingness to live as Adam and Eve were unwilling to live. It is the acceptance of subservience and subordination to God as master. Heaven is the renunciation of the pride that led to the fall in the first place. And even though there are no gardens, fruits, or springs, there is music in heaven because most of the time is taken up in singing selfless praises to God for his justice and mercy.[89] But even the great Milton found it difficult to present the eternal life with God as something appealing. In commenting on *Paradise Lost*, William Blake observed that things get interesting only when Satan appears on the scene.[90] But if heaven seems dull, we are told that this is due only to the fact that we are so flawed and selfish that we cannot fathom the bliss of the soul in its selfless adoration of God.[91]

All this adoration of God in heaven may not be as selfless as it is reputed to be. After all, those in heaven will be exceedingly grateful that they are not in hell. And just to make sure they are grateful, heaven will have a perfect view of the torments of hell. Indeed, one of the most significant aspects of the Christian heaven is watching the torments of the damned. Jonathan Edwards describes the joys of heaven as follows:

> The sight of hell's torments will exalt the happiness of the saints forever. It will not only make them more sensible of the greatness and freeness of the grace of God in their happiness, but it will really make their happiness the greater, as it will make them more sensible of their own happiness; it will give them a more lively relish of it; it will make them prize it more. When they see others . . . plunged in such misery, and they so distinguished, O it will make them sensible how happy they are.[92]

It is difficult not to conclude that the Christian heaven is so dull that unless the elect are constantly reminded of the alternative, they cannot relish it.

There is no need to rely on radical Puritans (such as Edwards) to illustrate the sadistic pleasures of heaven. Saint Thomas Aquinas thought that watching the torments of those in hell is integral to the pleasure of being in heaven.[93] He claimed that being "allowed to see perfectly the suffering of the damned" will make the happiness of the saints "more delightful to them" and enable them to "render more copious thanks to God."[94] But will they have no pity or compassion on the damned? In responding to this question, Aquinas explains that to have pity is to share in the unhappiness of another, "but the blessed cannot share in any unhappiness. Therefore they do not pity the afflictions of the damned."[95] On the contrary, he tells us that the "blessed will rejoice in the punishment of the wicked" as a manifestation of the justice of God.[96]

Augustine also takes it for granted that witnessing the torments of hell is integral to the pleasures of heaven. The only difficulties that concern him are logistical. Exactly how will the blessed witness the torments of the damned without themselves venturing into "outer darkness"?[97] God will arrange it somehow.

It would be a mistake to assume that Augustine, Aquinas, and Edwards were being perversely inventive. On the contrary, they were relying on the authority of the Gospels. In the Gospel of Luke, Jesus tells the story of a rich man and a beggar called Lazarus. The former was clothed in purple and fine linens and fared sumptuously. But Lazarus lived off the crumbs of the rich man's table and his body was covered with open sores that were licked by dogs. When Lazarus died, he went to heaven and rested in the bosom of Abraham, but the rich man went to hell. From there, he could see Lazarus in the bosom of Abraham, and from their vantage point in heaven they could see the rich man's tortured body very clearly. So the rich man cried out to them: "Father Abraham, have mercy on me, and send Lazarus that he may dip the tip of his finger in water, and cool my tongue; for I am tormented in this flame" (Luke 16:20–31). But Abraham refused. When the rich man realized that one moment's relief would not be granted, he begged for another favor. He asked if he could go back to earth just to warn his brothers. But that favor was also denied on the grounds that they have had ample warnings from Moses and the prophets, and one more warning will be to no avail.

The story of Lazarus makes it very clear that the blessed in heaven live in full view of the torments of those in hell. Yet they have no pity or compassion toward them. On the contrary, they see their torments as the manifestation of divine justice and they rejoice. But what kind of justice is this?

There is no indication in the story that the rich man exploited Lazarus or that the rich man contributed to the poverty of Lazarus. Nor is there any indication that the rich man was in any way responsible for the sores that covered Lazarus's body or for the dogs that licked them. On the contrary, the rich man allowed Lazarus to survive on the crumbs of his table. We are told that Lazarus was a beggar who had no trade, craft, or employment, by which to support himself, and this no doubt contributed to his plight.

It seems that divine justice is not just a matter of punishing actual sins, but also reversing the fates of Lazarus and the rich man. It has its roots in the desire to compensate those who have been slighted by fortune. The effect of the story is to console the poor and unfortunate by suggesting that they will have their rewards in heaven. But what is the nature of their rewards? They are not the wholesome or lusty pleasures that Muslims associate with heaven. Apart from singing hallelujahs in praise of God for having spared them, the only significant pleasure we hear about is the pleasure of watching the damned burn in hell. But people must acquire a taste for this sadistic pleasure. It is not an ordinary pleasure that people could naturally or spontaneously enjoy—like palm trees and pomegranates.

It is not surprising that when compared to the morality of a Nazi like Himmler, philosophers have found Christian morality to be wanting.[98] Himmler was wholeheartedly devoted to the Nazi cause. But he was worried that the extermination of the Jews would destroy the moral fiber of the Germans who have embarked on this hideous task. He was worried that the SS men would become coarse and callous ruffians, caring only for themselves, and incapable of being moved by sympathy or fellow feeling. According to Himmler's physician, Himmler suffered dreadfully from stomach convulsions, nightmares, and a host of other ailments.[99] It is difficult not to conclude that Himmler was more sensitive than the Christian saints and elect of God, not to mention God and his "angels."

The Christian heaven may not have originally been intended for sadists, who enjoy tormenting others, but anyone who spends much time there, let alone an eternity, is likely to become a callous ruffian with a taste for sadistic pleasures. The Christian preoccupation with torture—endless torture—casts a dark shadow not only on the elect but also on God and his angels.

6. How Glad are the Glad Tidings?

It may be objected that I have neglected the "glad tidings." But the fact is that the good news is premised on some *very bad news*. First, all of humanity is "justly" condemned to eternal torment for the sin of Adam and Eve. Second, only very few are destined to escape this dreadful fate. And even for this elect few, salvation will prove to be a very difficult matter indeed. Third, a very high price must be paid for the few to escape the deserved torment. So, what's the good news? Supposedly, the good news is that Jesus is willing to pay the ransom for our sins by his death and crucifixion. There seems to be little reason to rejoice. Indeed, it is more plausible to describe Jesus's message as the bad tidings. This unhappy news deserves closer scrutiny.

The first assumption that Jesus makes is that all humanity is "justly" condemned for the sins of their ancestors. Of course it is not clear that we are *justly* condemned. How is it fair to condemn an innocent generation for the iniquities of their ancestors? What is so just about visiting punishment on a whole community for the sins of the few? The God of the Old Testament had a penchant for that kind of justice: "I the Lord thy God am a jealous God, visiting the iniquity of the fathers upon the children unto the third and fourth generation of them that hate me" (Exodus 20:5). Time and again we hear: "the anger of the Lord was kindled against the children of Israel" (Joshua 7:1). Time and again, the anger falls on the whole community for the transgressions of some. For example, God punishes the entire house of Ali because his sons blasphemed against God, and Ali did not restrain them (I Samuel 3:13). And he delivered Israel to her enemies because of Ashan's transgression against His covenant (Joshua 7:1–12). And he brought a famine on Israel because Saul slew the Gibeonites despite God's order to spare them (II Samuel 21:2).

Some of the Hebrew prophets, such as Jeremiah, rightly objected to this divine justice and looked forward to a new covenant in which "everyone shall die for his own iniquity" (Jeremiah 31:30). Ezekiel echoes the same principle: "The son shall not bear the iniquity of the father, neither shall the father bear the iniquity of the son: the righteousness of the righteous shall be upon him, and the wickedness of the wicked shall be upon him" (Ezekiel 18:20).

In contrast to this more equitable vision of the divine covenant within Judaism, Jesus's doctrine is regressive. Jesus takes it for granted that all mankind are justly condemned for the sins of their ancestors—Adam and Eve. His God seems much less merciful than the God of Jeremiah and Ezekiel. The bad news of original sin (the sin of our ancestors for which we are condemned) is the basis of the good news—namely, that Jesus has come to pay the penalty for our sin. He has come to bear the punishment that we supposedly deserve.

It may be objected that the original sin is our own sin and not merely the sin of Adam and Eve.[100] The story of Adam and Eve may be understood figuratively, not literally. Taken literally, the story suggests that God is unjust because he insists on punishing us merely for being the descendants of Adam and Eve—which is to say that he is not punishing us for our own sins. But taken figuratively as a true myth or as a tale with a true moral, Adam and Eve represent all of humanity. The story tells us that any man and woman in their place would behave in the same way—they would disobey God. Indeed, we do so everyday. So understood, the story is a mirror of our own conduct. Far from being condemned to suffer for the sins of our ancestors, we are being punished only for our own sins. Church fathers such as Saint Augustine defend the justice of God by maintaining that no one is innocent; we all deserve to die. God is like a creditor and we are his debtors. If he decides to forgive the debts of some, those who have to pay have no basis of complaint.

This Neo-Platonic interpretation has some validity but it fails to improve God's sense of justice. If we accept the story of Adam and Eve as a true myth, then we are still left with a dilemma. If indeed everyone pays only for his or her own sin, then why are we all condemned to eternal torment? Even if we are all sinners, and there is not a single righteous man or woman in the whole world, it does not follow that we are all sinners to the same degree.

In its wisdom, the Catholic Church invented purgatory precisely as a solution to this problem—the problem of divine justice. In other words, the doctrine of Jesus was so unpalatable that the Church had to invent something else to live by. No doubt, the inventiveness of the Church has a great deal to do with the success of Christianity. But in condemning Luther, the Church was also condemning the harsh doctrines of Jesus that Luther embraced so heroically.

Like Jesus, Luther takes it for granted that we all merit eternal damnation. Be this as it may. That is the bad news. The good news is that Jesus has come to pay the "ransom" for our sins. Now, it does not seem fair for the innocent to pay for the sins of the guilty—but that is another matter. I will return to this question in section 8. The good news is that Jesus's death will release us from our supposed bondage. Not only are we saved from the eternal torment that we supposedly deserve, we are also liberated from the yoke of the Mosaic Law and all its cumbersome demands. And all we have to do is to believe in Jesus. Luther thinks that we should rejoice at such good news. But just how good is it?

7. The Angst of Salvation

Jesus says that everyone who believes in him will not perish. Faith is the key to salvation. But it is not that simple. Not everyone who hears the word of God and who wants to believe will be able to understand it. Even the disciples fail to understand the parables. In the parable of the sower, Jesus explains to them that it is not given to everyone to understand or to believe:

> Behold, a sower went forth to sow; and when he sowed, some seeds fell by the way side, and the fowls came and devoured them up: Some fell among stony places, where they had not much earth: and forthwith they sprung up, because they had no deepness of earth: And when the sun was up, they were scorched; and because they had no root, they withered

away. And some fell among thorns; and the thorns sprang up and choked them: But others fell into good ground, and brought forth fruit . . . Who hath ears to hear let him hear. (Matthew 13:3–9)

When the disciples ask him:

Why speakest thou unto them in parables? He answered and said unto them, Because it is given unto you to know the mysteries of the kingdom of heaven, but to them it is not given . . . Therefore speak I to them in parables: because they seeing see not; and hearing, they hear not, neither do they understand . . . But blessed are your eyes, for they see: and your ears, for they hear. (Matthew 13:10–16; also Luke 8:5–15; and Mark 4:3–20)

How can such an esoteric doctrine constitute happy news for all humanity? When Jesus explains the meaning of the parable to the disciples it becomes clear that the gladness of the glad tidings is highly overrated. The seeds are the word of God. The seeds that fall by the wayside represent those who hear the word of God but don't understand it because the devil comes along and plucks it out of their heart immediately. The seeds that fall on stony ground represent those who receive the word with joy but have no depth, so it can't take root, and at the first sign of persecution or trouble, they are no longer believers. And the seeds that fall among thorns represent those who are so preoccupied with the cares of this world that the word of God is choked out. But the seeds that fall on good ground represent those who hear and understand the word of God (Matthew 13:18–23). What is clear is that this is not a doctrine intended for humanity as a whole. It is very exclusive.

On another occasion, Jesus maintains that some people are congenitally incapable of understanding or believing him because they are children of the devil. It seems that some people are of the devil and others are of God:

Why do ye not understand my speech? *even* because ye cannot hear my word. Ye are of your father the devil, and the lusts of your father ye will do. He was a murderer from the beginning, and abode not in the truth, because there is no truth in him. When he speaketh a lie, he speaketh of his own: for he is a liar, and the father of it. And because I tell you the truth, ye believe me not . . . He that is of God heareth God's words: ye therefore hear them not, because ye are not of God. (John 8:43–47)

This flies in the face of the commonly held belief that Christianity is the religion of the universal brotherhood of man. The latter is premised on the belief that we are all the children of God; but this assumption is clearly contradicted by Jesus. All of us are not the children of God; some of us are the children of the devil and are predisposed to do the devil's bidding.

Another question remains: are we free to choose to be the children of God or the children of the devil? Jesus answers this question in the negative when he says:

> No man can come to me, except the Father which has sent me draw him: and I will raise him up at the last day. (John 6:44)

Saint Paul echoes the same view. He is convinced that salvation is through faith and that faith is itself a gift—our merits have nothing to do with being "God's elect." Indeed, Paul believes that election happens before birth or before we have done any good or evil (Romans 8:11; Romans 9:32). Realizing the harshness of this doctrine, Paul asks the obvious question: is God unrighteous? But the question makes him shudder. So he quickly says "God forbid" then adds: "For he saith to Moses, I will have mercy on whom I will have mercy, and I will have compassion on whom I will have compassion" (Romans 9:15). But quoting Moses is clearly no help.

If the choice between God and the devil is not ours to make, and there is nothing that we can do to avoid damnation or to secure salvation, then salvation must be an unmerited gift. And since no one is entitled to this gift, no one can complain about not receiving it. This raises the obvious question: to whom is this precious gift of understanding and hence salvation given? And is it bestowed on the few or the many? The disciples confront Jesus about this very issue:

> Lord, are there few that be saved? And he said unto them, Strive to enter at the strait gate: for many, I say unto you, will seek to enter in, and shall not be able. When once the master of the house is risen up, and hath shut to the door, and ye begin to stand without, and to knock at the door, saying, Lord, Lord, open unto us; and he shall answer and say unto you, I know you not whence ye are: Then shall ye begin to say, We have eaten and drunk in thy presence, and thou hast taught in our streets. But he shall say, I tell you, I know you not whence ye are; depart from me, all ye workers of iniquity. There shall be weeping and gnashing of teeth, when ye shall see Abraham, and Isaac, and Jacob, and all the prophets, in the kingdom of God, and you yourselves thrust out. (Luke 13:23–28)

And again Jesus says, "many are called, but few are chosen" (Mathew 22:14). Paul echoes the same view when he says: "Though the number of the children of Israel be as the sand of the sea, a *remnant* shall be saved" (Romans 9:27, my italics).

It is a mystery why the God of the New Testament is not more merciful and less inscrutable. The God of the Old Testament was better—less inscrutable *and* more merciful. He was a God that human beings could understand. He punished the children of Israel for their transgressions and not for doctrinal errors of belief. His wrath was kindled against Israel for misconduct or wrongdoing: "all that do unrighteously, are an abomination unto the Lord thy God" (Deuteronomy 25:16). If he was not merciful, that was usually because his people have not been faithful in worshipping him to the exclusion of all others or because they did not abide by His Law as well as they should. In the Old Testament, sins are actions, not beliefs. In contrast, the New Testament makes abiding by the Law secondary to believing in Jesus. And when believing in him is itself a gift of grace, we get a picture of a very remote, arbitrary, and inscrutable God who is also beyond reproach.

In the Old Testament, when God decided to destroy Sodom and Gomorrah, Abraham admonished him saying that he should not destroy the righteous with the wicked. He flattered God by saying that it is not fitting for God to behave that way. After all, "Shall not the Judge of all the earth do right?" (Genesis 18:25). God challenges him to find fifty righteous people, and He will spare the whole city for their sake. But Abraham bargains and brings God down to ten. But since ten righteous people could not be found, the city is destroyed:—however, Abraham's nephew, Lot, and his two daughters are spared. But the God of the New Testament is more remote and more inscrutable. No one can imagine bargaining with Him, let alone shaming Him by flattery into behaving better than He would have otherwise.

The simple reason for this difference is that Christians insist on both the absolute goodness of God as well as His complete omnipotence. But the goodness of God cannot be reconciled with His omnipotence. Job tries to accomplish this reconciliation, but in the end he admits that it is impossible.[101] The two come into conflict. Either He is good or He is omnipotent. The two can be maintained simultaneously only through obfuscation. God must be shrouded in mystery—His goodness must be deemed incomprehensible to the human intellect. Human rationality must be suspended in favor of blind faith in God's inscrutable ways.

Jesus leads the way. He acknowledges that his message contains much that is mysterious and incomprehensible. But he also promises to uncover all the mystery in the fullness of time: "For there is nothing covered that shall not be revealed; neither hid, that shall not be known" (Luke 12:2; Luke 8:17). Meanwhile, we have to accept and believe without understanding. Jesus requires mindless, devoted, zealous, and unquestioning disciples. The analogy of the shepherd (himself) and his sheep (the believers) is appropriate (John 10:11). Equally appropriate is the analogy of likening believers to little children: "except ye be converted, and become as little children, ye shall not enter into the kingdom of heaven" (Mathew 18:3; Mark 10:15). Sheepish conformity and unquestioning obedience are identified with the meek and good whose reward will be in heaven. In contrast, intelligent skepticism is met with threats of eternal damnation.

The God of the New Testament is not only more remote and inscrutable, he is also less merciful than the God of the Old Testament. When we discover that all but a few are destined for damnation for the sins of Adam and Eve, we must surmise that this is not a God of mercy, love, or forgiveness. He has condemned humanity to eternal torment for the sins of their ancestors. And there is nothing we can do to appease His wrath. He will have mercy on whom he will have mercy. And Jesus tells us that very few will be saved:

> Enter ye in at the strait gate: for wide is the gate, and broad is the way, that leadeth to destruction, and many there be which go in thereat: Because strait is the gate, and narrow is the way, which leadeth unto life, and few there be that find it. (Matthew 7:13–14)

It seems that the strait gate is so elusive that very few will find it. And even those who knew Jesus and followed him may be shut out. Maybe they did not understand him properly or maybe the devil snatched the word of God from their heart. Even the "very elect" may be deceived by "false prophets" who will come in "sheep's clothing" and whose message and works will sound alarmingly like the real thing. For they will prophesy in the name of Jesus, cast out devils in his name, cleanse lepers in his name, and do many other wonderful miracles, just as Jesus did (Matthew 7:15–22; Matthew 24:24; Mark 13:6).

If all our efforts to follow Jesus are in vain; if we are doomed to be confounded by devils and deceived by false prophets, then how can we be held responsible for our lack of understanding? Or for our iniquity? Or for our fate? When Jesus was dying on the cross, he said to God: "Father, forgive them; for they know not what they do" (Luke 23:34). Did he finally realize the injustice of it all?

The picture that emerges is one of a full-fledged metaphysics of terror that has inspired great literature and great angst in the history of

Western civilization. How will God choose the few who will be saved? Is there nothing one can do to merit election? Does election have anything to do with one's merits, good works, faith, or repentance? Why are some the lucky recipients of God's grace while others are not? Where is the justice in that?

Sigmund Freud thought that the appeal of religion lies in human insecurity and the desire for protection from the violence and unpredictability of nature. Religion supposedly replaces the lost protection of an earthly father with the protection of a more powerful heavenly father.[102] In other words, religion is a childish instinct that humanity will eventually outgrow. But the Freudian view cannot account for the terrifying specter of Christian metaphysics. Christianity does not create a comforting vision of existence, but quite the reverse. What emerges is a harsh, inscrutable, and arbitrary God, who is not so much a source of comfort but of angst.

John Bunyan's *The Pilgrim's Progress* is a classic depiction of Christian anxiety over salvation.[103] This is a story of men who are mere pilgrims in this world—they abandon mother, father, wife, and children to embark on a solitary journey to the Celestial City. They are in flight from the City of Destruction and the perdition to which the rest of humanity is destined. Bunyan presents a most unflattering picture of humanity "in bondage to sin." It is a story about men who are not free. It is not a story about men who are in a position to choose between good and evil. It is not a depiction of humanity reveling in wanton, loose, and carnal pleasures out of choice. It is not a story about men who are undone by their own iniquity and who deserve their terrible fate. The story is much more tragic. It is the story of men who, contrary to their best judgments and their deepest yearnings are wedded to their wicked ways, and therefore are destined for perdition.

The most tragic figures in Bunyan's tale are the ones who have been converted and no longer revel in their sinfulness, but are filled with self-loathing. And despite their best efforts, they cannot transcend their bondage to sin. There is absolutely nothing they can do to transcend their own iniquity. The pilgrims—Christian, Hopeful, and Faithful—are totally at the mercy of God's grace for their salvation. But this is not to say that the pilgrims sit around and do nothing. They are in a constant state of angst. Their journey is arduous; their faith is constantly being tested; and the obstacles in their path are staggering.

In Bunyan's story, a character whose name is Ignorance makes some excellent objections to the cosmic vision of the pilgrims. His objections are reminiscent of the objections that Pelagius made against Augustine.[104]

But the pilgrims think him ignorant. Yet, his dreadful fate in the story is the best argument against this terrorist metaphysics. His terrible fate reveals the cruelty of the pilgrim's God. Indeed, it is a serious indictment of His justice as well as His goodness.

Ignorance is a good man who strives for the Celestial City just as hard as Christian and Hopeful. But he has a serious theological difference with them. He believes that his conversion to Christianity allows him to be righteous, and that Jesus will plead on his behalf to make his actions acceptable to God. His interpretation of the Gospels is sunny. He believes that as a result of the Fall, we are in bondage to sin; but through faith in Christ, we are born again, released from our bondage, and free once again to choose between righteousness and iniquity.[105]

In contrast, Christian is convinced that it is not our righteousness that assures us a place in heaven but it is Christ's righteousness. In this way, Christian gets himself tangled in the usual puzzle. Are our actions irrelevant to our salvation? And if so, on what grounds does God save some but not others? Augustine's answer is that we are all equally deserving of death. God can do what he wants. He is the creditor and we have no reason to complain if the debts of others are wiped out. The idea of meriting salvation is out of the question, Ignorance must be rebuked.

Nevertheless, implicit in Bunyan's tale is that Christian and Hopeful somehow *deserve* their election because of the strength of their faith against the most formidable obstacles. There is only one way to reach salvation, and that is filled with terrors, traps, trials, snares, and monumental difficulties. At every turn the pilgrims encounter monsters, such as Pagan and Pope who dwell in the cave, Lord Lecherous, Mr. Liar, Mr. Turn-coat, Mr. Worldly-wiseman, and other "workers of iniquity." The pilgrims must make their way to God out of a world peopled with rogues and scoundrels whose supreme preoccupation is to cheat and deceive the pilgrims, ridicule them, pillory them, and fill them with gnawing doubt. Their torments are so formidable that they can only pray to God to deliver them from the next "uncircumcised philistine."

Reaching the Celestial City is not easy. And that is fair enough. But as Bunyan admits, Christian and Hopeful come to a point in their journey where there are two equally straight roads, and they are puzzled as to which is the right one. It seems to me that if their God was rational, just, and good, He would accept both roads as equally right and make sure that they both lead to the Gates of the Celestial City. But this is not the case. Ignorance chose one of the straight roads, but clearly it was the "wrong" road. Even though he took no shortcuts and made the same arduous journey as Christian, he was not granted admission into the Gates of the Celestial City. Not only was he turned away, he was led directly to Hell from a hidden gate that is alarmingly close to the gates of the Celestial City.[106] The message is that there is a route directly to Hell, even from the gates of Heaven. This means that there is only *one* right way to arrive at the gates of the Celestial City, and it is not the way that Ignorance chose to take. Bunyan implies that his ignorance rests in his pride, which consists in taking credit for his righteousness. But as we have seen, Ignorance humbly asks Christ to plead on his behalf so that his righteous deeds are accepted. This hardly qualifies as arrogance. Besides, what is so irrational about wanting his good deeds accepted? It seems that Ignorance is cast out because he is not groveling and self-loathing enough to satisfy God. Clearly, this is a God who loves mindless sycophants. In a Heaven lined with gold, He struts around with a great deal of pomp and ceremony—trumpets blazing and worshipers singing His praises. His contempt for His creatures is so great that even their righteousness "stinks in his nostrils."[107]

We find the same contempt for righteousness in Bunyan's autobiography. He recounts a significant spiritual experience of hearing the poor women of Bedford conversing among themselves about God and His effect on their spirit and His warning against the temptations of Satan. Supreme among these temptations is the temptation to cherish righteousness. On the contrary, the women of Bedford taught him that spiritual rebirth presupposed recognition of one's own wretchedness of heart, and contempt and abhorrence of one's own righteousness "as filthy, and insufficient" to be of any use.[108]

Jonathan Edwards also shows the same contempt for righteousness. He rails against the "legal spirit" that leads men to trust their own righteousness or to think that righteousness is the route to heaven. Such men are fools who think that they have something of their own that would make them shine in the sight of God. These "poor deluded wretches" are nothing but "a smoke in his nose, and are many of them more odious to him, than the most impure beast in Sodom."[109] These people are on "the high road to hell."[110]

Edwards makes it clear that the elect are not chosen for their righteousness but simply out of the sheer mercy of God:

> When they shall see how great the misery is from which God hath saved them, and how great a difference he hath made between their state, and the state of others, who were by nature, and perhaps by practice, no more sinful and ill deserving than they, it will give them a sense of the wonderfulness of God's grace to them.[111]

There may be *absolutely no moral difference* between the saved and the damned. Far from impressing us with the grace of God, Edwards paints a picture that makes God seem cruel, arbitrary, and inscrutable.

Wittingly or unwittingly, Jesus, Luther, Bunyan, and Edwards provide a portrait of a wrathful, unjust, cruel, and capricious God. He is revolted by sinful humanity, but he is unwilling to take any responsibility for the evils of his creation. He blames humanity. But how responsible for wickedness is a humanity that is "in bondage to sin"? Is it fair to punish men who so desperately wish to be good but are not free to act according to their own best desires, even when these desires are stronger than all competing desires? How can such men be condemned to death? Where is the justice of God?

Besides his wrath and injustice toward humanity at large, this God is particularly cruel to those who love and believe in him. Despite all the anguish, risks, temptations, and suffering they endure for their God, Christian, Faithful, and Hopeful, are the models of anxiety. They have no idea if they will be favorably received. Moreover, their God expects those who love and believe in him to accept His righteousness and mercy on faith. And He is continually tormenting his chosen ones just to test their faith—to see if they will curse him. We saw that Bunyan was himself overwhelmed by an irresistible urge to blaspheme. And now we know why.

The view that Christianity offers a kinder, gentler God than was found in the Old Testament is not supported by evidence. The wrath of the Christian God is manifest in the eternal torment to which He will condemn most of humanity, including many who believe in Him. The view that Christianity has replaced the capricious and arbitrary gods of paganism with a rational and just God is also unsupported by the evidence. The capriciousness of the Christian God where salvation is concerned is the source of the angst that has come to define Western civilization from Saint Paul to Heidegger.

8. The Ransom for Sin

All this bad news does not obliterate the loving sacrifice that defines Jesus—namely his willingness to suffer and die in our place. Jesus tells us that his death and torment on the cross is necessary to pay the "ransom" for our sins (Mathew 20:28). This is no doubt a beautiful gesture. But why is this sacrifice necessary? Who demands this dreadful ransom? Who is holding us hostage? And to whom is the ransom to be paid? Are we hostages of Satan? And is the ransom to be paid to the devil? Or is the ransom to be paid to God? Jesus does not say. But in the history of Christian doctrine, both views have been suggested.

Early Church fathers such as Irenaeus, Origen, and Gregory of Nyssa believed that the ransom was paid to the devil. Having fallen prey to the temptations of Satan, we have become enslaved to him. The fall was comparable to selling ourselves into slavery of our own free will. It was from this self-inflicted state of bondage that God intends to deliver us. But that was not an easy matter. Satan demanded the blood of Christ in exchange for releasing us from our captivity. According to Origen of Alexandria (185–254), the blood of Christ "was so precious that it alone would suffice for the redemption of all."[112] The atonement was an unfathomable action on the part of God to save us from our bondage and bring us back to Him—bring us home. Jesus comes to rescue us from sin, death, and the devil. His mission is to restore the original creation and reconcile us with God. Jesus could have defeated Satan in a violent struggle but He did not. Instead, he chose to pay the ransom money to win our lawful freedom.

Origen thought that God tricked Satan.[113] He let him think that he could have the soul of Christ in exchange for the souls of humankind. Satan agreed, but did not realize that he could not hang on to the sinless soul of Christ, and as a result, Satan was defeated and his sovereignty over mankind was ended.[114] The atonement was understood as a drama of the soul in its experience of unfathomable divine love.

This interpretation has unmistakable appeal. It makes the Christian God seem less remote, vengeful, and autocratic. It sets Christianity apart from other monotheistic religions by identifying God with His love and immediacy. God is experienced as a savior, rescuing us from a nightmare of our own making. There is an intimate, almost romantic relation between God and the soul.

This interpretation of Christianity has had some influence on the Eastern Church, but it has been largely ignored in the West.[115] One reason that the Western Church was reluctant to endorse it is that it takes the devil seriously, and therefore might open the door to dualism. But the Western Church was determined to avoid the slightest hint of dualism for fear of compromising the omnipotence of God. Saint Anselm and St. Thomas Aquinas vigorously opposed the idea that the ransom is paid to the devil. They denied that Satan had any claim. But unfortunately, their efforts have entangled God in infamy.

According to Aquinas, God requires the ransom for His "satisfaction."[116] He is in charge; He is omnipotent. Aquinas concedes that God could have forgiven our sins without any ransom, and that this would not have been contrary to His justice.[117] Instead, God the Father delivered his own son to pay for our sins.[118] And Aquinas believes that it was proper and fitting that Christ should die to "atone for the sin of our first parent."[119] With the disobedience of one man (Adam), all humanity was condemned and estranged from God. With the obedience of one man (Jesus), all humanity is reconciled to God. By his obedience—obedience unto death—Jesus pays the penalty for the sons and daughters of Adam, and makes their deliverance from eternal damnation possible.

To those who rightly objected that the innocent should not pay for the sins of the guilty but that the guilty should atone for their own sins, Aquinas responded: "He properly atones for an offense who offers something which the offended one loves equally, or even more than he detested the offense."[120] What is Jesus offering God that the latter loves more than he detests the offense? It can only be the suffering of His son on the cross. The implication is that God enjoyed the torture of his own son enough to cancel the sins of humanity. And in response to the very sensible objection that it was a "wicked and cruel act to hand over an innocent man to torment and death," Aquinas gives an equally poor response. He says that God "would not remit sins without penalty," and that no penalty that man could endure could "pay Him enough satisfaction."[121] It is difficult not to conclude that God gets more "satisfaction" from the torment of his own son than from the suffering of others.

The only sunny part of Aquinas's story is that the atonement of Christ was "sufficient and superabundant satisfaction for the sins of the whole human race."[122] This view is in marked contrast to the view of Augustine, Luther, Bunyan, and others that only a small portion of humanity is saved, because the mass of sin in the world is so great that even the precious blood of Christ is not enough to pay the ransom for all humanity.

Even though it is more charitable than Augustine's, Aquinas's juridical interpretation of the atonement involves two problematic principles. First, sins have a price that must be paid in suffering, self-abnegation, and self-mortification. Second, it is possible for the innocent to (willingly) pay the penalty for the guilty. The two principles were integral to the medieval system of penances and indulgences respectively. The penitential system involved elaborate catalogues of sins with the appropriate penance attached. One year on bread and water was not unusual as a penalty for fornication between consenting unmarried adults. Adultery was likely to be seven years on bread and water.[123] It is easy to see why sinners would be eager to avail themselves of some means of alleviating these temporal punishments. And this is where indulgences came to the rescue. Because the atonement of Christ for original sin was not only sufficient but "superabundant," the Church claimed to have at its disposal a "Treasury" that consisted of what was left over from the atonement of Christ as well as what was left over from the self-mortifications of the saints after they had finished paying for their own sins. This Treasury was clearly overflowing with riches, which the Church was generously willing to sell at a price. Indulgences did not wipe out the sin but they reduced the penalties dramatically.[124]

The idea that pain and torment are pleasing to God as a means of atoning for sin explains the prevalence of self-flagellations in the monastic orders of the Middle Ages (such as the early Franciscans), as well as the contagious outbreaks of penitential scourging in the population at large. The Brotherhood of the Cross (1349) is the most extreme version of the movement.[125] Stripped to the waist, members of the Brotherhood lashed themselves using scourges made of leather with iron tips that imbedded in the skin. They believed that their blood would mingle with the blood of Christ—the blood of salvation. In thirty days of lashing themselves twice a day, they could cleanse their soul of sin. The Church made every effort to suppress this fanatical mania that spread throughout Christendom.[126] But it must be admitted that the movement was a logical consequence of the medieval account of the atonement.[127]

With all his philosophical might, Aquinas was not able to paint the Passion of Christ in a better light. Unwittingly, he made God into a monstrous, bloodthirsty deity who delights in human agony and suffering—an omnipotent God who condemns all humanity to eternal torment for the sins of their ancestors. This is the "justice" that requires "satisfaction." He alone demands the ransom for sin. He alone insists on the death and torment of His son.

From this perspective, Christianity has failed to replace the hostile gods of primitive or pagan religion with a benevolent or loving God. A God who insists on eternal torment for the sins of our ancestors is neither loving nor just.[128] A God who insists on *eternal* punishment is neither good nor merciful. Why must humanity be eternally tormented? Surely, no justice requires that.

When compared to primitive men who practice human sacrifices, the God of Christian orthodoxy fares badly. In primitive tribes, a king sacrifices his firstborn to appease hostile gods; he accepts a personal tragedy in order to avoid an even greater calamity for his people—drought, famine, or plague. When Agamemnon sacrificed his daughter Iphigenia, he did not have his own "satisfaction" in mind. The gods forced him to choose between his daughter and the favorable winds that would ensure the success of the Greek expedition against Troy. The fact that Iphigenia was willing to sacrifice herself for the greater cause did not ameliorate her father's dreadful plight. He acted only under compulsion. He accepted a terrible personal fate for the sake of Greece. In contrast, the Christian God is not compelled. The decision to sacrifice His son is gratuitous. It is therefore difficult to avoid the conclusion that He traded the pleasure of tormenting a small proportion of humanity for the pleasure of witnessing the torment of His own son.[129] Such a God can hardly count as an improvement on the gods of pagan antiquity.

Christianity prides itself on its allegedly superior conception of God as good, just, and merciful. It contrasts its benevolent God to the capricious and wrathful God of the Old Testament as well as to the morally crude gods of paganism. Christianity claims to replace the hostile gods of antiquity with a loving, merciful, and benevolent God—a God of love and forgiveness. But these claims do not bear up in the face of the evidence. The orthodox interpretation of the doctrine of the atonement underscores the belief in a universe governed by hostile forces.

It may be objected that the Father and the Son are one and the same, and that it is God who sacrificed himself for humanity. But it is difficult for Aquinas to fall back on the Incarnation to save his God from infamy. After all, the Incarnation plays no significant role in his account of the atonement. On the contrary, Jesus is treated as the new man whose obedience replaced Adam's disobedience. It was as a man that Jesus makes amends on behalf of mankind.[130] Besides, the identity of Father and Son is not believable. The Father seems terrible but the Son appears to be the incarnation of love, forgiveness, and self-sacrifice. He is willing to pay the ransom for our sins—the ransom on which his Father insists.[131] The two seem very different indeed. This was also Arius's point.

It may well be that the mystical union of Father and Son is the secret strength of Christianity. It has the effect of concealing the harshness of the Christian God. The Father hides behind the Son, and the Son hides behind the Father. The Father conceals His cruel nature by his identity with the loving Son. By the same token, the Son conceals his intolerance, his autocratic character, and his vengefulness by claiming to be merely the messenger of his Father in heaven. The identity of Father and Son explains the two-facedness of Christianity. Christians come to power by claiming to represent the Son, but once in power, they act like the Father.[132]

In its effort to defend the goodness of God, the Church has generally found refuge in obscurantism. It has relied on the mystery and inscrutability of God. It has argued that the human mind cannot grasp the mystery of the creator. What seems cruel and wicked to us will in the fullness of time be revealed to be part of God's grand plan, which is good and just. Jesus made similar claims in the Gospels. He bid his disciples to believe, even if they could not understand, and he promised to reveal everything that has been "kept secret from the foundation of the world" (Mathew 13:35). "For nothing is secret, that shall not be made manifest; neither *any thing* hid, that shall not be known and come aboard" (Luke 8:17; Luke 12:2). Jesus also promised that the suspense will not last too long; he promised that "this generation shall not pass away, till all be fulfilled" (Luke 21:32). But this has turned out to be false. The world did not come to an end as anticipated and the mysteries have not been cleared up but have been extended indefinitely. But so much mystery and obscurity is positively harmful. It does not succeed in making God's goodness transparent. A God that does cruel and wicked things that will somehow lead to good consequences sets a bad example. And people eventually imitate their God.

9. Conclusion

If we look at our sacred texts impartially as outsiders, the picture is utterly terrifying. We see a religion with a fiendish understanding of reality. We find ourselves in a world where we have all been condemned to eternal torment merely for being the descendants of Adam and Eve and there is no way by which we can win our salvation. We are subject to a God who alone decides our fate according to criteria that are utterly incomprehensible. We find ourselves in a world where demons pluck the word of God out of the hearts of those who want to hear it. Even the "very elect" are subject to the perils of false prophets who deceive them and rob them of eternal life. And many of those who think that they have lived righteously (and have done everything that they could to secure their salvation) find themselves shut out. No wonder there is so much "wailing and gnashing of teeth." And in the end, the mass of humanity is damned to eternal torment, while the elect sit on the right hand of their God and join him in the sadistic pleasure of witnessing the eternal torments of humanity. It is not clear why any of this is good news.

Contrary to what Garry Wills and other apologists believe, there is nothing pluralistic, tolerant, modest, or moderate about Christianity or its founder.[133] Apologists cannot resort to an original, pristine, or untarnished Christianity. If there is a pristine, untarnished Christianity it belongs to

Jesus as portrayed in the Gospels. But an impartial examination reveals that the religion of Jesus, like Jesus himself, is neither moderate nor tolerant. Those who deny that Christianity is as dark as I have made it out to be must face the fact that these texts are integral components of Christianity. They are not the invention of Saint Paul, Augustine, Luther, or Calvin; they have their source in the sayings of Jesus as presented in the four Gospels. Those who try to represent Christianity in ways that do not entail these distasteful elements have to face the fact that these doctrines are not just the embellishments of zealous believers but are integral components of the sacred texts.

My argument is directed not only at Christian apologists but also at the critics of Christianity. Even the most vociferous critics assume that the religion of Jesus was dramatically perverted by his followers. They exempt Jesus from their censure and attribute all the defects of Christianity to the Church, to Saint Paul, or to Augustine. My point is that the harshest doctrines of Paul, Augustine, Aquinas, Luther, Calvin, Milton, Bunyan, Edwards, and others have their origins in what Jesus is reputed to have said in the Gospels.

The immodesty, intolerance, and vindictiveness of Jesus's words cannot be separated from the barbarous history of the Church and its long record of persecution—of Jews, Moslems, heretics, scientists, women, and freethinkers. And why would Jesus expect something better? How can his doctrine be institutionalized without creating something monstrous? How can it be politicized without inviting disaster?

PART II
POLITICS OF TERROR

The Christian approach to politics has been championed in the twentieth century for its modesty and moderation. Supposedly, it has the merit of forcing us to face the fact that human beings are wicked, and therefore, coercive measures are necessary to bridle evil and give humanity a modest peace. Christianity, the argument goes, presents us with the harsh truth, free of illusions. Consequently, it eschews utopian schemes as fantasies that wreak havoc on the world because they attempt to achieve the impossible. In light of our flawed humanity, Christianity counsels us to lower our expectations of politics, eschew radical politics, resign ourselves to the injustices of the world, and aspire only to what is humanly possible. Politics can provide peace and order to a wicked world but it cannot create heaven on earth nor can it provide salvation. Only Christ can save us. In light of the murderous utopian idealism of the twentieth century, this sober message has its appeal.

Saint Augustine has provided the classic version of this politics of resignation. In section 1, "Treachery with a Clear Conscience," I argue that the politics of resignation is not as sober as it appears. On the contrary, it is an active and energetic complicity in the evils of the world. And without being uncharitable, I describe it as an invitation to treachery with a clear conscience.

In our time, a modern Augustinian has defended the politics of resignation as a remedy for the radical utopian politics of the twentieth century. In section 2, "Augustinian Chic," I show why Eric Voegelin's stylish version of the theory is not an improvement on Augustine's. Even though Voegelin sings the praises of resignation to the evils of the world, he is not willing to resign himself to the evils of liberalism—*these* must be eliminated. So, which evils are Christians resigned to, and which are they determined to overcome? I am inclined to think that Christians are resigned to the world only when it is dreadfully wicked. They become militant when the world seems free and life is easy.

It is important not to confuse the politics of resignation with political realism. In my view, political realism is flawed but is not unreasonable. What concerns me is the effect that Christian theology has on political realism. In section 3, "Political Realism with a Twist," I argue that Christianity makes political realism a much bleaker doctrine than its secular incarnation requires. Realism in general is an effort to live in the face of reality without illusions. But what is the reality to which Christianity hopes to reconcile us? And, is resignation to tyranny and injustice an appropriate political posture?

I will argue that Christians are too arrogant to be resigned. Section 4, "Christian Arrogance," examines the losing battle against pride. Despite all their efforts to overcome pride, Christians succumb to a brand of arrogance that is truly extravagant. Resignation is a convenient posture only when they are powerless, but when in power, Christian resignation turns to militancy. Section 5, "Christian Militancy," shows how the possession of the one and only truth necessary for salvation, invites a militant, aggressive, and violent approach to politics.

Resignation and militancy have long been recognized as the twin pillars of Christian politics. It is tempting to think that this contradiction mirrors the contrast between God the Son and God the Father. While the Son represents love, forgiveness, meekness, resignation, and surrender, the Father represents power, authority, wrath, retribution, and justice. Christians use the rhetoric of the Son when they are politically powerless. But once in power, their rhetoric and conduct assumes the harsh and autocratic tendencies of the Father. Nothing succeeds like contradiction. Just as the severity of the Father is hidden behind the gentleness of the Son, so the posture of humble resignation conceals the militant spirit.

There is much truth in this view of Christian politics. But on closer examination, the Son is as harsh and as autocratic as his father. By the same token, resignation and militancy are not as opposed as they appear. The goals of both policies are the same—they are merely different means (suited to diverse circumstances) to achieve the same ends. They delight in the same harsh and oppressive reality. Only the latter can keep humanity cognizant of its need for redemption.

In section 6, "Against Christianity in Politics," I summarize the reasons for my opposition to the involvement of Christianity in politics.

1. Treachery with a Clear Conscience

At the heart of early Christian thought is a dualism between the sacred and the profane worlds—Augustine referred to these domains as the heavenly and the earthly city, the City of God and the City of Man. True justice, peace, love, and community are possible only in the heavenly city. The mundane world in which we live, the world in which politics is relevant, is fallen and flawed. It is not capable of peace, love, or justice.[1] No effort on our part can bring it in line with God's moral requirements.

As a powerless and persecuted sect in Rome, Christians could wash their hands of this world and await divine redemption in the next. But when Christians found themselves in positions of power and influence, they were in desperate need for a political philosophy. This seemed like a brilliant opportunity for Christians to humanize the world and prove their love for humanity and for justice. But instead of inspiring Christians with the spirit of social justice, Augustine assured them that they have no moral obligations to improve the world or make it more just. On the contrary, he declared that they must resign themselves to the ways of the world.

This politics of resignation is best illustrated in Augustine's advice to a Christian judge who is confronted with the Roman practice of torturing witnesses and criminal suspects in courts of law to make them confess "the truth." What could a Christian judge do about such abominable practices? How should a Christian judge behave? How can he use his power and his influence? This was a new experience for Christians, and they needed advice on how to handle their newly acquired powers.

Far from opposing these abhorrent practices, Augustine maintained that these evils were integral components of the temporal order. And Christians need not meddle with or try to change these evils, even when they have the power to do so. The rationale is that Christians are not part of the earthly city, but merely pilgrims, strangers, and sojourners in this world. So, it is not their duty to right the wrongs of this world; besides, it is impossible to right the wrongs of the world, even if they wanted to. The only sensible thing to do is to resign themselves to the evils of the world. Augustine argued that a righteous and godly judge, in a position of power, need not make any effort to discontinue these terrible Roman practices. On the contrary, Augustine insisted that a good and wise judge need not shrink from the darkness in which human society is necessarily shrouded. As Augustine wrote, the wise and godly ruler

> . . . thinks it no wickedness that innocent witnesses are tortured . . . or that the accused are put to the torture, so that they are often overcome with anguish, and, though innocent, make false confessions regarding themselves, and are punished; or though they be not condemned to die,

they often die during, or in consequence of, the torture; . . . These numerous and important evils he does not consider sins; for the wise judge does these things not with the intention of doing harm . . . he is compelled to torture and punish the innocent because his office and his ignorance constrain him.[2]

It may be argued that this understanding of Christianity leaves the world unchanged; it leaves the world as it found it, and that this is as it should be. Christianity does not promise to remake the world, bring heaven down to earth, or accomplish the impossible, because it is fully cognizant of the imperfections of man. But this argument is not persuasive. The example reveals something else.

My point is not that the moral ideals and principles of Christianity are so remote that they leave the world exactly as they found it. My point is that Christian principles lower the standards of morality in politics. By perverting natural human decency, they leave the world a much worse place than it was before the advent of Christian high-mindedness. In the absence of Christianity, a pagan man of decency may come to power now and again and temporarily provide relief from the usual abominations. But with Augustinian Christians in power, no such relief is to be expected.

The otherworldliness of Augustine's Christian principles allows him to make drastic compromises with ordinary standards of justice and decency. Such an understanding of Christianity not only undermines virtue, it invites depravity. I contend that it is the sort of picture of Christian piety that inflames the anticlerical imagination—from Lessing's Patriarch of Jerusalem to Dostoevsky's Grand Inquisitor.[3]

Augustine's political philosophy is often compared with Machiavelli's, but to my mind there is a very significant difference. Machiavelli believed that the moral standards that apply to private life do not apply to politics. In politics, the preservation of the state is the only good. This supreme end justifies the employment of whatever means are necessary. This is why Machiavelli maintained that a prince may have to do many evil and despicable things for the sake of his country, so he had better be a man who loves his country more than his soul; for the sorts of things he must do will surely compromise the purity of his soul and his chances for salvation. In contrast, Augustine's godly ruler is in the enviable position of not having to choose between his country and his soul. Nor does Augustine even pretend that the evils involved are necessary for maintaining order in a sinful world. Augustine assures the godly ruler that the necessary, as well as the not so necessary evils that he performs in his line of duty, are not wicked. I am not suggesting that Augustine's godly ruler is a Machiavellian prince—he is much more loathsome. The evils he commands are unnecessary; and even if they were necessary evils, Augustine's godly ruler would still be a ghastly spectacle—a Machiavellian prince with a clear conscience!

One thing is undeniable: the rule of the godly is much more grotesque than that of the godless. With his eyes set on heaven, the godly ruler has little use for this world. Indeed, the more grisly the world gets, the more he likes it because it is more in need of salvation. Besides, in the face of so much devastation, faith in a good and just God is truly heroic.

It is generally believed that the radical transcendence of God (and of the good) drains Christianity of all earthly significance and makes its adherents nihilistic and indifferent to the world. Supposedly, they leave the world as they found it. But this is not the case. The politics of resignation is an active and malevolent complicity with the evils of the world. It does not leave the world as it found it—but makes a definite contribution to injustice. By silencing the natural pangs of conscience, it makes human beings more wicked than nature intended. It is therefore nothing less than an invitation to treachery.

2. Augustinian Chic

It would be a mistake to assume that Augustinian politics is a thing of the past and has no contemporary relevance. The Christian rhetoric of resignation is always appealing in times when human beings despair of politics. And there is no doubt that politics in the twentieth century has inspired despair.

Although intellectually murky, and not particularly well known, modern day Augustinian and German émigré, Eric Voegelin, has a devoted following among Christian intellectuals who are disenchanted with modern secular society. Although Voegelin's message is thoroughly Augustinian, it is peppered with enough existential *angst* and smothered in enough jargon to make it seem terribly chic.

Voegelin surmises that radical politics, from the Puritan Revolution to the horrors of Nazism and Stalinism, have their source in the inability to accept the God-given world (the "first reality") with all its shortcomings. Instead, human beings want to invent a new world (a "second reality") according to their own lights.[4]

Voegelin regards the history of the West as a progressive development that reaches a climax in "sotereological truth" (i.e. Christianity) and then begins a steady and seemingly endless decline characterized by a variety of hideously deformed modes of consciousness, which Voegelin analyses in terms of "Gnostic" mass movements. The latter are not otherworldly enough and are therefore, in Voegelin's estimation, incapable of coping with transcendent reality.[5] Modern politics, modern technology, and modern life in general, are all denounced as Gnostic. But what is Gnosticism?

Historically speaking, Gnosticism is a Christian heresy of the third century. The Gnostic writings challenged the Church's authoritative interpretations of the Bible.[6] For example, they wondered why a good God would prevent Adam and Eve from eating of the tree of knowledge of good and evil. Why would He not want them to know the difference and freely choose the good? Why would a good God want Adam and Eve to remain childlike and to follow his commands without understanding? Why indeed?

The Gnostics rejected the literal reading of the story of Genesis and suggested that it be read symbolically as a myth with a true and deep meaning. They thought that the story was a drama of the soul—the drama of self-knowledge and awakening. Eve was the voice of the spirit. Acting on behalf of the true God, she sought the knowledge of good and evil. In coming to know Eve, Adam achieves self-knowledge, because she is his true self. Despite variations on this theme, the Gnostic reading is a dramatic contrast to the misogynistic interpretation of Augustine and the established Church.

According to the orthodox view, the moral of the story is that men must be warned against women because they are the source of evil and must be subordinated to men as a punishment for their wickedness. Augustine explains that Adam fell because he failed to subordinate Eve, who is inferior and carnal by nature. And this should be a lesson to all men who care to preserve their homes from being perverted and destroyed.[7] In contrast to orthodox misogyny, the Gnostics denied that women have a special predilection for evil. On the contrary, they insisted that evil is an equal opportunity employer.

The Gnostics struggled against the demonization of knowledge, wisdom, and femininity in the orthodox reading of Genesis. They rightly believed that the orthodox reading celebrates ignorance and blind superstition—qualities that enhance the power of priests and other self-appointed mediators between man and God. This may explain why the Church burned their writings. But much to the delight of scholars and thinkers, many of the Gnostic writings have been recently rediscovered.[8]

The Gnostics also rejected the Augustinian view of God as radically transcendent. Instead, they saw the divine as hidden deep within human nature—a spiritual potential to be discovered. This is precisely the position that Hegel adopted and Voegelin denounced as the "immanentization of the Christian eschaton," a deformation of the Christian truth and a revolt against the human condition. For Voegelin, God must remain transcendent and wholly other, while man must remain without understanding, suspended between hope and fear, tormented by existential *angst*.[9] In short, Voegelin sides with Augustine and the Church against the Gnostic heretics. But he makes no attempt to answer the difficult challenges they pose to his orthodoxy.

Voegelin used Gnosticism as a general term of abuse. He used it to describe every attempt that was, in his estimation, a revolt against the first reality (in which God is other and man is the victim of existential *angst*) in favor of the second reality (in which God is not so remote and man is at home in the world).[10] He applied the term to Communism, Stalinism, Fascism, and secular modernity (because modernity ostensibly rebels against the divine order and endeavors to create a new reality with the help of technology). This use of the term may be questionable but it reveals the extent to which Voegelin identified any departure from his own vision as a collapse into complete depravity.

Voegelin acknowledges that Christianity is indirectly responsible for the Gnostic deformity of consciousness. The cultural success of Christianity invites this deformity of consciousness because the rigors of faith are so great and so arduous that the masses are tempted to escape the hardship and uncertainty by adhering to the fantasy of the second reality.[11] Supposedly, the *angst* involved in the true understanding of the human condition is too heavy a burden for ordinary humanity; efforts to escape from it are therefore inevitable. Voegelin reckons that the Christian faith is so heroic that it is unsuitable for mass culture. Accordingly, he turns Christianity into an elite affair.

Several comments and criticisms are in order. First, there is no doubt that Voegelin's diatribes against the radical politics of modernity are a corrective to the inclination to look to politics for the redemption and transfiguration of the world. Voegelin rightly warns that those who expect too much of politics will inevitably become mired in terror and irrationality. But it is also the case that Voegelin himself demands too much of politics, as I will show.

Second, Voegelin's assumption that the evils of totalitarianism are a consequence of the modern rejection of transcendence and the desire to bring heaven to earth misses the mark. This analysis has the effect of attributing all the evils of the world to those who wish to improve the human condition. In my view, attributing the horrors of totalitarianism to a Promethean love of humanity gives the likes of Hitler and Stalin too much credit. By painting them as zealous but misguided humanitarians, we fail to notice the often shockingly gratuitous nature of the evils they inflicted.

Third, even if all the evils of the world have their source in the belief in radical immanence or the quest for an earthly paradise, it does not follow that belief in radical transcendence is the solution. As I have shown in my discussion of Augustine, belief in radical transcendence leads to morally obscene conclusions. And it is not surprising that Voegelin appeals to the political right in America. He appeals to those who resist political initiatives to improve life in this world—less poverty, greater freedom, and more sexual equality.

Fourth, Voegelin's world is as dualistic as the world of Augustine, the Manicheans, and the Gnostics. It is made up of the first reality and the second reality, the searchers for truth and the rebels against reality, formative consciousness (consciousness formed by the truth) and deformed consciousness (consciousness formed by untruth), the spiritually healthy and the spiritually diseased, the truth-tellers and the pathological liars, those who live in openness toward the divine ground of being and those who do not. Is reality that simple? Is every departure from radical transcendence, the work of the devil? Is every effort to improve the world that God gave us, a libidinal quest for Gnostic self-salvation?

It seems to me that Voegelin's work invites a myopic conservatism that condemns every effort to improve human life as an unspeakable cosmic impiety and a Promethean revolt against the gods. The result is a conservatism that is sensitive to the evils of rebels and revolutionaries but oblivious to the evils enshrined in the status quo—evils as grotesque as torturing innocent witnesses. This is the logic of a politics that is nourished by the philosophy of radical transcendence.

Fifth, Voegelin's work is plagued with the same incoherence that is characteristic of Augustinian thought—the tendency to shift from political disengagement to political militancy when it suits the faith.[12] This shiftiness is illustrated in Voegelin's response to liberalism in general and to Hobbes in particular. On one hand, Voegelin accuses Hobbes of being a Gnostic who thinks that politics can save us from the evils of life; but on the other hand, he rejects the minimalism of Hobbes's politics because it turns political life into an "empty vessel."[13]

These two criticisms are incompatible. If Hobbes is a Gnostic, then he is, on Voegelin's own account, someone who expects too much from politics—he expects it to bring heaven to earth, to create a life of ease and pleasure, free of cares, evils, and injustices. And if that is the case, then it is not reasonable to reject his political philosophy for being minimalist.

The truth of the matter is that Voegelin's objection to Hobbes is also an objection to secular liberal politics, which limits itself to the task of preventing harm and eschews the project of promoting any particular conception of the good. But Voegelin is unwilling to leave the world totally unsanctified. He objects to the sort of society suggested by Hobbes, a society limited to avoiding the worst evil or *summum malum*—violent death. He thinks that settling for peace and order is not enough. Politics must do more—it must be a participation in transcendent truth and goodness, it must embrace the *summum bonum*. Voegelin argues that failing to do so "suppress(es) the apparent freedom of the spirit and its order."[14] In other words, political minimalism leads to a mutilated form of consciousness.

Had he been consistent, Voegelin would have embraced the "empty vessel." But Voegelin is no more consistent than Augustine. Objecting to minimalism in politics is not an appropriate posture for an Augustinian. After all, politics is only meant to bridle evil by resorting to an even greater evil. Hobbes is simply being true to Augustine. Indeed, Hobbes would be quite justified in turning the charge of Gnosticism against Voegelin. To demand more than an empty vessel is to revolt against the order of God—to reject the God-given condition of human existence—the first reality.

It is Voegelin who is a Gnostic. It is Voegelin who lacks the heroic stamina that the Christian experience of transcendence requires. It is Voegelin who needs to sanctify the political by wedding it to the divine. It is Voegelin who accords Augustinian theology Koranic status and denounces every departure from it as demonic. It is Voegelin who demands too much of politics. To require the political order to be a microcosm of the transcendent order or a microcosm of the soul in its openness to God is to ask too much. How can such a demand be compatible with the painful awareness of the imperfection of man and the world? And what about those who do not share our formative consciousness? What were the persecution of heretics and the burning of witches but an effort to stamp out manifestations of deformed consciousness?

Voegelin insists on the representation of the divine. But who is fit to represent the divine in this world? Voegelin betrays more than a little nostalgia for the Middle Ages when he describes the Church as a "flash of eternity in time" that clearly satisfies his conception of political representation.[15] Voegelin fails to recognize that God cannot be politically represented without being defiled. In fact, the whole idea of the representation of the divine is nothing but a swindle and a pretext for treacherous, unscrupulous, and unlimited power.

Finally, it may be objected that Voegelin is not a Christian at all, let alone an Augustinian. In my view, it is not necessary to believe in Christian dogma in order to be an Augustinian. The doctrinal beliefs of Christianity (the divinity of Jesus, the Virgin Birth, and the Immaculate Conception) are not at issue. What is at issue is the Christian sensibility: the extreme deprecation of the world, the excessive otherworldliness, the radical transcendence, the profound dualism, the emphasis on original sin (Voegelin likes to call it *superbia*), the abysmal helplessness of man, and the inscrutability of God. I contend that the moral and political implications of this sensibility are not as innocuous as the self-righteousness of their adherents would lead one to believe. On the contrary, this Christian sensibility leads to morally repulsive conclusions. In the end, the world is made up of the city of God and the city of man, the godly and the ungodly, formative consciousness and deformed consciousness, the spiritually healthy and the spiritually diseased. These are distinctions with grave political implications. They are certainly not a recipe for a free or tolerant society.

The excesses of Augustinian Christianity are not remote and isolated phenomena. Nor are they exclusively Christian. They are echoed in the dramatic resurgence of religious fundamentalism in our time—Islamic Fundamentalism in the Middle East, Jewish Fundamentalism in Israel, Hindu Fundamentalism in India, and Christian Fundamentalism in the United States.[16] Like Augustine and Voegelin, these fundamentalists are not satisfied with an empty vessel. They are eager to use political power to establish the state of God. There is no dearth of godliness in the politics of our time. It is therefore difficult to believe those who insist that our troubles are connected to our godlessness.

In the absence of any spontaneous concord regarding the authenticity of revelation and in light of a plurality of conflicting claims about transcendent truth, the state must remain an empty vessel if any degree of earthly peace is to be achieved.

3. Political Realism with a Twist

It is important not to confuse the Christian politics of resignation with political realism. Simply stated, political realism is the view that the foundation of political order is not justice or truth, but power. In domestic affairs, politics relies on a monopoly over force to create a modicum of order. But international political life will always be characterized by conflict, hatred, and antagonism. There never was and never will be universal peace, justice, order, and goodwill. Utopian dreams are just that—dreams. War is a permanent feature of international affairs. Some version or other of this view has been held by Machiavelli, Hobbes, Freud, Carl Schmitt, Hans Morgenthau, Samuel Huntington, Henry Kissinger, and others.

It is often believed that political realism has its intellectual roots in moral skepticism—if there is no truth and no justice, then power is the only basis of order.[17] But it is a mistake to assume that political realism depends on moral skepticism. On the contrary, it is quite compatible with the moral absolutism of Christianity. There is truth and justice, but they belong to God. Fallen humanity cannot live according to the precepts of truth and justice.[18] Threats of terror are necessary to bridle evil in this world. In fact, Augustine is usually considered one of the classic exponents of the doctrine. But in my view, the alliance of Christian beliefs with political realism makes the doctrine much harsher than its secular incarnation requires. Nevertheless, Augustine provides political realism with one of its earliest and clearest expressions.

Nothing captures the essence of political realism more clearly than the tale told by Augustine of the pirate who was captured by Alexander the great. When the pirate appeared before Alexander, the emperor asked him what he meant by all his piracy? The pirate responded indignantly, saying: what do *you* mean by all *your* piracy? Just because I do it with a little ship and you do it with a great fleet, you are called an emperor while I am called a petty thief. But in truth, there is no difference between us, other than a difference of scale and hardware. You are not morally better than I am, just much better equipped. Augustine marveled at the astuteness of the pirate's response. He agreed wholeheartedly with the pirate. After all "what are kingdoms but gangs of criminals on a large scale? What are criminal gangs but petty kingdoms?"[19] The difference between Alexander and the pirate is not a difference of kind, but of magnitude. The message is that the function of politics is not to uphold justice but to bridle evil. This can be accomplished only with even greater evil. Social order is founded on terror of sufficient magnitude to subdue all others.

After the collapse of the Soviet Union, many Russians longed for the days of Stalin. It was not that they had forgotten his criminal brutality; they simply recognized that it is easier to withstand the treachery of one mega-criminal than to contend with an abundance of petty criminals.

The same logic has been applied globally. A universal tyrant, powerful enough to subdue all others, may be the secret to global peace and order. If history is understood as a long string of wars between competing powers, then the emergence of a single superpower, a global tyrant, whose power is unmatched, can be understood as the end of history. Alexandre Kojève predicted this scenario.[20] And when the Soviet Union collapsed, Francis Fukuyama popularized Kojève's views in his *End of History and the Last Man*.[21] As the world's only superpower, the United States certainly considers herself to be the global policeman. But she is reluctant to conceive of herself as the universal tyrant. She prefers to think of herself as the Zion that lights up the entire world. Hardheaded realists see it differently.

In its secular form, political realism is largely descriptive. But Christian theology turns it into a doctrine of sacred terror. Augustine argued that tyrants are sent by God to punish us for our sins. And because of the ubiquity of sin, all tyranny is a deserved punishment for sin. Rebelling against the tyrant is rebelling against the justice of God. Augustine used the same argument to advocate the submission of women to abusive husbands— namely that an abusive husband was a deserved punishment for sin—and heaven knows women are much more wicked than men.[22] But surely, so much submissiveness is bound to encourage bullies—tyrants and husbands alike.

Eric Voegelin used the same reasoning to make a spurious distinction between tyranny and Caesarism. He claimed that Christianity provided a deeper understanding of tyranny than pagan antiquity because it introduced the concept of Caesarism. The latter is a tyranny that is justified by the decadence and corruption of a people who deserve a tyrannical government that would punish their iniquity and whip them into shape. But the distinction between tyranny and Caesarism is a bogus distinction that serves only to conceal and justify tyranny.[23]

Starting from the Augustinian assumption that human nature is fallen, that sin is ubiquitous, and that the wages of sin are suffering and death, it is logical to conclude that mankind deserves a politics of terror and brutality. At the very least, human life must be punctuated at regular intervals with "Caesarism." But why settle only for Caesars and tyrants? Why not include revolutionaries and terrorists? Unlike Augustine and Voegelin, Joseph De Maistre (1753–1821), the famous French reactionary, had the courage and veracity to draw the logical conclusions from his own Augustinian assumptions. Maistre surmised that if history is the work of divine Providence, then the revolutionary is as much the product of divine wrath as the tyrant. It makes no sense to hail tyrants as instruments of God but reject revolutionaries or terrorists as instruments of God. In the aftermath of the French Revolution of 1789, Maistre declared that the Revolution and its Terror were divinely ordained as a punishment for the sins of the clergy and the aristocracy.

Maistre was a staunch monarchist and papist, so it was inconceivable to him that God might be on the side of the revolutionaries. He assumed that once the crimes of the regime are expiated (no one knows how long that may take), then the monarchy and the ancien régime would be restored. In other words, Maistre approved only of revolutionary terror, not revolutionary success. When he stated unequivocally that "men are too wicked to be free,"[24] he was not describing an empirical state of affairs, he was making a judgment on humanity—the judgment that is the basis of Christian political thought from Augustine to Voegelin—human beings are wicked, and they deserve tyranny and terror.

The trouble with the doctrine of God's historical Providence is that it compounds the difficulty of defending the justice of God. The problem is that terror, tyranny, war, and revolutions punish the innocent along with the guilty. Augustine resolved the dilemma by declaring that no one is innocent and that everyone deserves death. But Maistre took a more credible approach. He argued that the accumulated suffering of the innocent serves the same function as the death of Christ—it pays the ransom for sin:

> the righteous, suffering willingly, made amends not only for themselves but also for the culpable who, of themselves, could not expiate themselves.[25]

Like Augustine, Maistre believed that the sins of the world are so great that no amount of innocent suffering, not even the suffering of Christ, is enough to pay the debt involved. Maistre imagined that when the mass of sin in the world had accumulated to a degree that is intolerable to the deity, then the "the avenging angel" of heaven strikes the nations of the world with a mad frenzy and "bathes them in blood."[26] War is the result. And war is about killing the innocent—the soldier kills another soldier—a human being who has done him no harm. The guilty are looked after by the executioner. But we don't need too many executioners. However, we need lots of soldiers.[27] We need those who are willing to sacrifice innocent lives, including their own, "in order to find expiation."[28] The result is that:

> The whole earth, continually steeped in blood, is nothing but an immense alter on which every living thing must be sacrificed without end, without restraint, without respite, until the consummation of the world, the extinction of evil, the death of death.[29]

Maistre must be admired for not shrinking from the logic of his Augustinian assumptions, which invite an enthusiastic endorsement of innocent suffering as a means to expiation.

One of the curious things about the Christian metaphysics of terror is that it defeats the conservative edifice that political realism attempts to erect. The conservative rejection of revolutionary zeal is intended to exchange the impolitic, endless, and unattainable demand for freedom, equality, and prosperity with peace, order, and stability. But this rationale dissolves in a world that demands the endless sacrifice of every living thing without respite or restraint. Where there is so much carnage there can be little peace, order, and stability. The conservative rationale crumbles. So, why not risk the joys of freedom even if only for one glorious moment? What do we have to lose?

Christianity prides itself on its allegedly superior conception of God as good, just, and merciful. It contrasts its benevolent God with the capricious and wrathful God of the Old Testament as well as with the morally crude gods of paganism. The trouble is that Christianity has not succeeded in introducing a loving and benevolent God to replace the hostile gods of antiquity. Maistre was speaking candidly when he said that we live "under the hand of an *angry power*" that must be constantly appeased.[30] If the universe is indeed as gruesome and ghastly as so many Christians imagine, then our humanity must compel us to renounce it as a model for our own conduct. Only defiance and contempt for this inhuman universe can be compatible with our humanity. No one understood this better than Albert Camus. Convinced of the cold indifference of the universe to all our most cherished values—justice, love, compassion—Camus counseled revolt against the absurd. Instead of the Cartesian slogan, "I think therefore I am," Camus declared "we rebel therefore we are." What he meant was that our humanity consists in defiance of the absurd inhumanity of the universe.[31] Imitation of a God who punishes infants for their inherited sins, or who demands innocent blood as a means of expiation, is bound to turn men into monsters.

In conclusion, what concerns me is not the truth or falsehood of political realism but what Christianity does to political realism. The Christian metaphysics of terror makes political realism a gloomier doctrine than its secular incarnation requires. It turns it into a doctrine of sacred terror. The Christian politics of resignation paints a picture of reality that is dark and fiendish because only a world of endless suffering can satisfy the infinite need for expiation. Then it tells us that this is the God-given reality from which there can be no escape. Any effort to improve on this reality is sacrilege—it is an effort to escape our deserved punishment, replace God, and create a world in our own image. Far from being resigned, the politics of resignation is active because human complicity is necessary to make the world terrifying enough. The politics of resignation needs the brutality of tyrants, terrorists, and revolutionaries. In the absence of the latter, we can resign ourselves to the grotesque rule of the godly and their frightful distinctions between formative and deformed consciousness. The one thing that the Christian politics of resignation cannot abide is a successful revolution because it might give the world a short reprieve from wretchedness. In this severe and censorious political vision, humanity is unworthy of the briefest interlude of happiness. The smallest triumph over abject despair, the smallest celebration of human power or goodness, is construed as a sin against God—the sin of pride.

4. Christian Arrogance

Human depravity is pivotal to the understanding of the politics of Christianity. But of all the vices of human nature, nothing has inspired the antipathy of Christians more than pride. Christianity has made a special enemy out of pride because it regards it as the root of all sin, since it was the source of Eve's temptation and the demise of all humanity.[32] But despite its antipathy to pride, Christianity has cultivated its own brand of arrogance, which it mistakes for humility. It is no exaggeration to say that Christianity has succumbed to a form of arrogance that is extravagant in its recklessness and conceit.

In order to undermine pride, Augustine, Luther, and others relied on belief in the bondage of the will to sin. The doctrine was made famous by Augustine's interpretation of the Fall. According to Augustine, human beings were created free to choose between good and evil. But after the Fall, the freedom of the will is forfeited and human beings are in a state of "bondage to sin."[33] Martin Luther echoed the same doctrine in his "Bondage of the Will."[34] So did John Calvin.[35] This meant that human nature is so flawed that it cannot be a guide to what is morally good and right. There is an unbridgeable gulf between our nature and inclinations on one hand, and the moral law of God on the other; human nature is at odds with the moral law. And even when we desire the good, the will is unable to choose it. The will is broken, flawed, and not able to function. It chooses what it does not want. Human beings cannot trust themselves to live as they wish to live. In their fallen condition, they are incapable of choosing the good—at least not without God's miraculous intervention. They can act righteously only by the grace of God. Supernatural assistance is necessary to bridge the gulf between human nature and the moral law. All human virtue is therefore a gift of grace.

In this way, Augustine, Luther, Calvin, and others thought that human beings would not be puffed up by their virtues. But in an effort to insure that people did not take pride in their virtues, advocates of this doctrine managed to undermine people's responsibility for their deeds in general and their wickedness in particular. If the will is in bondage to sin, then it is not free to choose between good and evil. And if it is not free, it cannot be held responsible. This was the argument made by Pelagius (354–420) and his defenders.[36] They rightly maintained that if we are in bondage to sin, then we are not free, and hence are not responsible. The Pelagians won the philosophical debate, but the Church condemned them as heretics and excommunicated bishops who agreed with them. Meanwhile, Augustine was championed as a saint. Hundreds of years later, Erasmus was still defending human freedom against Luther's Augustinian gloom. All of Erasmus's books were condemned by the Church and placed on the Index of forbidden books in 1559. Pelagius, Erasmus, and their supporters were right in thinking that the bondage of the will is objectionable. But the doctrine is not a departure from the Gospels. On the contrary, it is compatible with the view of faith as a gift of grace, examined earlier. If faith is the fount of virtue, and faith is a gift of grace, it follows that virtue is itself a gift of grace. The passive implications of the doctrine are morally objectionable and they fly in the face of our personal experience of freedom. Nevertheless, the doctrine is not as incoherent as it sounds.

At first blush, bondage to sin sounds contradictory. Being in bondage indicates being held captive. But sin indicates freedom because you are to blame for your sin, and you can't be blamed if you can't help it. But bondage to sin is not as contradictory as it sounds—it is like being an alcoholic. Initially, drinking is a choice, but when you get hooked, you keep drinking even when you do not want to. Once you are hooked, your initial freedom is compromised.

The Christian message is that we are all alcoholics. The difference is that some of us recognize the fact and seek treatment. But the rest are in denial. Christians are the alcoholics who admit it and seek help. What they discover is that there is no cure (at least in this world)—once an alcoholic, always an alcoholic. But there is a treatment that relieves the symptoms. That treatment is the grace of God, which is symbolized by the water and blood that flowed out of the wounds of Christ when he was on the cross.

Nothing could have pleased the Church more than Augustine's assertion that the blood and water flowing out of the wounds of Christ are the sacraments of the Church. Augustine declares bluntly, "outside the Church sins are not remitted."[37] In other words, the Church has exclusive dominion over the remedy that we all need so desperately—the blood and water of life. How brilliant! No greater scam could have been conceived. And it worked—at least until Luther uncovered the swindle.

Luther balked at the idea that the Church has exclusive rights to the dissemination of God's grace. But he did not change the fundamentals of Christian theology. We are all in bondage to sin, and the sooner we admit it the better. We must repent and seek the treatment we desperately need. Those who refuse to admit that they are in bondage to sin, those who refuse to admit that they are sick, those who refuse to repent, are not Christians. They obstinately believe that they have done nothing to repent for. But in truth, they are like self-deluded alcoholics who are intoxicated with pride. They are too evil to repent. C. S. Lewis says bluntly that Christianity has nothing to offer to those who have nothing to repent for. But then he tells us that it takes a good man to repent. And this implies that thinking you have nothing to repent for just goes to show that you are not good.[38] In other words, those who refuse to plead guilty, those who refuse to accept the Christian picture of the world, must be hopelessly wedded to wickedness.

We are back to the idea that not believing what Christians believe makes you evil, regardless of how you conduct yourself. Demonizing the opposition is an age-old Christian tactic; it has its foundation in the identity of sin with unbelief, which was used so successfully by Jesus, as we have seen.[39] If you admit your wickedness and repent, you will be saved; if you do not admit your wickedness and refuse to repent, you will be damned. These are the only two options.

The trouble with this doctrine is that it fails to accomplish what it sets out to do—namely to undermine pride. Instead, the doctrine accounts for the distinctive brand of Christian arrogance. The alcoholics who know that they are alcoholics and must seek treatment cannot help feeling superior to the alcoholics who are in denial. Being in denial is being in a state of *false consciousness*. The latter is not a concept invented by Hegel, Marx, the Critical Theorists of the Frankfurt School, or the postmoderns; it has its origins in Christianity. In its modern and post-modern incarnation, false consciousness indicates a lack of awareness, naiveté, and simplicity. Those who suffer from false consciousness are deceived by the structures of power. In its modern and postmodern incarnation, false consciousness is forgivable because the structures of power that operate to conceal the truth are so formidable. But the original or Christian version of false consciousness is more vicious. The Christian version not only discredits and silences the opposition—it demonizes it. The Christian version of false consciousness implies not only blindness and stupidity but an intentional rejection of the truth, a love of wickedness, and a moral pathology.

Christians have no intention of priding themselves on their monopoly over truth. They humbly attribute their wisdom to God. In their quest for humility, they imitate the "humility" of Jesus, who claimed to be merely the agent of his Father in heaven. The result is a tendency to identify their perspective, judgments, and preferences with those of God. This sort of arrogance is what Christians mistake for humility. And anyone who disagrees with them is in denial of the God-given truth. And this purposeful denial is wickedness.

Augustine displayed this Christian brand of arrogance when he declared that his interpretations of the Scriptures were directly inspired by God. He humbly took no responsibility for his often bizarre renditions; instead, he admonished his critics saying: "they should stop blaming me and ask God to give them vision."[40] In the end, Augustine won the argument because the Christian emperors silenced his opponents by the coercive force of law.[41]

On another occasion, Augustine described the "stupidity" of his intellectual opponents in their refusal to yield to the "force of truth." This resistance to truth is a "monstrous moral fault," which has its source in "irresponsible frivolity" and "malignant spite" that is "in defiance of their own conscience." And as if stupidity, deceit, and wickedness did not suffice, Augustine attributes to his intellectual opponents a "raging madness," and a "disease proof against all efforts to treat it."[42] And even though Augustine describes himself as blessed by God, possessor of truth, and a "physician," he is powerless to provide a remedy for the "incurable" disease from which his opponents suffer. In short, by refusing to yield to his point of view, his intellectual opponents prove themselves to be stupid and wicked liars who are the victims of a sickness that is of their own making.

Martin Luther used the same tactics in his dispute with Erasmus over the freedom of the will. In "Bondage of the Will," Luther accused his intellectual opponent of wickedness, and repeatedly begged Erasmus to "repent" his sin.[43] And what is Erasmus guilty of? His sin was not believing what Luther believed. In contrast to Luther, Erasmus believed that the will is free and not "in bondage to sin." And this is what Luther found "really unpardonable." Because Luther believed that salvation depends on faith not works, errors in faith cannot be tolerated because they are supposedly deadly. We are back to the doctrine of sin as unbelief, which was discussed in Part I. Having the wrong beliefs is the Christian definition of wickedness; sin consists in not believing what Christians believe. Accordingly, Luther begs Erasmus again and again to repent. It is worth noting that when the Church condemned Galileo Galilei in 1633 for claiming that the earth revolved around the sun, his tormentors were not satisfied to punish and silence him, they demanded that he repent his "error."

The same tactics are used by Eric Voegelin against his intellectual opponents. Those who disagree with him (Marx, Hegel, and others) are denounced as liars, swindlers, and enemies of God. Voegelin accuses his opponents of suffering from a "neuropathological disorder" or a "spiritual disease," which leads to their willful, knowing, and malicious subversion of the truth of God.

When Voegelin denounces his intellectual opponents as victims of a disease beyond their control *and* as demonic rebels against the order of God, he is involved in a paradox. But this is not a paradox peculiar to Voegelin. As we have seen, it is the Christian version of *false consciousness*. It involves condemning one's intellectual opponents not just because they are blind, mistaken, or unperceptive, but also because they are wicked liars, swindlers, and serpentine deceivers of mankind. Voegelin's entourage continues the practice. They denounce their intellectual opponents as pathological liars, and describe themselves as the "defenders of civilization" (the slogan of the Voegelin Society). The subtle implication is that if you are not with them, then you are some sort of savage—certainly not a defender of civilization.

The ability to see one's intellectual opponents as representatives of the forces of darkness, the insistence that they are purposefully rebelling against the truth of God, the conviction that they know the truth and are being perversely obstinate, the demand that they repent, are not just the foundations of political extremism and intolerance but also the basis of totalitarian regimes that aspire to thought-control.

In conclusion, despite all their efforts to avoid pride, Christians have succumbed to an extravagant conceit that makes them believe that those who disagree with them are guilty of the most absurd and criminal resistance to truth. It is impossible for so much arrogance to inspire resignation to the world as it is. Once in positions of power, Christians cannot resist using the coercive mechanisms of the state for their own ends—ends that are often bereft of moderation or restraint. It is no coincidence that the history of the temporal power of the Church is a long train of abominations.

5. Christian Militancy

It is generally recognized that the Christian political ethos suffers from a serious inconsistency. On one hand, it is passive and resigned to the will of God, it washes its hands from the world, and it espouses a totally apolitical posture. But on the other hand, it yields to the temptations of its own arrogance, succumbs to a self-righteous militancy, and uses the power of the state to create a Christian commonwealth.[44] But in my view, these two postures are not as different as they appear. As we have seen, the resignation that Augustine espouses is not particularly passive; on the contrary, it is active in its complicity with injustice. Both postures—resignation and militancy—pose as humble submission to the will of God but they are equally energetic, zealous, and malevolent.

No sooner did the Christians become powerful in Rome, then they abandoned their pacifism in favor of militancy. Again Augustine provided the necessary arguments. Augustine's position on war shifted dramatically in the course of his long career. At first, he took a position that was consistent with his posture of resignation. He argued that since all political rulers are from God, Christians have an obligation to fight in all wars authorized by the powers that be.[45] At first, he maintained that all these wars are unjust, but that is irrelevant to the political obligation of Christians. After all, injustice is the way of the world, as we have seen in the discussion of torture. When the Bible says, "Render unto Caesar what is Caesar's and unto God what is God's," Augustine interprets this to mean that we should pay taxes to Caesar to finance his wars, which are generally wars of aggression.[46] War is one of the evils of this world, and like other evils we can do nothing except go along with it, all the while reassuring ourselves that we are ostensibly the humble servants of God's unfathomable will.

But Augustine had a change of heart. Instead of looking at all wars as reflections of the rapacity and injustice of the world, he introduced a distinction between just and unjust wars. He argued that all wars couldn't be unjust since God himself commanded the Israelites to wage righteous wars that would crush the wicked and humble the proud.[47] Some may think that this Old Testament view comes into conflict with the New Testament, which counsels us to turn the other cheek. But Augustine assures us that there is no conflict and that the New Testament injunction is not intended to refer to our actions but only to the "inward disposition of the heart."[48] We are to repay evil with good only in the first instance, in order to shame the wicked into changing their ways. But if this fails, then we are entitled to use force and correct them with a "benevolent severity" that is "contrary to their wishes."[49] In this way, "wars might be waged by the good" in order to bring the "unbridled lust of men" under the yoke of a just or Christian government that could abolish or at least suppress them.[50]

Augustine is not content to resign himself to the evils of the world and leave salvation to God. He counsels wars of aggression against infidels to save their souls. In waging such wars, Augustine assures us that we are complying with the New Testament injunction to "do violence to no man."⁵¹ In waging such wars, Christians are merely imitating the benevolence of God, who crushes the wicked and humbles the proud in order to save their souls. The only caveat is that in waging these "just" wars, we should make sure that we do not take too much pleasure in the violence and carnage of war. For the evil of war, according to Augustine, is the "love of violence, revengeful cruelty, fierce and implacable enmity, wild resistance, and the lust for power."⁵² In other words, we can kill and plunder as long as we intend to save souls and don't take too much pleasure in the plundering. Clearly, this is a classic justification of Christianity's militant and crusading spirit.

Augustine's position justifies not only the Crusades but also the Inquisition. His position on war is consistent with his position on heretics—namely that it is legitimate to correct them, and by "afflictions and terrors of a temporal kind," coerce them into joining the Church, which is supposedly the root of all life.⁵³ It is for their own benefit that heathens and heretics are crushed. In both cases, wickedness is defined as not believing what Christians believe, and that is deemed sufficient reason for the affliction of otherwise innocent people.

Long before the Inquisition was officially established, Augustine was very active in rooting out heretical beliefs and insuring that their advocates were condemned and excommunicated by the pope. Bishop Julian of Eclanum is one example; he was convinced by Pelagius's views on the freedom of the will. But Augustine was a tireless defender of the doctrine of original sin and the bondage of the will, against his Pelagian opponents. The Council of Carthage (411) condemned Pelagian teachings, but when the doctrines of Pelagius were accepted by John, bishop of Jerusalem, as compatible with the teaching of the Church, another Council of Carthage (416) repeated the condemnation as did the Council of Milevis (416). Augustine was present at the latter Council. But it took yet another Council of Carthage (418) and a letter writing campaign to Pope Zosimus to have all Pelagian teachings denounced as heretical. When Julian of Eclanum led a group of dissident bishops against the pope's ruling, he was excommunicated and deposed.⁵⁴ Augustine was not satisfied with the freedom to worship, write, and debate; he wanted dominion. He was not satisfied with refuting his intellectual opponents; he wanted them destroyed.

Bishop Julian of Eclanum was merely guilty of not sharing the opinions of Augustine and the Church authorities who were captivated by his supposed genius. Julian argued that the doctrine of original sin had the effect of making God the persecutor of the newborn. Julian was right. The doctrine did lead to barbarous practices. For example, it became a custom for women who died while pregnant to be cut open and the unbaptized child removed so that the mother could be buried in the consecrated cemetery of the church. This gruesome exercise was defended well into the twelfth century by respected Christian theologians such as Johannes Beleth (d. 1165).[55]

I do not mean to demonize Augustine, since he was not necessarily more fanatical than those who came before him or after him. His zeal and his lack of moderation will always be the supreme hazards of Christian faith. And when such zeal is allied with political power, it invites catastrophe.

After Emperor Constantine "converted" to Christianity, he issued the Edict of Milan (313), which gave all Roman citizens the freedom to worship as they pleased. But this liberty was short-lived.[56] Then as now, Christians were not satisfied with freedom of religion; they wanted dominion. Constantine relented. As Edward Gibbon remarks, "with the knowledge of truth the emperor imbibed the maxims of persecution."[57] After only twelve short years of religious freedom, the Council of Nicea (325) outlawed paganism, and the persecution of pagans, Jews, heretics, dissenters, women, and freethinkers began and continued until the modern era.

Christian emperors who followed Constantine were no improvement. Like Constantine, they used the legal system to enforce the beliefs and inclinations of the new religion. Here are some examples from the Theodosian Code, which is a compilation of the laws passed by Constantine I, Theodosius II (emperor in the East from 408–450), Valentinian III (emperor in the West from 419–455), and other Christian emperors:

1. Pagan rites and worship were prohibited because they departed from the "true religion" or Catholic faith, with their "heathen enormities," and their "natural insanities and stubborn insolence."[58]
2. Jews were prohibited from building new synagogues.[59]
3. Jews were prohibited from marrying Christians and vice versa.[60]
4. Jews were prohibited from having Christian slaves.[61]
5. Jews were prohibited from being members of the imperial service.[62]
6. Adultery was made into a public crime, as if chastity were itself under public guardianship; adulterers were considered "opprobrious and nefarious criminals" deserving "exquisite punishment."[63]
7. In the investigation of adultery, it was decreed: "torture must be employed without impunity to anyone, provided that they were at

the house at the time when the adultery is said to have been committed."[64] In other words, merely being in a house where adultery may have been committed, made you an accomplice in the crime.

8. The distinction between rape and fornication was blurred so that consent was made irrelevant and the "ravisher" and the "ravished" parties were punished equally. Although women who were unwilling got lighter penalties than those who consented—the former lost all their inheritance while the latter merited "exquisite punishments," which included death, exile, and confiscation of property.[65]

9. Nurses, maids, orderlies, and others who offered incitement to rapists or opportunities to fornicators were punished by having molten lead poured down their throats.[66]

10. Anyone who assisted rapists and fornicators, without distinction to sex, was to be consumed by fire.[67]

11. Heretics were to be exiled, their property confiscated, their churches and places of worship were to be handed over to the Catholic Church or the "true religion." They were not permitted to meet either in public or in private. This applied to Arians, Manichaeans, Montanists, Priscillianists, Novatians, Sabbatians, Eunomians, Donatists, and other "diverse and perfidious sects, who are driven by the insanity of a miserable conspiracy against God, . . . "[68]

12. Any of these "demented" and "damned" breed of "heretical monsters," including Jews, who dared to "seduce a slave or freeborn person, . . . from the worship of the Christian religion to an impious sect or ritual, he shall suffer capital punishment, together with the forfeiture of his fortune."[69]

Clearly, the spirit of Christian charity did not extend to pagans, Jews, heretics, fornicators, or anyone who might have harbored a belief in the salubrious effects of fornication and turned a blind eye to it.

Augustine pays great tribute to Constantine and Theodosius for their "endeavors to help the Church against the ungodly by just and compassionate legislation."[70] In Augustine's vocabulary, vile and oppressive laws are miraculously transformed into "just and compassionate legislation" because they further the interests of the Catholic Church and silence all her opponents and critics.

It may be argued that the support for the oppressive laws of the Christian emperors was due to the fact that Christianity was but a fledgling and insecure religion. But this is not the case. The establishment of Christianity as the unchallenged religion of Europe throughout the

Middle Ages did not temper its politics. Jews continued to be persecuted, as were heretics, who were no longer banished or exiled but were burned alive—many of these were women who were accused of consorting with the devil. Nor did the Protestant Reformation constitute progress. Luther and Calvin represent the two sides of the Christian approach to politics—resignation and militancy.

Luther was rightly repelled by the worldliness of the Catholic Church and supported the retreat of the Church from the secular and profane. He adopted the posture of resignation to the powers that be and counseled dutiful obedience to kings as well as tyrants on the grounds that they are both from God. In my view, even when this posture of resignation does not invite treachery, it is politically dangerous because it encourages tyranny. And there is no doubt that one of the attractions of the new religion for Constantine was the fact that it made submission to temporal rulers a religious duty.

In contrast to Luther, Calvin defended theocratic rule.[71] He thought that the task of the magistrate is to enforce the religious teachings of the Church. The function of the state is to implement the laws of God as found in the Bible and to institute the reign of God on earth. As a French Protestant, he was persecuted in France. When he was welcomed to Geneva in 1451, he set out to reform its government and its laws according to his interpretation of the ordinances of God. He created a legal system that sought to control every aspect of life. The result was his infamous reign of terror in Geneva. Even learned men such as Michael Servetus could not rely on Calvin's protection. After being condemned to death by the Spanish Inquisition for his two books on the Trinity, Servetus managed to escape from prison and made his way to Geneva, thinking that Calvin would protect him. But Calvin had him arrested, tried, condemned, and burned in 1553.

By undermining the authority of the Catholic Church, the Reformation inadvertently contributed to the development of liberty and democracy in the West. But it is a mistake to assume that the rise of liberal and democratic institutions is the legacy of Christianity. There is no doubt that the Gospels were egalitarian in spirit, but the Church managed to censor the good book in favor of its own hierarchical organization. And when it comes to liberty, it must be admitted that Christianity has always been inimical to the freedom of thought and action. For one thing, the religion requires the blind acceptance of incomprehensible mysteries, such as the trinity, the Incarnation, and the virgin birth. Moreover, freedom from external restraints does not bode well with a morally flawed creature such as man. As Maistre candidly declared, man is too wicked to be free. It is therefore only logical to surmise that the triumph of freedom and egalitarianism in the West was won in spite of Christianity and not because of it.

In conclusion, any effort to re-empower the Churches, any effort to bestow them with even a modest degree of political power, must have its roots in historical amnesia—unless of course, we believe that human beings deserve to be wretched.

6. Against Christianity in Politics

It is time for me to enumerate the reasons that I am against Christianity in politics. I would like to make it clear that my objections are not based on contingent historical crimes—crimes committed by bad people hiding behind religion. On the contrary, my claim is that most of the political crimes committed in the name of Christianity are the logical consequences of its doctrines. And it is the latter that I find destructive of politics.

First, even when it does not invite active complicity in the injustices of the world, Christianity encourages resignation to evil—either as the deserved punishment for sin or because this world is a matter of indifference. Even Reinhold Niebuhr, who has made a heroic effort to avoid the political extremes of despondency on one hand and self-righteous militancy on the other, admits that the radical pessimism about human nature inclines toward the capitulation to tyranny; and he goes so far as to suggest that the Nazi tyranny was connected to the prevalence of Reformation Christianity in Germany.[72] By its resignation, passivity, and otherworldliness, Christianity serves tyranny. No one can deny the significant role that Christianity has played in the history of European colonialism. In his novel, *The River Between*, Ngũgĩ provides a penetrating analysis of the role of Christianity in the colonization of Africa. First, the missionaries arrive to teach a passive, submissive, and otherworldly faith; when the people learn to resign themselves to tyranny and misfortune and to accept their destiny without a fight, then the white man arrives and takes over the land.[73]

Second, the Christian preoccupation with sin and the need for expiation has the effect of reconciling us to the suffering of the innocent. The claim that no one is innocent is not believable. A more likely reason for tolerating the suffering of the innocent is the precedent set by Jesus, whereby the innocent pays for the sins of the guilty. This is a dangerous precedent, which can confound justice. But worst of all, it fosters a zest for innocent suffering, as Maistre so clearly illustrates.

Third, Christianity has a profoundly singular conception of the good that encourages a militant and crusading spirit, while discouraging tolerance, plurality, and diversity. In a recently published directive, the Vatican has warned Catholic politicians around the world not to be lured by liberal tolerance and pluralism into condoning abortion, same-sex marriages, or euthanasia. Such directives are not without a threat to believers. If Catholic politicians have a loyalty to the Vatican that supercedes their loyalty to the constitutions and values of their own countries, then they cannot be trusted with public office in democratic societies. And it explains why John Locke refused to extend toleration to Catholics in his famous *Letter Concerning Toleration.*

Jesus did not intend his religion to be the foundation of political order or the basis of a political philosophy. And clearly, his religion is supremely unsuitable for such a task. The function of politics is to create order in the midst of plurality and diversity. Politics is about insuring peace and civility in the absence of any agreement about the nature of ultimate reality. The supreme political virtues are moderation and a certain degree of tolerance—not tolerance of tyranny and gross injustice—but tolerance of the plurality of the good, tolerance of a plurality of beliefs about ultimate reality, tolerance of the many roads to righteousness, and tolerance of private vice.

Jesus could not tolerate the idea that his vision was not the truth incarnate, or that his way was not the only right way, or that he was not the only path to God. But he also knew that his intransigence, his singular understanding of the good, and his intolerance of competing views, would not bring peace but the sword: "Think not that I am come to send peace on earth: I came not to send peace, but a sword" (Mathew 10:34). He knew that his doctrines would create enmity and division not only among fellow citizens but even within families:

> Suppose ye that I am come to give peace on earth? I tell you, Nay; but rather division: . . . The father shall be divided against the son, and the son against the father; the mother against the daughter and the daughter against the mother. (Luke 12:51–53)

The implication is that all this strife is worth the cost because absolute truth is at stake. But tolerance and diversity presuppose a certain skepticism regarding the human ability to grasp the nature of ultimate reality, coupled with recognition that there is a plurality of competing goods. As long as its conception of the good remains profoundly singular, Christianity cannot overcome Manichean dualism and the radical strife it involves. Dualism is a necessary concomitant of the singular conception of the good. The latter is not exclusive to Christianity; but Christianity has brought it to new heights of absurdity and intolerance.

Fourth, the harshness of Jesus's message has often been overlooked in favor of his message of love and forgiveness. The moral teachings of Jesus can be understood as a heroic ethic that transcends natural justice. Natural justice does not require living with an abusive husband; it does not require putting up with a chronically unfaithful wife. But the heroic ethic of Jesus may inspire forgiveness and love that may, with time and patience, transform the transgressor. But this heroic ethic cannot be the basis of a legal system or a foreign policy; natural justice, not Christian love, must be the guide to law and politics. Natural justice does not require us to turn the other cheek, go the extra mile, and not resist evil; on the contrary, it allows us to avenge ourselves within reason. It even praises us when we fight against injustice and refuse to be passive in the face of iniquity. Politics is primarily about resisting evil.

No Christian country has ever followed the moral teaching of Jesus, simply because it is politically disastrous. To take it seriously as a political doctrine would mean giving free reign to tyranny, oppression, and brutality. Not surprisingly, the Romans recognized that such an otherworldly religion could not defend the Empire. Christianity had to give up the injunction—"resist not evil"—as soon as it became the official religion of the Empire. But in its zealotry, it defined evil as rejecting the doctrinal beliefs of Christianity.

Fifth, the Christian conception of virtue as an inner disposition of soul cannot infiltrate politics without making the latter totalitarian in the literal sense of the word. Christianity is not satisfied with outward conformity; it demands heartfelt convictions; it is not limited to the public realm but pervades every aspect of life—worship, belief, education, entertainment, business, family, and intimate relations. But law and politics can only require outward conformity. They cannot demand particular sentiments. They cannot command the heart. And when they try to, they become monstrous. Unfortunately, the conception of virtue as an inner disposition of the heart is irresistible to society. Society is rarely satisfied with people who behave decently as upright and honorable citizens. Society insists on changing attitudes—it insists on particular beliefs, sentiments, and dispositions. In that sense, society is by nature totalitarian.

The Christian idea that you must believe in order to be saved is one of the problems: "He that believeth on the Son hath everlasting life: and he that believeth not the Son shall not see life; but the wrath of God abideth on him" (John 3:36). This emphasis on right belief accounts for most of the excesses of Christianity. It is not that Christians disdain good conduct or think it irrelevant, it is just that they cannot imagine good conduct having a source in anything other than the correct beliefs, which they define as *their* beliefs. And when those who are not believers do good works, Christians are blind to their virtues; they are certain that their good works stink in the nostrils of God. They condemn them as arrogant sinners suffering from a spiritual disease that leads them to refuse to acknowledge what they know is the truth or they condemn them as crypto-Pelagians who think they can earn their way to heaven by their good works. Historically and theologically, Christians have confused wickedness with not believing what Christians believe.

What the Inquisition and the secular dystopias of the twentieth century have in common is the primacy of belief and the desire to control not only action, but thought. The totalitarian movements of the twentieth century are modeled on the Christian Inquisition. Like the latter, they are not satisfied with conduct, they insist on the right beliefs and dispositions. Like the Inquisitorial trials in the Middle Ages, the purge trials of Stalin during the 1930s and the mass murders of Pol Pot in Cambodia during the 1970s, were not about conduct, but belief. We are only beginning to realize that such efforts cannot avoid courting disaster. When politics preoccupies itself with beliefs and inner dispositions and not with conduct, the result is not utopia but dystopia. The literature of the twentieth century testifies to the horrors of totalitarian rule: Arthur Koestler's *Darkness at Noon*, Aldoux Huxley's *Brave New World*, George Orwell's *1984*, Yevgeny Zamyatin's *We*, and others. Equally terrifying fictions can be written about the Inquisition and the witch trials in Rome, Spain, England, and New England. Regimes that aspire to thought-control, whether Christian or secular, are never satisfied with prohibitions and punishments. They demand repentance and confession. The Church was not satisfied to silence Galileo, it insisted that he repent, confess, and acknowledge his sin.

It may be argued that Christianity has evolved, and has changed for the better. Many Christians have adopted social democracy. And that is true. It may even be argued that social democracy is compatible with the Christian insistence on equality before God and concern for the poor. It may be argued that institutions like slavery are incompatible with the principle of equality before the law, even if the early Christians did not realize it. There is no doubt that the Christian insistence on equality before God has lent support to the principle of equality before the law. However, equality before God is equally compatible with slavery in this world, especially when the otherworldliness of Christianity and the decrepitude of human nature are emphasized. The Christian emphasis on the radically fallen nature of the world makes life in this world unsuitable for principles of justice such as equality before the law. Christian principles are interpreted as transcending the profane world; they are intended only for the world to come. So it cannot be argued that equality before the law is *required* by Christianity. On the contrary, Christian beliefs can serve to undermine the implementation of this rational principle of justice.

I am not suggesting that Christianity has never inspired anyone to do good work in public life—witness the Social Gospel movement, the Red Cross, the Salvation Army, and their concern for the poor and downtrodden. Walter Rauschenbusch (1861–1918), the American clergyman, was inspired by his faith to play a leading role in the Social Gospel movement, which tried to remedy the abuses of capitalism and industrialism by insisting on better working conditions, one day off during the week, the right of every worker to a living wage, and the abolition of child labor. James Shaver Woodsworth (1874–1942), Canadian politician and Methodist minister, was inspired by his faith to devote himself to labor and welfare causes, and when Canada's New Democratic Party was founded in 1932 (a party that was inspired by the Social Gospel movement), he became its parliamentary leader. William Wilberforce (1759–1833), a British politician, was inspired by his faith to join the campaign for the abolition of slavery, and devoted his efforts to the suppression of the institution throughout the British Empire; a bill to that effect was passed by the British Parliament a month after his death. Martin Luther King (1929–68), a Baptist minister, opponent of segregation, and leader of the Civil Rights Movement, was inspired by his faith to call for justice and mutual understanding. But who is listening to Christian democrats? Who is listening to Christians with a social conscience?

The most vocal Christians of our time are members of the Religious Right. And far from undermining the harshest features of Christianity, they highlight them. It is not equality before God that inspires their political principles; it is not the message of love and forgiveness that guides their policies. On the contrary, it is the harsh, vengeful, ruthless, and merciless features of the faith that attract them. They are defenders of the rich, not the poor—supposedly on the ground that the rich deserve their riches because of their industry, sobriety, and abstinence, while the poor deserve their poverty because they are slothful, indolent, and self-indulgent. Even Augustine is likely to balk at such nonsense. But he is not likely to dissent from their use of Christianity to support capital punishment, to condemn any hint of diplomacy or dovishness in foreign policy, to justify intolerance toward homosexuals, to denounce the equality of the sexes, and to deprecate plurality as moral relativism.[74]

I am certain that Augustine (for one) would wholeheartedly share in the right-wing diatribes against a liberal culture that provides so many opportunities for freedom and pleasure. My point is that these harsh and intolerant versions of the faith are as soundly rooted in the sacred texts (and their canonical interpreters) as any dovish Social Gospel understanding of the faith might be.

PART III
ETHIC OF LOVE

It may be argued that Christianity was not intended as a standard for politics but as a guide to private life, and that Jesus was primarily a great moral teacher. Indeed, those who deny that Jesus was God incarnate, and even those who recognize the defects of his theology, often acknowledge the wisdom of his ethic of love.[1]

What is curious about Christianity and what probably accounts for its resilience, is its ability to balance a harsh metaphysic with an apparently genial morality. In what follows, I intend to show that the ethic of love is not as genial as it appears nor is it as opposed to the metaphysics of terror, as it seems. On the contrary, it has bequeathed to the West a concept of morality as an inner state of siege. And this view of morality assumes that morality is antithetical to natural human inclinations. This conflict between human nature and morality is at the root of the Western assumption that terror—spiritual, political, and psychological—is at the heart of the civilizing process. The assumption is that to be civilized, man must be spiritually terrified, politically oppressed, or psychologically brutalized. And as I will show in the next chapter, this attitude invites a revolt against morality itself.

1. The Morality of Jesus

There are four aspects of the moral teaching of Jesus that deserve critical analysis. First, his moral teaching is profoundly otherworldly, which is to say that his ethic cannot be totally separated from his theology. The focus of his moral teaching is on the world to come, not on this world, which is worthless and is about to be destroyed anyway.[2] He entreats people to sell all they have, distribute it to the poor, and follow him (Luke 18:22). Since "it is easier for a camel to go through the eye of a needle, than for a rich man to enter into the kingdom of God" (Matthew 19:24), it follows that this world and its riches must be obstacles to spiritual fulfillment.

Jesus tells his listeners not to concern themselves with the mundanities of life (i.e., what to eat, drink, or wear). Instead, he tells them to think of themselves as ravens or lilies:

> Consider the ravens: for they neither sow nor reap; which neither have storehouse nor barn; and God feedeth them: how much more are ye better than the fowls? . . . Consider the lilies how they grow: they toil not, they spin not; and yet I say unto you, that Solomon in all his glory was not arrayed like one of these. If then God so clothe the grass, which is today in the field, and tomorrow is cast into the oven; how much more will he clothe you, O ye of little faith? And seek not ye what ye shall eat, or what ye shall drink, neither be ye of doubtful mind. For all these things do the nations of the world seek after: and your father knoweth that ye have need of these things. But rather seek ye the kingdom of God; and all these things shall be added unto you. (Luke 12:24–33; also Matthew 6:25–26)

The idea is not to be too preoccupied with our mortal life, but to attend to our spiritual needs instead. Jesus is recommending a carefree attitude to life: "take therefore no thought for the morrow" (Matthew 6:34). He thinks that we can attain this carefree existence if we trust in God and believe that he will look after us as he does the lilies in the field.

The advice is well taken, but if taken too seriously, it is fraught with danger. It suggests that it is not necessary to sow, spin, or toil, and that we should model ourselves after the ravens and lilies of the field. If taken to heart, this advice may encourage indolence, sloth, and dependence on others to minister to our needs. At the very least, it sanctions a happy-go-lucky approach to life that shuns work, toil, self-sufficiency, and responsibility.

This carefree existence was suitable to Jesus and his disciples because they had a special calling, but it is a poor model for others. Jesus and his disciples traveled and preached, and relied on others to minister to their needs. They were not exactly freeloaders, because people clearly loved to hear Jesus teach and were happy to provide for him and his disciples in exchange.

The example of the two sisters, Mary and Martha, is illustrative. As Jesus traveled, he came to a village where a woman named Martha received him in her house. She had a sister called Mary who sat at Jesus's feet and listened to him, but did nothing to help Martha who was busy ministering to the needs of Jesus and his entourage. When Martha appeals to Jesus and tells him to bid her sister give her some help, Jesus says: "Martha, Martha, thou art careful and troubled about many things: But one thing is needful: and Mary hath chosen that good part, which shall not be taken away from her" (Luke 10:38–42). In other words, Mary has the right priorities. Nevertheless, Jesus and his disciples depended on the likes of Martha to look after their needs—because they were neither ravens nor lilies.

The second important feature of Jesus's moral teaching appears in his famous Sermon on the Mount:

> Ye have heard that it hath been said, An eye for an eye, and a tooth for a tooth: But I say unto you, That ye resist not evil: but whosoever shall smite thee on thy right cheek, turn to him the other also. And if any man will sue thee at law, and take away thy coat, let him have thy cloak also. And whosoever shall compel thee to go a mile, go with him twain … Ye have heard that it hath been said, Thou shalt love thy neighbour and hate thine enemy. But I say unto you Love your enemies, bless them that curse you, do good to them that hate you, and pray for them which despitefully use you, and persecute you. (Matthew 5:38–48)

Instead of exploding over the smallest abuse or insult, Jesus recommends turning the other cheek, going the extra mile, loving our enemies, and not resisting evil. This sounds like a noble ethic that sets a very high standard of conduct, which is altogether antithetical to the violence and belligerence of the pagan preoccupation with honor and valor.

However, it is a mistake to exaggerate the nobility or the novelty of this ethic. First, it does not surrender vengeance as I have pointed out earlier. On the contrary, it replaces human vengeance with a divine vengeance that is much greater and much more effective. Second, long before Jesus, the Hebrew prophets had repudiated revenge without any assurances of rewards in heaven or the more efficacious revenge of God in the beyond. Long before Jesus, Chinese moralists such as Lao-Tsze recommended kindness to enemies.[3] Likewise, the mythical Hindu legislator and author of "The Laws of Manu" advocated blessing those who curse you.[4]

Long before Jesus, Socrates also repudiated revenge. He taught that it is better to suffer evil than to do evil. But the Socratic doctrine is superior to that of Jesus's in two ways. First, it does not depend on the expectation of some reward in the afterlife but on the happiness and inner peace that is constitutive of the virtuous life in this world. Second, the Socratic doctrine is more reasonable. As a principle of action, "resist not evil" is morally and politically disastrous; it could encourage bullies and inspire tyrants. As a principle of action, it implies that it is not morally blameworthy to be passive in the face of gross injustices. In contrast, Socrates does not tell us not to resist evil; he simply tells us that when we are forced to choose between doing and suffering evil, we should choose the latter. Socrates was himself in that position when Critias, the leader of the thirty tyrants of Athens, asked him to arrest an innocent citizen. He refused, and took the chance that he would suffer harm at the hands of the tyrants.[5]

The third aspect of Jesus's moral teaching is the golden rule: "Therefore all things whatsoever ye would that men should do to you, do ye even so to them; for this is the law and the prophets" (Matthew 7:12). This may be a noble rule to live by as long as we do not take it too literally. It would certainly be a bad policy to assume that everyone has the same tastes and pleasures as ourselves. It may lead some to do all sorts of things that accord with their own tastes and pleasures but are most unpleasant to others. It has certainly led Christians to torment nonbelievers in order to save their souls. It has inspired Pope Pius IX to kidnap a Jewish child so that he can grow up a believer and go to heaven.[6] The negative version of the golden rule, formulated before Jesus by the famous Rabbi Hillel, is a somewhat safer guide to action. It tells us not to do to others what we would not like done to ourselves. This version is subject to similar misunderstandings as the positive version of the rule, but it is slightly safer because there is generally more agreement on the *summum mallum* than on the *summum bonum*, as Hobbes has argued so convincingly.

The fourth aspect of Jesus's moral teaching is perhaps the most significant, most difficult, and most far-reaching of all. Jesus stressed the importance of thoughts and feelings for the moral life. He rejected the view that righteousness consists merely in the outward conformity of actions to God's rules. Instead, he insisted that virtue is an inner disposition of mind. It is not just a question of doing the right thing, but doing it willingly and with a glad heart.

Jesus knew that the moral standard he demanded is more difficult than the one that Moses required. For example, he replaced polygamy with monogamy; he condemned the cavalier attitude to divorce, and declared that marriage is sacred and indissoluble. When the Jews, including his own disciples, challenged him, saying that Moses allowed divorce as well as a plurality of wives, he told them that this was never right, it was just allowed because of the "hardness of your hearts" (Matthew 19:8). He clearly believed that he was setting a higher moral standard than Moses—and he was.

The new ethic raises several questions. Is this a fair and reasonable ethic in view of human abilities? Or are its demands impossible and unfair? Is it merely a prudential ethic as critics have maintained? Does this ethic of love come into conflict with the metaphysics of terror or is it intimately connected with it? Is it the sort of ethic that trumps fate and eschews tragedy as Nietzsche has maintained? And, can the ethic of Jesus be separated from the sexual obsessions of the Church and its tendency to confuse ethics with asceticism? I will address these questions in what follows.

2. Sins of Thought

Jesus sets a standard of piety that surpasses the mechanical worshipper who goes through the motions but his heart is not in it. But is the emphasis on inner purity of heart a fair and reasonable standard for morality? Predictably, there have been two answers to this question: yes and no. Interestingly, both of these answers have come from within the Christian tradition itself. One is provided by Thomas Aquinas and the other by Martin Luther. And for different reasons, I think that they are both objectionable.

On the face of it, it seems that the Old and New Testaments come into conflict, especially where the question of polygamy is concerned. The Old Testament approves of it, while the New Testament does not. Jesus was confronted with this contradiction by his disciples, and he responded by saying that his own ethic is the right one, and has existed from time immemorial. If it comes into conflict with the ethic of Moses, it is merely because Moses was cognizant of human frailty and limited moral capacities. Moses allowed what was never right from the start only because of the "hardness of your hearts," as Jesus put it.

The obvious question is why was Jesus not also mindful of human shortcomings? In the course of elaborating on what Jesus says, Aquinas develops a more detailed answer that addresses this question in a way that may seem surprising for a pre-Hegelian writer. He claims that there is no contradiction or conflict between the morality of the Old and the New Testament; the two moralities differ because they are applicable to two different stages in the development of humanity. The Law of Moses was suitable to the crude and coarse condition of humanity in its early stage of development. The Law was intended to train, habituate, and educate humanity, just as we would educate a child by habituating it to virtue. In time, the Law had the effect of improving human nature.[7] The implication is that the latter is not static but is progressive; it lends itself to improvement. This progress in human consciousness makes it possible for human beings to live according to a higher and more difficult law, which God saw fit to provide in the New Testament. In other words, God gives man rules according to His perception of human abilities in the course of history. Jesus does not fashion a law that revolves around the "hardness" of the human heart, supposedly because the Law of Moses has triumphed over that hardness.

There are some serious objections to be made to these claims. In the first place, the question of polygamy is fundamental. The disciples are shocked when Jesus rejects polygamy and then proceeds to make marriage so sacred and indissoluble that only adultery would justify divorce. Among the Jews, a man did not need a reason to divorce any one of his wives.[8] The situation is the same among Muslims. I don't think that it is very controversial to say that polygamy is not fair to women. By the same token, I think that it is not an unreasonable arrangement in conditions where men are scarce because the natural balance between the sexes has been destroyed by war or some other calamity. It would be more consistent with the Thomistic view to argue that different marital arrangements are legitimate or reasonable under different circumstances and conditions, and that polygamy, monogamy, and polyandry are all reasonable arrangements depending on the circumstances. But that is not what Aquinas says.

Instead, Aquinas claims that humanity has advanced to a stage of development that makes it receptive to the higher moral law, the true morality. But clearly, this claim is spurious. The Romans observed monogamy, at the same time that the Jews practiced polygamy. So, it cannot be said of humanity as a whole, that the Law of Moses has improved them and made them ready to accept the higher law. Aquinas's quasi-Hegelian response fails because the Romans had already accepted that law, long before Jesus came along. What the Romans did not share is the idea that marriage is indissoluble. Neither Jesus nor Aquinas provides any argument to support the superiority of this principle. Marriage is the sort of association whose goals and ends are frustrated if the parties are not agreeable. The indissolubility of marriage has been the source of great misery and unhappiness in the history of the West since the ascendancy of Christianity. First, the ascendancy of such a harsh, caustic, and unreasonable dogma cannot be considered a superior morality that has existed from time immemorial, and was merely waiting for a great moralist and the moral development of mankind.

Second, as attractive as it is, the idea of virtue as an inner disposition of mind has limits. And Jesus pushes it beyond its reasonable limits. In his Sermon on the Mount, he explains the difference between the Law of Moses and the new morality. The Old Law says "thou shalt not commit adultery: But I say unto you that whosoever looketh on a woman to lust after her hath committed adultery already with her in his heart"

(Matthew 5:28). There are two ways to interpret what Jesus means. He could be saying that committing adultery in thought is *a sin*, but not a sin that is equal to the deed. Or, he could mean that the sins of thought and deed are identical.

No matter how we interpret what Jesus said, we must conclude that we should aspire to have no lustful thoughts or impulses. If we take this seriously, we would embark on a most hazardous path. In a desperate effort to eliminate illicit desires and to blunt unwanted impulses, human beings would be tempted to create a society in which anything that might trigger temptation is eliminated. Because sensuality is the enemy, the visual world and the people in it must be dull and colorless so as not to stimulate our senses and accidentally trigger unwanted desires. Architecture, decor, and clothing must be carefully monitored. Beauty becomes the enemy. Those responsible for beautifying the world or stimulating the senses must be repressed. Men naturally blame women, who become the evil temptresses in league with the devil. And this justifies their repression and subordination. In Islamic society, the bourka has been resorted to as the solution. The result is the creation of a world that is as drab as it is repressive and unjust. Besides, this strategy backfires. The total absence of environmental stimulus means that there is less opportunity for individuals to exercise self-control. Plato pointed to this problem in the context of the prohibition of wine in Sparta. And we have seen it as a problem for Afghani women who have regained the freedom to walk unveiled but are too afraid to do so because they have such a low estimation of the capacity of their men for self-restraint.

It may be argued that no system of law that has any claim to sophistication could rely exclusively on external conduct in defining crime. Even a pagan such as Aristotle identified several degrees of culpability depending on the state of mind associated with the act. He claimed that causing harm accidentally without the intention to harm and without any possibility of anticipating that the action in question would lead to harm, is a misfortune.[9] For example, I see a long lost friend, and I am so happy to see her, that I clap her on the back somewhat enthusiastically and as a result, she has a heart attack and dies. That is a great misfortune. But if I go shopping on a hot day and lock my children and dog in the car with the windows closed, then come back two hours later to find that they have expired, that is culpable behavior, even if it comes out of ignorance and not out of malice or any intention to harm. I am culpable because I should have known better. Such colossal ignorance does not serve as an excuse. Even worse is a crime that is done knowingly and with malice. But the worst crimes of all are those that proceed not only from malicious intentions but also from bad characters who are habitually malicious, cowardly, intemperate, and unjust. Therefore, the Jesus ethic is not unique in recognizing thoughts as integral to morality. Even Aristotle cannot dispense with thoughts in his account of crime and the equitable degrees of culpability that are to be attached to it. And our own legal system recognizes this fact in asserting that there can be no crime in the absence of a guilty mind, or *mens rea*.

In response to this objection, it must be said that intention and other mental states are relevant in defining crime and in determining the extent of culpability involved. But in so doing, we are not confusing thoughts *alone* with sins or crimes. There must first be *an action* or some actual harm done, before the relevance of thoughts and intentions comes into play. Thoughts are relevant *only* when actual harm has been done. But Jesus made thoughts alone, in the absence of any external manifestation, culpable. In so doing, he undermined the difference between thoughts and acts. This has had some far-reaching consequences.

When the Catholic Church invented an elaborate system of penance, it compiled sins and their appropriate penalties in penitentials, such as the famous penitential of Theodore. When a sin was confessed to a priest, he would consult one of these widely used penitentials and prescribe the appropriate penance as a voluntary atonement. What is significant is that in the penitential of Theodore, the distinction between thoughts and acts was obliterated. And this tells us something about how the words of Jesus were understood. Thoughts were to be punished with the same severity as if they were acts. In other words, it does not matter whether you committed adultery in your heart or in actuality—the penalty was the same. If you've had the thought, you've already committed the sin. This is not only unfair—it also invites depravity. If you have had the thought, you are just as culpable as if you had committed the act. So, you might as well enjoy the real thing. In either case, the penance recommended by Theodore was seven years on bread and water.[10]

As Walter Kaufmann has rightly maintained, the distinction between thoughts or impulses and acts is critical for morality.[11] The moral individual does not act on every impulse, every inclination, or every fleeting desire. Morality presupposes the ability to judge one's desires, inclinations, instincts, and impulses and to repress some while affirming others, or to reject them at certain times and affirm them at the appropriate times. Like animals, human beings have instincts; but unlike animals, human beings are free to choose when to yield to their instincts and when to repress them. It is unjust to make the mere fact of having instincts, impulses, or thoughts, blameworthy. We are not free to choose our instincts, and sometimes we are not free to choose our impulses, thoughts, desires, or dreams, but we are free to choose which impulses, thoughts, or desires we will act on. It is impossible to be moral if the mere having of an instinct, an impulse, or a fleeting thought or desire, makes us blameworthy.

On the most charitable interpretation, Jesus blurred the distinction between thoughts and acts, and some of his followers collapsed the distinction altogether. By the end of the tenth century, penitentials were not only part of ecclesiastical discipline, but also integral to Anglo-Saxon law. First, the priest prescribed the penance as a "voluntary" atonement; then, the judicial officer prescribed it as a punishment under law. The refusal of the sinner to submit to the judicial penalty led to the excommunication of the sinner from the Church.[12] Therefore, Church and state worked hand in hand. The Church used the secular powers to enforce its penalties and that meant that they were very far from being voluntary atonements for sin. The criminalization of sin was complete.

The Protestant Reformation ended the penitential system and undermined the power of the priests, but the sins of thought continued to have a central place in Protestant morality. Luther replaced the thought-control of the Church with self-repression and self-policing. This obsessiveness about the sins of thought manifested itself in Protestant diaries and spiritual memoirs.

In *The Puritan Family*, Edmund Morgan begins his book with a dramatic statement that captures the character of Puritan society:

> There was a type of man whom the Puritans never tired of denouncing. He was a good citizen, a man who obeyed the laws, carried out his social obligations, and never injured others. The Puritans called him a "civil man," and admitted that he was "outwardly just, temperate, chaste, careful to follow his worldly businesses, will not hurt as much as his neighbours dog, payes every man his owne, and lives of his owne; no drunkard, adulterer or quareller; loves to live peaceably and quietly among his neighbours." This man, this paragon of social virtue, the Puritans said was on his way to Hell, and their preachers continually reminded him of it.[13]

Good conduct was not enough for the Puritans, just as it was not enough for Jesus. What mattered were thoughts, feelings, and inner dispositions—these defined the truly virtuous man. The "civil man" is just an imposter. But how can we tell the difference between the real thing and the subterfuge? Either we should invent criteria to make the distinction or we should leave it to God.

The Puritans insisted on making the distinction. They surmised that the difference between genuine virtue and the mere appearance of virtue must rest in faith. Genuine good conduct can only come out of faith—their faith, the true faith. As I have argued earlier, the idea is not peculiar to the Puritans; Jesus also emphasized the importance of believing in him as fundamental to good conduct; and as we have seen, he thought of unbelief itself as sin. When this idea inspires those in power, like the Puritans of New England, its ramifications are dark—sectarian intolerance, political oppression of unbelievers, thought-control, witch-hunting, and endless soul-searching on the part of the faithful themselves. All these were features of Puritan society in England and New England.

In defense of Jesus, it must be pointed out that he was not establishing a legal system but a moral one. In contrast to the Puritans and other Christians in positions of power, Jesus thought that we should leave it to God to penetrate the heart and decide who is truly virtuous and who is an imposter. This dovetails with Jesus's view that we should not make a show of our virtue, but keep it secret: "let not thy left hand know what thy right hand doeth" (Matthew 6:3). But it remains the case that a preoccupation with sins of thought is dangerous when it triumphs socially and politically. No society can be free if it criminalizes thoughts, ideas, beliefs, feelings, fantasies, and dispositions. Truth itself would be sacrificed. Science would be impossible. Accepted falsehoods would be preferable to new and unsettling truths. This is the sort of intellectual tyranny that was established by the Church. Galileo was tried by the Inquisition (1633) and forced to repudiate his work in support of the Copernican system. Even then, he was put under house arrest, and the teaching and exploration of his ideas were banned. Under these conditions, philosophy is compelled to conceal itself; as a result, it deteriorates into a collection of cultish beliefs disseminated by esoteric writers of dubious intellect. If fantasies can be sins, then art, literature, and film—creativity itself—must be shunned for posing serious dangers to the purity of one's soul.

A free society must be satisfied with civil conduct intended to conform to public order and decency; it should not insist on conformity of thoughts, feelings, and attitudes. I am not denying the importance of thoughts, feelings, and dispositions for a rich and genuine morality. I am not saying that people cannot or should not repress their base inclinations. I am not saying that moral education should make no effort to influence feelings and dispositions, especially at an early age. I am not suggesting that we should indulge in murderous or lascivious thoughts without self-restraint. As Luther once remarked in reference to pornography, "Man cannot prevent a bird from flying over his head but he can stop it from building a nest in his hair."[14]

My objection to the Christian sensibility is that it is a poor foundation for morality. Moral virtue involves a certain confidence in oneself, which is antithetical to the anxiety created by the preoccupation with the sins of thought. By blurring the distinction between thoughts and acts, Jesus sets the stage for the self-doubt and self-mortification, which were to become the hallmarks of Christian morality. In my view, a virtuous person is not one who must overcome a titanic struggle over the forces of evil in her heart, before finally doing the right thing.

A virtuous person is someone for whom good conduct comes easily and naturally; he is someone who takes pleasure in doing the right thing; a moral person is someone who recognizes that good conduct is integral to his happiness and fulfillment. But Jesus did not connect his morality to happiness or fulfillment in this world.

In the final analysis, a morality of love is unfair, because love needs to be spontaneous and free; not even God can demand it. An ethic of love cannot be required for salvation. Law—whether human or divine, cannot command love because love is incompatible with threats of punishment or promises of reward.

No one recognized this more poignantly than the Prophet Muhammad. The Prophet had a very large polygamous household. But he was painfully aware of the Islamic restriction on polygamy—the husband is required by God to treat all his wives equally and justly. Being a just man, Muhammad had no difficulty treating his wives equally and justly. But in his heart, he had a special love for Aisha. So he begged God not to demand the impossible by commanding his heart; he begged God not to require what was not in his (Muhammad's) power.[15] In other words, the Prophet was clearly warning God not to command what could not be commanded. He was asking God to be satisfied with the outward conformity of his actions to His law. But Jesus was not satisfied with outward conformity to divine injunctions. Jesus demanded what is not necessarily in our power to deliver.

It may be argued that the Prophet failed to distinguish between *eros* and *agape*. *Eros* is erotic love, but *agape* is the kind of love that God has for humanity. It is the kind of love that is independent of our merits. It is the kind of love that is dependent on the will to love; it is about loving rather than being in love or falling in love. It is a heroic sort of love that reflects more on the lover than on the beloved. And while that kind of love has a role to play in marriage, it is not the only kind of love that a wife would care to have from her husband. But in the context of Muhammad's large polygamous household, it is probably the only kind of love that most of the wives could expect. But some were fortunate enough to have more. I am not suggesting that *eros* is superior to *agape*. It is the combination that is really delightful. The distinction between the two forms of love is itself a testimony to the Christian abhorrence of the body. It assumes that love is either spiritual and exalted or lustful and depraved. But in truth, a combination of the two is a very common experience indeed. But that combination was not always in Muhammad's power to give, at least not in equal measure to all his wives. But only God could have known what was in his heart. And that is why he rightly begged God not to demand more than was humanly possible.

3. A Tragic Ethos

Jesus is often criticized for providing what is merely a prudential ethic— an ethic that relies heavily on rewards and punishments.[16] Righteousness is not endorsed as an end in itself, or for the pleasure it gives to the giver in this world. It is not for love of God that we are asked to do good deeds. Nor is giving to others recommended for the sake of others, but rather only for the sake of one's own salvation. The idea is profoundly self-centered. And as we have seen, this selfishness colors not only our relations with strangers but also our relations with our family, whose welfare is ignored in the quest for personal salvation. It must be admitted that this is not the basis of a very elevated morality.

The critics seem to have a point. The ethic of Jesus relies heavily on a selfish preoccupation with self-salvation. Jesus assures the listeners of the Sermon on the Mount that "great is your reward in heaven," (Matthew 5:12). He also says, "Sell that ye have, and give alms; provide yourselves bags which wax not old, a treasure in the heavens that faileth not, where no thief approacheth, neither moth corrupteth" (Luke 12:33). And this is repeated again and again as we have seen in the discussions of heaven and hell earlier. Righteousness is endorsed merely for the sake of getting to heaven or escaping the torments of hell. There seems to be no inherent rewards in the ethic of love itself. It is never endorsed for its own sake or for the pleasure it gives the giver or the receiver. On the contrary, we find clear indications that fidelity to the ethic of Jesus is likely to cause us grief in this world: "And ye shall be hated of all men for my name's sake: but he that shall endure unto the end, the same shall be saved" (Mark 13:13). Jesus clearly anticipates the persecution of his followers.[17]

When we read the Epistles of Saint Paul, we find the same tormented sensibility that considers the righteous path so difficult and filled with sorrow that the faithful can do little more than hang on and hope that the end is near. And Paul does his best to reassure them that it is, and that their heavenly father will soon reward them for their ordeal.

All this evidence notwithstanding, the critics who regard Christian ethics as prudential are only partly right. The Catholic Church substituted the morality of Jesus with a tame and prudential ethic that was more palatable. If the Jesus ethic was merely a prudential ethic, then it would be simple and fair. But the Jesus ethic is neither simple nor fair. It is not just about being rewarded for living righteously or doing good work. It is about having particular beliefs, sentiments, and dispositions without which all the good work in the world is worthless. In its wisdom, the Church turned Christianity into a quiet and comforting religion. The criticism that the ethic of Jesus is merely prudential applies to the simplified version of the ethic espoused by the Catholic Church but it does not apply to the ethic as presented by Jesus in the Gospels or as understood by Augustine, Luther, Calvin, or Bunyan.

The religion of Jesus is not about earning your way to heaven by doing good works. Righteousness may be a necessary condition for salvation but it is by no means sufficient. Jesus does not offer a quiet and comforting religion but a religion filled with angst. More than any others, Luther and Bunyan understood fully that the Jesus ethic was more terrifying than prudential. And they were rightly critical of the Church for turning the religion of Jesus into something Pharisaic, which is to say, prudential. As I will show, these heroic writers embraced the Jesus ethic in all its gloominess. And what they embraced was neither comforting nor prudential.

4. Inner State of Siege

In contrast to the progressive optimism of Saint Thomas Aquinas, Martin Luther denies that the Law of Moses has played any role in the improvement of humanity. He bluntly states that the Law has never improved anyone. The Mosaic Law is dreadful and onerous—circumcision, dietary restrictions, ceremonies, and the like. As human beings, we instinctively hate the Law. Who can love it? But thanks to Jesus, we have been liberated from the Law. Therein lies Christian liberty.[18] We no longer have to justify ourselves by our own righteousness or adherence to the Law. The whole matter was impossible in any case. As long as our salvation depended on our own efforts, we were doomed. Christ came to save us from this terrible predicament. But at the same time, Jesus requires what is equally impossible.

One cannot help admire Luther for confronting the most grievous and unpalatable aspects of Christianity with unflinching courage and veracity. His conclusions are often dreadful but not illogical. Luther surmised that virtue properly understood, which is to say, as understood by Jesus, is humanly unattainable. Speaking from personal experience, he writes:

> Though I lived as a monk without reproach, I felt that I was a sinner before God with an extremely disturbed conscience. . . . I did not love, yes, I hated the righteous God who punishes sinners, and secretly, if not blasphemously, . . . I was angry with God, and said, 'As if, indeed, it is not enough, that miserable sinners, eternally lost through original sin, are crushed by every kind of calamity by the law of the Decalogue, without having God add pain to pain by the gospel and also by the gospel threatening us with his righteousness and wrath!'[19]

Luther acknowledges the truth about the God of the New Testament—namely, that He is much more wrathful than the God of the Old Testament—and *He* was no picnic. First, God gives us the arduous Decalogue or commandments; then in the New Testament, He tells us that we are required to follow His commandments with a loving heart. Ordinary laws require nothing of the sort. You can keep ordinary laws simply by doing what they enjoin, even if you have no heart in it. But God's laws are different. They cannot be fulfilled merely by compliance with their demands. They require an inner disposition of love; they require a glad heart free from all compulsion, threats, and fear. They require a genuine love of what the Law demands. "God judges according to your inmost convictions; His law must be fulfilled in your heart, and cannot be obeyed if you merely perform certain acts."[20] Jesus made that very clear.

Luther thought that all our efforts to obey the Law of God are in vain. Everything that we can do by our own strength to meet the demands of the Law is worthless as long as we hate the Law and feel it as a constraint. And in the depths of our hearts, we all hate the Law. No man does good work "without a certain reluctance and unwillingness in his heart."[21] The reason is that the commandments are deeply at odds with our nature.

In a dramatic inversion of the Socratic dictum, Luther claims that no one does good willingly. So, the idea of adhering to the Law of God with a loving heart is utterly preposterous. We end up hating the Law even more. And as a result, the Law serves only to multiply our guilt. We are doomed; our plight is hopeless; we are congenitally incapable of meeting God's demands. And that is particularly true of those of us who are unfortunate enough to be in bondage to Satan, and not in bondage to

God. And it is not our choice, whether we belong to Satan or to God; in either case, it is God's doing.[22] Then, He adds insult to injury by condemning us to eternal damnation for our failure. Yet, that failure was inevitable in view of the incongruity between the Law and our nature. What kind of a God is this? And how does Luther propose to reconcile himself with such a miserable God?

All His injustice notwithstanding, God nevertheless makes a gesture of totally undeserved love that is utterly staggering. By an extraordinary gift of grace, He makes it possible for *some* to do what the Law requires, without constraint and with a glad heart. For these lucky few, it is "as if neither the law nor its penalties existed. But this joy, this unconstrained love, is put into our hearts by the Holy Spirit, as Saint Paul says in chapter 5 [Romans 5:5]. But the Holy Spirit is given only in, with, and through, faith in Jesus Christ ..."[23] In other words, only those who have the gift of faith are capable of virtue.

This priceless gift of faith, which makes possible obedience to the law, is not conferred all at once, but in two stages. The first stage is conferred here on earth, and the rest of the gift is delivered in the beyond. So, what is the nature of the gift? And how do we know when it has been conferred? It seems to consist in the experience of the Holy Spirit. The descent of the Spirit in one's heart is transformative. Suddenly we love the Law that we once hated. We are gripped by a desire to act according to the Law. But not because of the rewards and punishments attached to the Law—not at all. It is as if the Law and its accompanying threats and rewards did not exist. But unfortunately, this love of the Law, this desire to do its bidding with a glad heart, without any expectation of reward, is not accompanied by the ability to do so. The descent of the Spirit is a surprising introduction of a foreign agent into the heart of man. The Spirit is at odds with human nature because the latter is antithetical to the Law. The result is that the Spirit wars against the flesh, and the flesh against the Spirit.

It is important not to confuse the conflict between the flesh and the Spirit with the old Platonic conflict between reason and the appetites. The latter conflict is between two parts of the human being. It testifies to the experience of having conflicting desires. Plato thought that the rational desires are superior or better in guiding life toward happiness and fulfillment. He thought that the rule of the passions will insure perpetual inner conflict; in contrast, the triumph of reason (and justice) will result in inner peace and harmony, so that the psyche will no longer be divided against itself. But the conflict between the flesh and the Spirit is another matter. Flesh represents the entirety of man—*body and soul*. Spirit is a divine spark that is no part of man. The descent of the Spirit into the soul is the introduction of a *foreign element* that inspires man to good, contrary to his natural inclinations. The descent of the Spirit does not result in inner peace and harmony, but quite the reverse. The result of the presence of the Spirit in the soul is an inner state of siege, war, and turmoil, in which the Spirit wars against the flesh and the flesh against the Spirit. In this way, morality is denatured; far from being the natural condition of health and happiness, the object of morality is to thwart nature.

Despite the gift of grace, Luther regards morality as a titanic inner struggle against the forces of darkness. It is a mistake to think that the gift of grace confers the ability to do good effortlessly. Effortless virtue is not possible in this life. Fasting and other labors continue to be necessary to subdue the flesh to the demands of the Spirit. Complete subservience of the flesh to the Spirit is accomplished only in the beyond, and that is the second and final installment of the gift of grace.

For this gift, Luther is profoundly grateful. But neither his gratitude nor the gift can alter the basic facts of the situation. We still have a God who demands from us what we are inherently incapable of doing and who punishes us with hitherto unmatched severity for our totally predictable and inescapable failure. The fact that he exempts a few from his wrath does not alter matters. Just because He is nice to Luther and a few others does not make Him a decent fellow.

If you are a child, and your father is very kind and gentle to you, you will love him with all your heart and you will believe that a better man has never walked the earth. One day, you find yourself kidnapped by gangsters, bound and gagged in a dark and dingy place. They seem determined to kill you, but not before they have some fun torturing you in this dungeon. A feeling of terror and despair descends upon you, such as you have never known before. And just when you thought your plight was utterly hope-less, your father appears on the scene and saves your life by doing something totally unexpected, dramatic, risky, and full of love and largess. So, he becomes an even bigger hero in your childish heart. But when you grow up, you discover that all along, your father was a mafia boss who is wanted by the police and is implicated in many crimes. Your kidnapping as a child starts to make sense to you. It is the sort of thing that would happen to a child whose father is in this nasty business. Nevertheless, you still love him because he is your father, but you would be fooling yourself if you thought that, all the evidence against him notwithstanding, he was a very decent fellow. Luther is paradigmatic of this sort of self-delusion.

It remains the case that Luther's love of God is based on self-interest. Luther loves God because God saves him from the dreadful plight to which others are subject. So, despite his heroic efforts, Luther does not succeed either in defending the goodness of God or in transcending the prudential ethic.

It seems to me that Bunyan tackles the difficulty with more fortitude. He lacks Luther's self-assurance of being one of the elect. He suspects that he will be damned no matter how hard he tries to be virtuous. But he resolves to love God regardless of God's cruel and capricious conduct. In a sense, he turns the tables on God. It is Bunyan who gives God a gift of grace—an unconditional love that is totally undeserved.

Far from softening the metaphysics of terror, the ethic of love makes the cruelty and injustice of God even more manifest. How can such a savage God inspire believers to virtue?

Clearly, the success of Christianity was partly due to the fact that the morality of Jesus was suppressed by the Catholic Church. It was transformed into a garden-variety prudential ethic, which is less exalted but more palatable. Only someone with the veracity of Luther or Bunyan could resurrect the ethic of Jesus in all its harshness. And only someone with the piety of Luther or the courage of Bunyan could embrace such a bleak morality.

In my view, Nietzsche totally misses the mark in thinking that Christianity trumps fate and destroys the tragic sensibility. Tragedy presupposes a universe that is totally indifferent to the human need for justice. The dreadful fates of the tragic heroes and heroines had no connection to their merits. In spite of her shortcomings, Antigone did not deserve to be buried alive. And Oedipus did not deserve his fate either. The fact that Oedipus had no intention of killing his father and marrying his mother seems to be irrelevant. His purity of heart makes no difference; he is punished for what he did, and not what he intended. Nietzsche wrongly assumes that Christianity destroys the truth of tragedy by taming reality and by pretending that a just God is in his heaven and all is well with the world. He wrongly assumes that a just God reigns over the Christian universe. But the truth is that the universe is as indifferent to justice as it has ever been.

Far from taming reality, Christianity makes it much more fiendish. And that is precisely why it has inspired so much art and literature. Instead of denouncing it, Nietzsche should have praised it for upping the ante where art and the tragic sensibility are concerned.

When seen in the light of the metaphysics of terror, the morality of Jesus is the farthest thing from a prudential morality; it is a supremely tragic ethic. If the essence of tragedy is a discrepancy between one's merits and one's fate, then the morality of Jesus is tragic indeed. If the substance of tragedy is a deep awareness of the indifference of the universe to the values that human beings hold dear, especially justice, then the Christian sensibility is tragic in the classic sense of the term. What could be gloomier than being condemned to eternal torment merely for being human? What could be more indifferent to justice than being saved from this dreadful fate by the capricious will of a God who is indifferent to our merits?

Does it make any sense to talk of a tragic ethic? The tragic sensibility presupposes a conflict between reality on one hand and the human demand for justice on the other. To act morally is not to imitate the cold indifference of the world. On the contrary, it is to affirm something in our humanity that is in conflict with the harsh universe. When Bunyan decides to love God, regardless of the latter's conduct, he affirms something in himself that stands in marked contrast to the cruelty of God. He rejects the idea that morality is the imitation of God—an idea that accounts for much of the horror done in the name of religion. All of Bunyan's humility notwithstanding, he affirms a morality that is superior to God's—a morality that is uniquely human. So understood, morality is man's gift of grace to the world. Unwittingly, Bunyan reclaims the pagan pride in morality as a human phenomenon and not as the imitation of God or nature. Bunyan does not understand what he has done nor does he express it as I have expressed it.

What is wrong with the morality of Jesus is not its lack of tragic gloom. It is rich in that. The harm it has inflicted has been largely psychological. Jesus raised the moral standard to unnatural heights without providing any confidence that human goodness is up to the task. On the contrary, he maintained that human wickedness is so great that it deserves eternal torment. It is no wonder that Luther despaired of the possibility of virtue. It is no wonder that Paul, Augustine, Luther, and Bunyan saw morality in terms of an inner struggle of the Spirit against the flesh. So understood, morality is an imposition, an inner state of siege, the internalization of an alien force that is hostile to natural human instincts and desires.

It may be argued that the understanding of morality as an inner state of siege may be avoided if we understand the descent of the Spirit into the soul, not as an act of sabotage but as the act of divine salvation—an act by which God reclaims us as his own. In other words, the descent of the Holy Spirit may be understood as a return to our true nature or our true self as children of God—a return to the self that was forfeited by the Fall. Indeed this is how the matter was understood by Origen of Alexandria and Saint Gregory of Nyssa. But this charitable interpretation is not the one that prevailed, because it is not altogether true to the sacred texts, especially the Epistles of Saint Paul. The latter's ingenious substitution of Jewish or bodily circumcision with the Christian "circumcision of the heart" highlights the agony involved in the experience of conversion.

5. More Than a Hint of Asceticism

The view of morality as the enemy of the natural instincts has the effect of confusing morality with asceticism. Morality is about good conduct or righteousness broadly understood. The moral life is neither devoted to the single-minded pursuit of pleasure nor is it antithetical to pleasure. Pleasure and duty are not identical, but they often overlap. To juxtapose them is to deny that it is possible to take pleasure in one's duty or in doing the right thing. Nevertheless, morality requires a willingness to forgo personal pleasure for the benefit of another.

In contrast to morality, asceticism confuses virtue with self-mortification, which benefits no one. Asceticism is hostile to pleasure in general and to sexual pleasure in particular. Because sexual pleasure is not necessary for the survival of the individual, it is singled out as a special target for ascetic vilification. And there is more than a hint of asceticism in the morality of Jesus.

It is fashionable among biblical scholars to criticize the treacherous history of the Church's sexual morality as if it had nothing to do with Jesus, the Gospels, or the true spirit of Christianity.[24] But this is clearly false.

In the context of a discussion of marriage with his disciples, Jesus asserted that marriage is a partnership in which husband and wife become one flesh, and this partnership is indissoluble—except by adultery (Matthew 19:11–12). The disciples are appalled at the strictness of this teaching in comparison to the Mosaic Law, which allows a man to have more than one wife and to dismiss a wife at his whim. Indignant, the apostles conclude that it is better not to marry all. And Jesus takes this opportunity to remark casually that it is not a bad idea to become a "eunuch for the kingdom of heaven's sake" (Matthew 19:12). We need not take Jesus literally to be suggesting self-castration. Understood figuratively, the reference to eunuchs is a reference to celibacy, not to castration. In other words, sexual abstinence would help in getting to heaven. But he does not make it mandatory; he considers it optional: "He that is able to receive it, let him receive it."[25] In short, those who can be (figuratively speaking) eunuchs should do it for the sake of heaven. In preferring celibacy to marriage, the Church is merely following the teaching of Jesus.

I wholeheartedly agree with Augustine in thinking that the words of Jesus imply that the celibate have an advantage where the kingdom of heaven is involved. As Augustine says: "what truer, what clearer words could have been spoken?"[26]

On another occasion, when Jesus was discussing life after the resurrection, he said that marriage does not exist in heaven. In heaven, people live like angels and they "neither marry, nor are given in marriage" (Matthew 22:30; Luke 20:27). The implication is that celibacy is superior to marriage because it is akin to the blessed life of the angels. It follows that those who practice it in this world are likely to be more fit for the world to come. It is difficult to avoid the conclusion that celibacy is more heavenly.

On yet another occasion, Jesus betrays a definite hostility to procreation. When he is led away to his crucifixion, he anticipates the day when "they shall say, Blessed are the barren, and the wombs that never bare, and the paps which never gave suck" (Luke 23:29). This is probably a reference to the spiritual kingdom to come, but it also reveals a hostility toward procreation that dovetails with his general indifference toward family life, including his own family, as we have seen.

It is important to note that Jesus presents celibacy merely as an option or a special sacrifice for heaven's sake. But in view of the fact that heaven is so elusive, and in view of who Jesus was believed to be, the smallest hint from Him was bound to have enormous ramifications. It is therefore not surprising that the fathers of the Church insisted on the moral superiority of the virginal life, and regarded carnal intercourse with a certain horror; they identified it with pollution, impurity, sin, and filth. And they were convinced that such "pollution" hindered the contemplation of God,[27] and made man more vulnerable to the machinations of the devil.[28] Accordingly, they recommended avoiding all "impure" looks, kisses, or touches.[29] Saint Gregory of Nyssa claimed that even "*thought* of the flesh" must be put aside,[30] to insure that the soul is not involved in anything that is "opposed to salvation."[31] And Aquinas quoted Augustine with approval saying: "I consider that nothing so casts down the manly mind from its heights as the fondling of women, and those bodily contacts which belong to the married state."[32] It was only natural for the Church to demand the highest standard of morality from the spiritual leaders of society. But the consequences were disastrous. The crimes and vices of enforced celibacy have filled volumes of history books and sold millions of newspapers.

Throughout this book, I have argued that Jesus cannot be totally absolved of the grim history of the Church. I am not suggesting that he is responsible for all of the atrocities done in his name; however, it remains the case that his doctrines are zealous, immoderate, and unwise. And when given the opportunity to triumph, they necessarily wreak havoc on the world. His preference for celibacy is one example. This is not the place to enumerate the horrors of the Church's celibate policy. But it is important to provide some objections to the quest for virginity, and the severe sexual repressions without which it cannot be accomplished.

First, men who consider their sexuality as the greatest threat to their salvation cannot regard women with a simulacrum of objective detachment, let alone with any humanity. When sex is identified with sin in the minds of men, women generally bear the burden of this vilification. The devotion to celibacy has led the Church to heap extravagant aspersions on the female sex. This antipathy to womanhood reached its climax in the infamous "Witch-Bull" of Pope Innocent VIII (1484) and its closely associated *Malleus Maleficarum* or "The Hammer of Witches," written by two zealous Dominican inquisitors hired by the pope to track down witches. This was a self-help manual for ambitious inquisitors who wanted to enhance their careers and improve their statistics on how many witches they managed to hunt down in their service to the pope. It contained step-by-step instructions on how to find witches, interrogate them, torture them, and make them confess: Yes, I had carnal relations with demons. Yes, I made a pact with the devil. Yes, I sealed the pact with the infamous kiss on the devil's posterior. Yes, yes, yes! On such unassailable evidence, these "witches" were burned alive.[33] But there were those who proclaimed their innocence in the face of formidable instruments of torture. Such great courage was considered definitive proof that they were guilty as charged. How else could they stand to be torn limb from limb if the devil did not contrive to make them insensible to the torture?

Jesus did not harbor the irrational aversion to women that has been so characteristic of the Church. He had many female disciples and was favorably disposed to all mankind. Nevertheless, he cannot be totally absolved of the terrors committed in the quest for the celibate and virginal ideal that he inspired. The Church's preoccupation with celibacy has led to a plethora of personal and institutional vices, not to mention crimes. Not least among these evils is the harm done by the grotesque vilification of the female sex that a celibate ideal requires.

It is also the case that Jesus encouraged the understanding of the world as filled with malevolent demons that conspire to snatch the words of God from our hearts and minds and threaten our salvation; this is the vision of the world on which belief in witches is based. It is not surprising that Aquinas declared that believing in demons was integral to the Catholic faith. The Church went a step further by declaring that denying the existence of witches was heretical and was probably an indication that the doubter was a witch herself. Jesus had no intention of demonizing and persecuting women, but this is precisely what his religion has done. The idea that Christianity has been a liberating force in the lives of women is one of those enduring fictions with no basis in reality.

The second case against the quest of virtue through sexual abstinence is that it generally backfires. Aquinas argued that the virginal life leaves one free for the contemplation of God. But far from silencing concupiscence, the life of the monk strengthens it. Even in his old age, Saint Augustine complained of "nocturnal pollutions." Saint Jerome beat his chest with a stone to drive away the evil desire he had for a dancing girl he saw in Rome. Saint Francis tried to cool the lust that burned within him by caressing figures made of snow. Saint Benedict stripped himself naked and rolled around in thorny bushes to chastise his body for its lust. Saint Bernard was prone to so much self-flagellation that his body reeked (probably with infections) so no one could stand to be near him.[34] Pascal wore a belt with metal spikes and tightened it whenever his passions got out of control. All this frustrated desire may serve only to stoke the flames of hell.

It seems to me that the radical thwarting of this natural instinct results in an obsessive fascination with sex that is likely to interfere with contemplation in general and the contemplation of God in particular. Aquinas spent a great deal of time defining the six different species of lust, identifying lustful looks and lustful kisses, determining the degrees of sinfulness of different sexual positions, deciding when the sexual intercourse of married couples was a venial sin and when it was a mortal sin. By the same token, Augustine spent much time imagining the sex life of Adam and Eve, cogitating on modes of generation in Paradise, wondering if the movement of the generative organ is not the symbol of the Fall, speculating on the venereal pleasures of the polygamous patriarchs, and worrying that the caresses of women might enfeeble the "manly mind" and threaten salvation. I venture to suggest that ordinary mortals who satisfy themselves now and again have much more leisure for the contemplation of higher things.

Finally, it is difficult not to conclude that what has made celibacy a virtue in the Christian tradition is the agony involved. As described by Saint Gregory, the goal of virginity is to unite oneself with God; this unity "comes from being *crucified* with Him" and sharing his anguish.[35] Celibacy is first and foremost about self-flagellation. And it is difficult to argue that this self-mortification pleases God without imputing to God a taste for sadistic pleasures.

In conclusion, the morality of Jesus has had some far-reaching consequences for Western civilization. It explains the prevalent confusion of
ethics and asceticism that is at the heart of the conception of morality as
an inner state of siege. As we shall see, this view of morality is reflected
in Freud's understanding of conscience as a "garrison in a conquered
city." The result is a conception of morality that is antithetical to human
nature and human instincts. Such a conception of morality fuels the view
that to be civilized, man must be tormented, brutalized, and repressed.
This underscores the assumption that human nature and civilization are
at odds, and that terror—physical, spiritual, and psychological—is the
secret to the success of civilization.

PART IV
PSYCHOLOGY OF TERROR

Wittingly or unwittingly, the ethic of love has contributed to the development of an inner state of siege—a psychology of terror—that accounts for the psychic neurosis of the West. In what follows, I will examine Freud's efforts to provide a remedy for the sort of pathology that Christian morality invites. I will show that Freud cannot provide an antidote to the Christian burden of guilt because he is trapped in the Christian horizon of moral thought. He shares the Christian emphasis on human depravity, the belief in original sin, the preoccupation with sins of thought, the pervasiveness of guilt, the need for expiation, the obsession with sex, and the confusion of ethics with asceticism. In short, Freud reinvents the austere Christian morality in a scientific guise.

In my view, none of this is good news for the moral and psychological health of a civilization. Far from inspiring piety, it inspires revolt—a Promethean revolt against God, a revolt that deprecates morality and makes evil heroic. This Promethean revolt reaches its climax in Nietzsche and his postmodern followers. But far from transcending the biblical horizon, this Promethean revolt accepts the fundamental premises of Christian thought, and responds to them in a way that is altogether understandable.

At the heart of the matter is the assumption that there is a conflict between human instincts and morality—human nature and civilization. By nature man is a wild and dangerous animal. Terror and brutality are necessary to civilize him and make him fit for society. The assumption is that the civilizing process is a process by which man is tamed, despoiled, and domesticated. In other words, terror and civilization are intimately linked because terror is the key to the civilizing process. This is the view that I intend to challenge.

1. Neurosis of the West

Christianity has bequeathed to Western civilization a conception of morality as a repressive internal policeman. Not only is this policeman concerned with monitoring our actions, but also our thoughts. The result is a pathological augmentation of guilt that Freud associates with neurosis. In other words, the Christian sensibility has created a psychic state of siege that is best described as the neurosis of the West. Freud was deeply cognizant of this neurosis and sought a remedy that would liberate the beleaguered psyche, but to no avail.

At first blush, Freud seems to offer an invaluable antidote to Christian guilt. It would seem that the thrust of his work has the effect of assuring us that we are normal, ordinary, and decent folk, even if we happened to have had bad dreams about killing a parent or having sexual relations with a sibling. He assures us that these dreadful dreams are part of our psychic makeup, which is not of our choosing. Supposedly, these are primitive impulses, which have been repressed into the unconscious, and bubble up in dreams. So we need not be alarmed. Nor should we think of ourselves as homicidal maniacs. But Freud cannot provide a remedy for the neurosis of the West, because he is in the grip of the neurosis himself, as we shall see.

In psychoanalytic terms, a neurosis is a mental disorder that has a wide variety of sources and symptoms. One of these sources is the repression of a dreadful or traumatic event, including thoughts and dreams. In one of his case studies, Freud describes the circumstances that led to the neurotic symptoms of his patient as follows:

> The patient was a girl, who had lost her beloved father after she had taken a share in nursing him ... Soon afterwards, her elder sister married, and her new brother-in-law aroused in her a peculiar feeling of sympathy which was easily masked under a disguise of family affection. Not long afterwards, her sister fell ill and died, in the absence of the patient and her mother. They were summoned in all haste without being given any information of the tragic event. When the girl reached the bedside of her dead sister, there came to her for a brief moment an idea that might be expressed in these words: "Now he is free and can marry me." We may assume with certainty that this idea, which betrayed to her consciousness the intense love for her brother-in-law of which she had not herself been conscious, was surrendered to repression a moment later, owing to a revolt of her feelings. The girl fell ill with severe hysterical symptoms.[1]

Freud explains that with analysis, this severely repressed thought was readmitted into consciousness with signs of the most violent emotions. But once brought into view what then? Freud tells us that it was dealt with appropriately and the girl became well again. But what does being dealt with appropriately mean? A rational approach would be to recognize this as a dreadful thought, but one on which she did not act and had no intention of acting. In this way, the guilt is recognized to be rationally groundless, and this recognition is likely to lead to its dissipation.

One might think that Freud would take this rational approach. But that is not so. Instead, Freud takes the guilt seriously. He believes that neurosis has its source in failing to admit the truth about our guilt. Somehow, the admission of guilt is itself the cure. Accepting our guilt is accepting the truth about ourselves, and that is the basis of the psychoanalytic cure.[2]

If Christian civilization as a whole is analogous to Freud's neurotic patient, then a rational antidote would require overturning the morality of Jesus. It would require a new understanding of morality—a sunnier and more naturalistic understanding. But Freud has no such remedy. Freud cannot provide Christian civilization with a remedy for its psychic pathologies because he is the heir of Christianity. Far from undermining Christian morality with his signature brand of rational secularism, Freud lends it scientific authority and makes it as influential in the modern secular world as it was in the Dark Ages. Nor does he deny his intellectual debt to Christianity. On the contrary, he declares Christianity to be true—historically and psychologically speaking. Far from rejecting original sin as preposterous, chimerical, and unfounded, Freud provides it with a historical and psychological justification.

2. Guilt, Original Sin, and Expiation

Christianity augments guilt by inventing the concept of original sin—the inherited sin against God. This is supposedly a terrible sin that requires expiation; but there is no hope that we can actually pay the penalty for such a great sin. Jesus offers to pay the penalty on our behalf, but that only serves to make us even more painfully aware of the magnitude of our sin. The debt on account of original sin, coupled with the debt on account of our own sins (thoughts as well as acts) makes the burden of guilt monumental. Morality becomes consumed by the need for expiation, and as a result, the distinction between morality and asceticism is blurred.

If Freud is right in thinking that a heightened sense of guilt is the cause of neurotic symptoms, then Christianity threatens our psychic health. The trouble is that Freud has no remedy; instead of undermining the idea of original sin, Freud gives it scientific credibility.

In *Moses and Monotheism*, Freud praises the Christian conception of original sin as historically and psychologically true.[3] According to Freud, the dawn of civilization began with the rule of a terrible, authoritarian, and castrating father over the horde. In the prehistory of mankind, the primeval father monopolized all the women in the clan, while castrating and repressing the sons. In time, his sons conspired against him, murdered him, and cannibalized his body.[4] The result of their deed was a strange ambivalence of feeling—joy and sadness. On one hand, the terrible deed liberated the sons from the castrating repressions of the father, but on the other hand, it filled them with remorse. For as much as they hated him, they also loved him—he was their father after all—a provider and protector. In time, the sorrow, pain, and guilt of this terrible deed was forgotten and buried deep in the unconscious. And then, the father was deified—he became a heavenly father.

According to Freud, the rule of the father is replaced by a period of matriarchal rule with its great mother deities, and its plurality of male gods who appear as sons, side by side with the great mothers.[5] The male gods are numerous, but they must share power, and must voluntarily accept the same limits that were previously imposed by the primeval father. A voluntary and mutual acceptance of the rules imposed by the father is the basis of civilized justice. First among these edicts is the prohibition on incest or the insistence on exogamy, which Freud defines as the "renunciation of the passionately desired mothers and sisters of the horde."[6] Totemism is devoted to that end. Two individuals belonging to the same totem cannot marry. Freud is convinced that the totem is a veiled substitute for the deposed father. The totem animal is the spiritual ancestor of the clan, and is worshiped. But once a year, the totem animal is killed and eaten by the clan, in what Freud believes to be a ritual repetition of the murder of the father. The totem feast survives in the Christian ritual of Holy Communion—the eating of the flesh and blood of the murdered Christ, our spiritual father and our God.[7] This cannibalistic act allows the prohibitions of the father to be internalized in the form of the superego.

So far, the story sounds progressive: once liberated from the primeval tyrant, human beings recognize the need for limits, and voluntarily accept them even in the absence of an external threat. We can also understand the story as a true myth in which our childish resentment toward the restrictions and repressions of our parents are overcome when we recognize the necessity and rationality of these restrictions for our own well-being as well as the well-being of our society. But Freud does not leave it at that. Instead, Freud regards the overthrow of matriarchal structures and the return to patriarchal religion in the form of Judaism to be a sign of further progress.

In Freud's view, Judaism is based on the return of the memory of a traumatic event and that traumatic event is the murder of the primeval father.[8] Nor is this traumatic event a fiction. Freud is certain that it refers to the historical killing of Moses. The memory of that killing is part of the "archaic heritage," which preserves in the mind of each generation "memories of what their ancestors have experienced."[9] Freud compares it to innate ideas. The Father religion reintroduces the repressions of the father and requires ever increasing and exacting instinctual renunciations. Freud surmises that circumcision is practiced in memory of the castration imposed by the primeval father.[10] In this way, the Jews reached new heights of "moral asceticism."[11] But why would new heights of asceticism be progressive?

The answer lies in the fact that Freud is trapped within the horizon of biblical thought. He thinks of morality in terms of asceticism—which is to say, instinctual renunciations and self-flagellating activities that may or may not benefit anyone, but supposedly please that dreadful God in heaven modeled after the primeval father. Freud praises this moral asceticism as an achievement—but it is not clear why. It is not clear why a rational or scientific mind, cognizant of the dangers of radical and unnecessary instinctual renunciations, would praise new heights of moral asceticism as an achievement.

Freud's praise of Judaism is modest in comparison to his praise for Christianity. He thinks that the success of Christianity is due to the fact that it has its "source in historical truth."[12] The Christian doctrine of original sin is both historically and psychologically true. Historically, it refers to the killing of the primeval father. Psychologically, it explains the burden of guilt that we have inherited as a result of that murder.[13]

Freud is convinced that the original sin must be the killing of the father. What else but a murder deserves death? Freud takes the killing of the father seriously, not as a myth, or even a true myth, but as a historical fact, integral to the history or prehistory of the human horde. What he admires about Christianity is that it tells the truth about our psychic history; it admits the murder of the father; it accepts the burden of guilt; and it recognizes the need for expiation. It is a religion of the Son who seeks reconciliation with the Father by atoning for the original patricide through his death on the cross. Nevertheless, even Christianity does not fully acknowledge the murder. The concept of original sin keeps the murder obscure. However, accepting the burden of our "archaic heritage" is a step in the right direction.

Freud gives Christianity too much credit. Notwithstanding their focus on original sin, Christians nevertheless regard themselves as innocent in comparison with Jews, whom they accuse of being the killers of God. Freud thinks that the accusation is true; and that the Jews would be better off acknowledging their guilt instead of denying and repressing it. Supposedly, the Jews would be less neurotic if they admitted their guilt. But what reason does Freud have for recommending the confession of all this imaginary guilt? Why is the acceptance of the archaic burden of guilt a step in the right direction?

It seems to me that there is an important distinction to be made between real and imaginary guilt. But Freud seems indifferent to the distinction. Real guilt has its source in actual deeds and transgressions, or in serious omissions. Imaginary guilt has its source in thoughts, dreams, impulses, and that mystical "archaic heritage." To consider all these on an equal par is a mistake. Jesus and Freud make the same mistake. For example, in his commentary on Hamlet, Freud tries to unlock the mystery of the play. Why is Hamlet so indecisive when it comes to avenging his father's murder? Why does he brood ineffectually? Why does he fail to act, even when he has all the evidence he needs? Simply stated, Freud's answer is that Hamlet cannot revenge himself against the man who killed his father and married his mother because that is precisely what Hamlet longed to do in his heart. In Freud's estimation, Hamlet is "*literally* no better than the sinner whom he is to punish."[14]

In truth, there is no reason for Hamlet to confuse himself with the murderer. There is a gulf that separates him from the murderer—that gulf is not his lack of courage (as Freud implies), but his decency. If Hamlet's malaise is due to recognition of archaic guilt, then Freud cannot provide a remedy. By the same token, he cannot provide a remedy for the archaic guilt of Christian civilization.

Far from transcending the burden of guilt on account of original sin, Freud augments the problem. Like the Christian theologians before him, he magnifies human depravity in a scientific guise. He tells us that we are all just like our primeval ancestors—remorseless killers. Supposedly, primeval man still survives in our unconscious: "judged by our unconscious wishful impulses, we ourselves are, like primeval man, a gang of murderers."[15]

Even if primeval man is as murderous as Freud claims, what proof is there that we are just as murderous as primeval man? The proof says Freud is in our thoughts, dreams, and unconscious—we are just as ready to annihilate our enemies—and even our loved ones, if they stand in our way. Now, supposing that we often wish that those who stand in our way would just disappear. Freud says *that* is a death wish and is proof that we are murderers. But is that fair? Is it fair to accuse people of being remorseless killers because they find others irritating? Or because they wish someone were dead or just out of the way, but have absolutely no intention of acting on such a wish? Is it reasonable to feel criminally liable on account of haphazard or fleeting thoughts and wishes—thoughts that we have no intention of acting on?

Let us take Pinocchio as an example. When Pinocchio was about to become a real boy, the Blue Fairy appointed Jiminy Cricket to be his conscience.[16] In the original story, Pinocchio runs way from his conscience. He feels guilty for doing this—and rightly so. But in the Walt Disney version, Pinocchio is abducted. What then is the source of his guilt? His guilt is unfounded. It can only be described as psychoanalytic guilt.[17] He feels guilty for being abducted because deep down he feels, as Hamlet did, that in his heart, he longed to run away from his conscience. If Pinocchio is not going to be hopelessly neurotic, then he must understand that a real boy must accept responsibility for his actions, not for his unconscious wishes.

Freud tells us that it is the function of the healthy ego to navigate between the repressions of the superego on one hand and the id's quest for pleasure on the other. But how can the ego protect itself against the tyranny of the superego without making a clear distinction between legitimate guilt, which is the result of wrongdoing and illegitimate feelings of guilt on account of dreams or unconscious wishes. How can the ego succeed in a climate in which thoughts and acts are equally culpable? Just admitting the guilt will not do. It matters a great deal whether our feeling of guilt has a basis in reality or not. We cannot simply say that all guilty feelings, qua feelings, are equally legitimate. Feelings are not all equally legitimate. Some are justified in view of the facts, and others are not. If reason judges our feelings to be unfounded and illegitimate, they will eventually fade. Our rational mind cannot dictate our emotional life, but it can certainly influence our feelings by legitimating or delegitimating them.

The failure to distinguish between legitimate and illegitimate feelings of guilt, leads Freud to take archaic guilt too seriously. He does not distinguish between guilt for our own wrongdoing and guilt on account of original sin. He assumes that the guilt is about feelings and feelings are all equally real. We just have to uncover the deadly deed that is the source of the guilt. And he thinks that he can relieve the burden of guilt by confession. Supposedly, the Christians confess, but the Jews refuse to confess and therefore live with their neurosis. But are Jews really more neurotic than Christians?

Thanks partly to Freud and to television talk shows, we have a confessional culture. But does public confession relieve the burden of guilt? And if the guilt is legitimate, why should it be alleviated just by confession? How can such a culture improve anyone? There is no evidence that a confessional culture improved Catholics. So why do we think it will do our secular society any good?

In conclusion, there is a simple reason why Freud cannot provide Christian civilization with an antidote against its burden of guilt: he is the heir of Christianity. He accepts the Christian idea of original sin, as the sin against God the Father. He thinks that the sin is inherited and is part of our psychic makeup. He does not care to make a distinction between acts and thoughts—he does not care to separate real murders from imaginary ones—he thinks that our unconscious thoughts reveal what we would be *really* like if it were not for the repressions of civilization. In this way, Freud provides the doctrine of original sin with a pseudo-rational, historical, and scientific justification. He also shares the Christian view that morality has its source in the acknowledgment of our wickedness, and the recognition of our guilt—a guilt that is defined as "repressed hostility to God."[18] And he thinks that such guilt requires expiation in the form of renunciation of instinctual gratification. In short, Freud shares the Christian view of morality as an ascetic renunciation of natural instincts, self-abnegation, and masochistic self-flagellation. And when he speaks of a "higher" morality, he means a morality with more exacting renunciations.

3. A Garrison Within

What passes for late modernity or postmodernity is not so much a departure from fundamental Christian assumptions, but their continuation in a new guise. This is no doubt an astonishing statement. But its meaning will become apparent if we attend to a most disturbing assumption that Nietzsche and Freud share with the dominant aspects of Christianity—namely, the assumption that there is a profound conflict between human nature or human instincts on one hand, and morality on the other. This view is at the heart of Western morality from Saint Paul to Nietzsche, Freud, and their postmodern followers.

As we have seen, in the conflict between the flesh and the Spirit, the latter is the alien voice of the Holy Spirit that inclines man to doing good contrary to his nature. Freud replaces the war between the flesh and the Spirit with the struggle between the id and the superego. Just as the Spirit is the alien voice of God, the superego is the alien voice of society. But the assumption is still the same—namely, that there is a conflict between human nature on one hand and the moral law on the other. No one articulated this thesis more clearly or more systematically than Freud.

In what follows, I will focus primarily on Freud's version of the thesis. The view that I am challenging is the view that conscience is an alien, hostile, and repressive force—the internalization of terror—the terror of civilization. I believe that this thesis leads to erroneous (but enduring) assumptions about the relation between human nature and civilization. Moreover, it seriously misconstrues the connection between terror and civilization.

At the heart of the matter is the evil of human nature that civilization must restrain. As Freud puts it, we are all descendants from "little sadists and animal tormentors."[19] When World War I broke out, people were shocked and disillusioned at the barbarism of their fellow human beings. But in commenting on the war, Freud argued that their disillusionment has its source in the assumption that it is possible to eradicate evil by education. But in Freud's view, there is no such thing as eradicating evil; the basic human instincts cannot be changed or improved. They can only be repressed. But they are always there, just below the surface, ready to wreak havoc on civilized life. In other words, one should not be shocked or surprised by barbaric conduct. That is par for the course. And those who think that wars and other atrocities can be eliminated are unwilling to face reality—the ineradicable savage reality of our nature.

In light of this fierce reality, terror is necessary to repress, tame, and domesticate man's savage instincts. It may be argued (as Thomas Hobbes did) that fear of punishment or the threat of violent death is a necessary and sufficient means to control human nature. But Hobbes was wrong. Fear of corporal punishment is not enough. As Nietzsche rightly observed, punishment succeeds primarily in hardening the criminal and making him resolve to proceed more cautiously.[20] Besides, those who rely on the fear of punishment as the foundation of civilization cannot explain why people comply with the law even when there is no chance of being found out. Nietzsche and Freud provide an explanation that eludes the likes of Hobbes.

The explanation is two-fold. First, civilization plays with our feeling of indebtedness. We are made to feel as deeply indebted to our civilization as to our father and protector. Second, like the father, civilization represses our natural or aggressive instincts. The idea is to make us feel that any transgression of its rules is akin to raising our hand against our benefactor, against our father, so that we are filled with feelings of remorse and self-hatred. In this way, our aggressive instincts, which cannot be eradicated, are turned inward, in the form of the self-immolating and self-censuring phenomenon of conscience. The genius of civilization rests in its capacity to turn our aggression against ourselves. It is not overt terror that succeeds, but the covert terror that is internalized in the form of conscience—*that* is the secret of the success of civilization. Notice that this explanation does not amount to saying that civilization internalizes its ideals and values.

Freud explains that the task of civilization is to render the aggressive instincts of the individual innocuous; otherwise, social life and the life of the individual are threatened. The strategy is as follows:

> His aggressiveness is interjected, internalized; it is, in point of fact, sent back to where it came from—that is, it is directed towards his own ego. There it is taken over by a portion of the ego, which sets itself over against the rest of the ego as the super-ego, and which now, in the form of "conscience," is ready to put into action against the ego the same harsh aggressiveness that the ego would have liked to satisfy upon other, extraneous individuals. The tension between the harsh super-ego and the ego that is subjected to it is called by us the sense of guilt; it expresses itself as a need for punishment. Civilization, therefore, obtains mastery over the individual's dangerous desire for aggression by weakening and disarming it and by setting an agency within him to watch over it, like *a garrison in a conquered city.*[21]

Conscience is a garrison within—the military metaphor underscores the violence involved. For Freud, civilization is an all-out war against the instincts. This psychological form of terror is far greater and considerably more effective than any threat of physical torment. Indeed, it is so successful that it punishes the individual not only for her misdeeds but also for her thoughts and wishes:

> the distinction, . . . between doing something bad and wishing to do it disappears entirely, since nothing can be hidden from the super-ego, not even thoughts.[22]

Conscience succeeds where punishment fails. However, the success of civilization is purchased at a price—a staggering price for the human psyche and its instincts. For conscience is not satisfied merely with the renunciation of the illicit desires, it demands that they no longer be desired. The forbidden thoughts, feelings, and desires must be banished. Conscience demands thought-control and censorship. Freud's conception of conscience has for its model the morality of Jesus. Like Jesus, Freud does not confine sin to actions. Conscience finds us culpable not only for our wrongdoing, but also for our thoughts, impulses, dreams, and fantasies.[23]

From Christianity to Freud, this view of civilization invites the same questions. What evidence is there that human nature and the moral law are antithetical? What evidence is there that civilization and the instincts are indeed deadly enemies? And even if there is an implacable conflict between civilization and the instincts, it remains a mystery as to why a wild and brutish animal would allow its nature to be subverted without any tangible selfish compensation. I will deal with these questions in what follows.

4. The Moses of Freud: A Criticism

The belief in the conflict between civilization and the instincts is best illustrated in Freud's imaginative interpretation of Michelangelo's controversial sculpture of Moses with the head of Pan.[24] This is not the hotheaded Moses of the Bible.[25] He is not angry with his people for partying, carrying on, and worshipping idols. He is calm, controlled, and reflective. And instead of breaking the tablets in a rage, he preserves them under his arm. Freud suggests that Moses must have had second thoughts about the Ten Commandments inscribed on these tablets. He must have been worried about the news he had to deliver. He must have suspected the exorbitant toll that these commandments will exact. He must have imagined the human cost involved. He must have calculated the price that the instincts will have to pay. This explains why he sits quietly, holding the tablets under his arm. These tablets contain the commandments that will launch civilization on its war against the instincts. And Freud is convinced that the worst suspicions of Moses have become a reality. The commandments have exacted a very high price indeed. So much so, that we find ourselves at great risk of being neurotics. But what evidence is there that civilization is built on the backs of the instincts? What evidence is there that human beings are murderous savages kept in check by the prohibitions of civilization?

It is my contention that the war of civilization against the instincts is the invention of Freud. But he did not invent it single-handedly; he inherited it from the Christian civilization that shaped him. In what follows, I will make *four* arguments against the view that civilization is built on the backs of the instincts, that human nature and civilization are profoundly antithetical, and that only spiritual, political, or psychological terror can civilize humanity.

First, let us start with the Ten Commandments (Exodus 20:1–17). Just how onerous are these commandments anyway?

1. Thou shalt have no other gods before me. If we are going to worship gods at all, it would be much easier to worship one god than a collection of different gods with different jurisdictions for different

purposes—the god of war, the goddess of wisdom, the god of the sea, and so on. Assuming (of course) that the one God does not make unreasonable demands. As it turned out, His preoccupation with foreskins was somewhat disconcerting. And now and again He made some unreasonable or unjust demands. But the commandment simply tells us not to worship other gods; it does not tell us to obey every one of His outlandish requests. And the Jews certainly questioned some of God's commands.

2. Thou shalt not make unto thee any graven images. That means no statues of bugs, beetles, or birds to grovel before—not even a statute of the one and only God. This is a very dignified existence. This God is clearly sublime. He wants love, devotion, and loyalty, not empty ceremonies and rituals.

3. Thou shalt not take the name of the Lord thy God in vain. This is a simple gesture of respect—it is quite understandable that God would feel that He is entitled to this sort of respect. In practice it means no swearing or cursing at God when things don't go the way you want them. Again this is a dignified way to live.

4. Remember the Sabbath day, and keep it holy. This is an enforced holiday. God must have suspected that deep down, we are all workaholics, and to save us from ourselves, he created the Sabbath.

5. Honor thy father and thy mother. Now, how hard is that? He is not telling us to love our enemies, he is just telling us to love and honor the two people who brought us into the world, cherished us, nourished us, and protected us. So, that's not a big deal; it is something we generally do anyway. Only teenagers rebel against their parents; so you might say that this is a teenage commandment. The rest of us follow the commandment as a matter of course.

6. Thou shalt not kill. This is not a blanket commandment. We are not prohibited from killing in self-defense. Nor does this commandment forbid slaughtering the Canaanites or the Philistines at the behest of God. The only thing it prohibits is arbitrary and capricious killing whenever we feel like it, in the absence of the command of God or the state. But who really wants to do that? Not many. And those who do are hardly deterred by fear of punishment. They do it anyway, and give journalists something to report to the rest of the sane population.

7. Thou shalt not commit adultery. Now, that should be of interest to Freud. There's his proof that civilization has launched a war against the instincts, especially the sexual instincts, which are the ones that really count in Freud's scheme of things. But what was adultery to the polygamous Israelites? For Israelite men, adultery was sleeping with

another man's wife. That did not preclude sleeping with unmarried or unattached women, or marrying more than one woman. Sleeping with an unmarried woman that was not your wife was not adultery. In other words, a man could not commit adultery against his own marriage, only against another man's marriage. The commandment against adultery is meant to protect the property that men have in their wives. The commandment is for your own self-protection. It is just a matter of prudence. If you want to sleep with a woman that's not your wife, make sure she is not another man's wife, otherwise, you can get yourself killed (Leviticus 20:10). However, the commandment does not apply to women in the same way. For a woman, sleeping with *any* man who was not her husband, whether he was married or unmarried, was adultery, and the penalty was death (Deuteronomy 22:22). Even a betrothed damsel who lies with a man other than her betrothed, is guilty of adultery, and should be stoned to death along with her partner (Deuteronomy 22:23).[26] Let's face it—the Old Testament is not famous for justice between the sexes.[27] Israelite women have every reason to object to this inequitable state of affairs. But Freud is in no position to object. He cannot argue that the unequal burden placed on women is unjust—not in view of his estimation of female sexuality, or lack thereof. If Freud is right in thinking that only men are sexual beings or have strong sexual drives that civilization can repress and sublimate, then women cannot complain of being unduly burdened by the commandment regarding adultery. If Freud is right in saying that only men are interested in sex, while women merely put up with it for the sake of offspring, then the prohibition of adultery, even though it is much stricter for women, is not particularly burdensome.[28] Freud's failure to comprehend the female psyche is legendary.[29]

8. Thou shalt not steal. Again we have a commandment that is not difficult to keep, as long as our own self-preservation is not at stake. A starving man who steals a loaf of bread is excused, in all but the most brutal societies. With the notable exception of Locke, philosophers consider property a political and not a natural right. And prior to Locke, most philosophers would have agreed with Aquinas in thinking that stealing is not wrong in a society where the laws of property were highly inequitable. But thanks to the fanatical admirers of Locke, we are living in a society that is more and more inclined to think of property rights as inviolable. Clearly, the commandment against stealing is set in the context of modestly adequate conventions about property rights.

9. Thou shalt not bear false witness against thy neighbor.[30] This seems to be a very important rule, and I am surprised it is not more prominently situated. It is a rule that cuts to the heart of justice. To bear false witness is a very serious matter that could have all sorts of dreadful consequences—the destruction of a good person's reputation or a miscarriage of justice that would put an innocent man to death for a crime he did not commit, and so on. Imagine bearing false witness in a court of law, and as a result, an innocent man was put to death. How will you feel about it for years to come? Whatever advantage you might have derived from the lie would be cancelled by the torments to which your conscience would subject you. Freud thinks that conscience is a mere social construct—the internalization of the terror of civilization. But this underestimates the pivotal place of justice in the human psyche.

10. Thou shalt not covet thy neighbor's house, wife, manservant, maidservant, ox, ass, or Ferrari. Here we have another good rule to live by—a rule that can only enhance our happiness. Those who are envious are unlikely to be happy. They are generally people who see only their misfortunes, but overlook all their blessings. In so doing, they fail to take advantage of the good fortune and opportunities that come their way. They are like the character in the song "If it weren't for bad luck, I would have no luck at all." The commandment is meant to protect us against this self-destructive envy. It also guards against the inclination to keep up with the Joneses. Like the Sabbath, the idea is to make us relax, and enjoy life, instead of driving ourselves to distraction, as we are wont to do.

Looked at impartially, the commandments are neither onerous nor taxing on our instincts, which is to say, on our quest for pleasure. On the contrary, they are easy because we are inclined to what they enjoin in any case. And those, to which we are not necessarily inclined, are wise and good, since they are designed to secure our happiness, not to frustrate it. So, the Moses of Freud's imagination need not have worried. The commandments can hardly be considered bad news. And the claim that they have exacted an exorbitant price from the instincts is highly exaggerated, and serves to justify repression. I have no intention of substituting the belief in the depravity of human nature with faith in its inherent goodness. Reality is much more complex, as I will show.

I turn now to my second argument. Freud is under the mistaken impression that the very existence of a rule is an indication that there is a strong instinct in favor of whatever is prohibited by the rule. He makes this point again and again throughout his writings. In *Totem and Taboo* he applies the thesis to the almost universal prohibition of incest.[31] He surmises that the existence of a strong taboo against incest in primitive societies is an indication that incestuous desires are among the oldest and strongest of human impulses. The prohibition frustrates the gratification of this strong desire or impulse. The desire is therefore repressed, but does not disappear. The repression leads to a "psychic fixation" on the prohibited desire. This fixation is a result of the "conflict between prohibition and impulse."[32] On one hand, the prohibited desire is very tempting—it is the highest pleasure. But on the other hand, it is abominated, because of the prohibition.

One need not resort to the study of exotic tribes in order to see the partial plausibility as well as the implausibility of what Freud is saying. One need only observe the celibate clergy in our own culture. The repression of the sexual instinct has led to a fixation on sexuality that has been well known long before the sexual abuse of boys became a matter of public concern and criminal investigation.

There is however, a huge difference between the prohibition of all sexual gratification, and the prohibition of sexual gratifications with certain persons—siblings, parents, or children. The impulse is not itself prohibited; it is merely directed toward exogamous relations, rather than incestuous ones. The existence of a prohibition is not in itself proof that the act prohibited constitutes a strong primal instinct, or that it is the locus of a powerful desire, or a deeply felt inclination. The fact that homosexuality is prohibited in many societies, does not mean that heterosexual desire is the artificial product of social coercion, or the rechanneling of the natural homosexual desire toward legitimate outlets. Yet this absurd understanding of sexuality follows logically from Freud's thesis.

Just because there are strong prohibitions against homosexuality and incest, it does not follow that the "prohibitions concerned actions for which there existed a strong desire."[33] The existence of the prohibition and even the existence of the dread of incest is not proof that incestuous desires hold a special fascination for human beings, or that incestuous desires are somehow integral to our instinctual makeup, or that they are the most powerful and primeval instincts. The only reason for holding such a view is that it lends support to Freud's darling thesis about the conflict between civilization and the instincts.

It would follow that everything that is strongly prohibited is an indication that it is among the strongest instincts and inclinations of mankind. It would follow that killing and homosexuality are very strong human inclinations. Freud thought that the aggressive instincts are natural—but why not homosexuality? His reasoning invites that conclusion. And it is precisely the prevalence of this sort of thinking that has led some to imagine that heterosexuality is itself an imposition of society that conceals the natural and instinctive inclination for homosexual intercourse.[34] It is useless to protest that most of us are inclined to neither homosexuality nor incest. The Freudian response is that the absence of the desires in question is an indication of the success with which civilization has expunged them by its repressive mechanisms. The result is that they exist only in the shadowy domain of the unconscious.

I am not siding with Edward Westermarck against Freud and James Frazer in the dispute over incest.[35] I find both positions equally implausible. The existence of a strong prohibition against incest is no indication that there is either a strong natural impulse in favor of incest (as Freud and Frazer contend) or an instinctive aversion to it (as Westermarck contends). Neither incest nor incest-dread is an instinct. Only sexual desire is instinctive. The propensity to satisfy that instinctual desire by resorting to siblings is neither totally absent nor particularly strong. But it is society that guides the instinct to its appropriate satisfaction. The marriage of brothers and sisters is not totally prohibited in every society under all circumstances. There are examples, such as the ancient Egyptians, where such marriages were encouraged in royal families. Even in the Bible, Sarah was both Abraham's half sister and his wife.

As Frazer and Freud have pointed out, if there is a strong natural aversion to incest, then there is no reason whatsoever for the prohibition. But there is reason for thinking that even where these desires exist, they are not very powerful, nor very difficult to repress. Inspired by Westermarck, anthropologists, such as Arthur Wolf, explain that children who grow up together from an early age develop a strong affection for one another that precludes the sort of fascination and mystique that accompanies sexual attraction. Using the study of Japanese customs, Arthur Wolf has pointed out that familiarity from an early age dampens sexual eroticism.[36] Havelock Ellis expressed similar views in his *Studies in the Psychology of Sex*.[37] It seems to me that if Freud was right, then the marriages of adopted children who grew up together but were not blood relatives, would be common—but it is not. Adopted children seem to have little desire for coupling, even though they are not blood relatives, and there are no obstacles to their union. This may explain why divine intervention was necessary for Sarah and Abraham to conceive.

If we deny that the prohibited desires are strong natural impulses, Freud responds that we are not aware of them because they have been so very successfully repressed by civilization, but they have not been eradicated; they are still there as part of the unconscious that erupts to the surface in dreams, jokes, or slips of the tongue. The denial of the desire is a testimony to the success of civilization in repressing the instincts. Freud is left to marvel at the power of civilization. He is in awe of its repressive capacities. So great are the latter, that the victim approves, cooperates, and acquiesces.

What makes Freud's explanation so appealing is the fact that it is so fantastic. But this imaginative explanation, and Freud is always brilliantly imaginative, cannot withstand much scrutiny. Freud assumes that a strong primal desire cannot be created nor destroyed. If you have a desire for x, and there is a very good reason why x is prohibited, and you understand the reason for the prohibition and concur with it, the desire nevertheless remains, and the lack of gratification merely strengthens it. It is never destroyed; it merely goes beneath the surface and wreaks havoc in the form of fixations and other neurotic symptoms. The argument assumes that desires are fixed. If taken seriously, this assumption would lead to the collapse of the whole advertising industry. If psychoanalysis is founded in self-knowledge, then it must acknowledge that our desires are not totally static, eternal, or unchanging; they are subject to considerable variation. Besides, there is a big difference between fundamental desires for food, drink, and sex, and desires for particular food, drink, or sexual partners, although I would admit that there may be more fastidiousness about sexual partners than food—but then again, not necessarily.

My third argument is that the conflict between human nature and civilization is highly exaggerated (if not totally fallacious) because it cannot explain the extent of our complicity with the schemes of civilization. Resorting to the concept of conscience as the internalization of terror cannot explain the success of civilization without undermining or totally denying the pleasure principle as something that genuinely operates on the psyche. If we really are programmed to pursue pleasure above all else, then we are unlikely to be so easily co-opted into the schemes of civilization when they involve such radical instinctual renunciations. Why do we not throw off the yoke of the superego when its repressions become intolerable? How long can civilization continue to succeed at the expense of the instincts? An edifice that defies nature will likely come crashing down. Freud resorts to delivering knowing premonitions of disaster—the animal is likely to revolt and all hell will break loose. But as civilization continues to march forward, Freud is left marveling.

In my view, there is no reason to marvel at the success of civilization. Far from being at war with the instincts, it answers a deep need in human beings—a need to live according to a grand vision, a life that counts as an achievement. Unlike animals, human beings have limited ability to affirm life—simple biological existence is not enough for them. They seek a life that is difficult and arduous, and is recognized as such. Instead of marveling at the capacity of civilization to repress our primitive impulses, it is more plausible to see the success of civilization as having its source in the fact that it offers us what we long for—and that includes rules and prohibitions. But if the Ten Commandments are any indication, the rules that make civilization possible are hardly onerous or repressive—unless we see human beings as murderous savages with an insatiable sexual appetite (directed primarily at family members) and a lust for killing (directed primarily at one's parents).

All this negativity about civilization, its terror, and its internalization of terror, is a legacy of Christianity. It is no exaggeration to say that our bravest iconoclasts are Christian in their understanding of civilization as the repression of human nature. And even when they abandon the concept of human nature as unfashionable and essentializing, they cannot abandon the concept of civilization as repression—as a garrison in a conquered city. Michel Foucault is a case in point. In his early studies of madness, punishment, and medicine, Foucault understood the power of civilization negatively, as what says no. But suddenly, he shifted gears; he decided that all this negativity could not explain the overwhelming capacity of civilization to control our discourses, our bodies, and even our gestures. Foucault thought that he had discovered the positivity of power:

> If power were never anything but repressive, if it never did anything but say no, do you really think one would be brought to obey it? What makes power hold good, what makes it accepted, is simply the fact that it doesn't weigh on us as a force that says no, but that it traverses and produces things, it induces pleasure, forms knowledge, produces discourse. It needs to be considered as a productive network which runs through the whole social body, much more than as a negative instance whose function is repression.[38]

Instead of repression, blockage, exclusion, and censorship, Foucault discovered the secret strength of power—its lightness, its positivity, and its non-obtrusiveness. It is these qualities that account for the capacity of power to "produce effects at the level of desire—and also at the level of knowledge."[39]

But on careful examination, it turns out that all this positivity is merely a ruse of power. It is a strategy of a new, more subtle, and less obtrusive form of control and manipulation. The new strategy of power is control via stimulation instead of repression. The strategy of power allows it to pose as a liberation movement. Go ahead, "get undressed— but be slim, good-looking, tanned!"[40] This may seem permissive, but Foucault thinks that it is just part of the unbearable sneakiness of power. The positivity of power is just a testimony to the potency of social control. So, the discovery of the positivity of power did not make Foucault any more cheerful or less melancholy. On the contrary, it made him suspect that the project of liberation was impossible. It made him feel that there can be struggle but never freedom. It convinced him that we are accomplices in our own demise; we are collaborators in the project of domination. The situation is more hopeless than could be imagined. The positivity of power is a testimony to the potency of social control—but now, the garrison within is no longer recognized for what it is—it is no longer experienced as oppressive.

So, despite his efforts, Foucault failed to escape negativity. He discovered the positivity of power only as a scam and a strategy in the project of control, manipulation, and repression. But it seems to me that introducing new positive strategies of power makes a mockery of the distinction between freedom and repression, self-restraint and coercion.

Why not abandon the negative view of civilization altogether? Why not see civilization as presenting us with something appealing that we love, and are willing to serve with devotion and even self-sacrifice. Why not affirm a genuine positivity or a true good? Conscience may not be a garrison within; it may be a self-imposed restraint that admonishes and even torments, because men and women cannot stand to live haplessly without purpose, without ideals, and without discipline. Civilization offers us a way of life that is as arduous as it is enchanting.

Far from subverting human inclinations, civilization succeeds so well because it goes with the grain—not against the grain. And that is why there is no reason to marvel at its astounding success. Civilization cannot succeed against all odds. It succeeds because it answers a deep need for discipline, a need to give life structure and meaning, a need to be admired, and to admire oneself. Civilization succeeds not because it is contrary to nature, but precisely because it appeals to certain fundamental aspects of our nature. In particular, it allows us to indulge our penchant for grand ideals, and to pursue these ideals without mercy and without restraint. Civilization provides us with the opportunity to live large; it provides us with grand visions or grand narratives that give significance to our lives.

Civilization makes it possible to conquer and colonize in the name of our ideals. But in so doing, it makes human beings more dangerous animals than need be. When we find a grand ideal to give significance to our lives, we are eager to share it with the world; and if the world is unwilling to receive it, we are ready to impose it on a recalcitrant and ignorant multitude. And if threatened by a competing ideal, we are ready to defend our ideals to the death.

I have no intention of substituting the belief in the depravity of human nature with faith in its inherent goodness. I have no intention of denying that terror and civilization are intimately linked. My claim is that the connection between them has been seriously misconstrued. In my view, human beings are not attracted to evil; they aspire to be part of something resplendent; they need to order their lives according to some grand ideals, some difficult principles, or some arduous rules; and this is why civilization must be understood as a search for ideals. It is not for love of evil or even love of self that human beings do wrong. The worst atrocities have their source in the zealous pursuit of a sublime ideal that is believed to be so majestic, so magnificent, and so grand, that it is worthy of every sacrifice, every hardship, and every abomination.

Civilization makes it possible to do things collectively; it makes it possible to act together in concert and with conviction. Such collective action may contribute to our well-being and our development but it also allows us to indulge in abominations that transcend the abilities or inclinations of primitive man. In particular, civilization provides the tools to fight, not just for survival, but also for the triumph of our ideals. In short, what makes us civilized is also what makes us terrible.

The problem is that Freud has misunderstood the nature of the danger involved. It is not a question of the revolt of the instincts; it is not the animal that we should fear; it is not the beast within that poses the danger; it is the civilized man. Civilization co-opts us into its schemes by allowing us to indulge our penchant for grand ideals. It allows us to colonize and conquer in the name of these ideals. Civilization arms us with weapons and with a clear conscience. Only civilized men have the technological as well as the psychological equipment to launch deadly and destructive wars of unimaginable cruelty and terror. Only the conviction that we are conquering in the name of something sublime and splendid allows us to ignore the barbarous ferocity of our conduct.

My fourth argument is that Freud naïvely allies civilization with pacifism and the savage instincts with war. In his exchange with Einstein on war, Freud interprets war as the revolt of the instincts against the repressions of civilization. But this dualism between civilization and the savage instincts is fallacious. There is nothing pacifistic about civilization. Besides, Freud's claims about the savage instincts do not stand up.

He tells us that primeval man survives in our unconscious and is never annihilated by cultural advancement, and that is why civilization must be constantly on guard against the beast within.[41] This primeval man, this beast within, is

> more cruel and more malignant than other animals. He liked to kill, and killed as a matter of course. The instinct which is said to restrain other animals from killing and devouring their own species need not be attributed to him.[42]

But something does not add up. On one hand, primeval man is a remorseless killer, but on the other hand, Freud tells us that anthropological studies of primitive man reveal that he is haunted by "an obscure sense of guilt" that leads him to fear the avenging spirits of his slain enemies.[43] Freud surmises that the fear of the spirits is merely a reflection of his own guilty conscience. But if primeval man is indeed a remorseless killer, then where does this guilt come from? In the case of the guilt connected to the killing of the primeval father, Freud has a ready answer. His answer is love. They hated the father, but they also loved him, and it was from this ambivalence of feeling that the remorse and guilt is explained. But how do we explain the remorse and guilt associated with killing enemies? How do we explain the extensive ceremonies of purification that these so-called savages—Australians, Bushmen, and Tierra del Fuegans—had to submit to in order to expiate their guilt? These savages had to atone for their crimes and implore their enemies for forgiveness. Only then were they allowed to touch their wives or return to their communities.[44] In civilized society there are no such rituals. Nor is there any guilt or remorse about the enemy, nor any desire to seek his forgiveness. Manifestations of guilt or remorse are dubbed "post-traumatic stress," and considered a sign of weakness. Civilized men are skilled at demonizing their enemies. The enemy is the other, the heathen, the unchristian, the uncivilized barbarian who deserves his fate for standing firm against the truth—the truth that only we civilized men represent. In light of his own evidence, Freud should have concluded that only civilized men could be murderous killers.

In conclusion, the assumption that human nature and civilization are at odds, and that human beings must therefore be terrorized spiritually, politically, or psychologically in order to be civilized, has very dire consequences. It leads to a fallacious understanding of the relation of terror and civilization. It assumes that terror and civilization are opposites. It assumes that civilization represents the right, the just, and the good. It assumes that the function of civilization is to subdue nature in general and the diabolical nature of man in particular. By exaggerating the evil of human nature, it justifies the endless terrors of civilization. But worst of all, it has the effect of mistaking all self-restraint and self-government for repression. In what follows, I will argue that this attitude incites a Promethean revolt—not only against God but also against morality itself.

5. A Promethean Revolt

At the heart of biblical religion is a profound deprecation of morality that inspires revolt. The Bible often presents moral goodness as mindless and unquestioning obedience to authority. And to make matters worse, God's prohibition of knowledge suggests an alliance between goodness and ignorance. If goodness is obedience—blind, mindless, stupefying submission, without understanding, then wickedness or disobedience is wisdom, defiance, courage, and audacity. In this light, Eve's transgression appears brave and bold; the Bible's effort to make her Fall the result of weakness and stupidity, fails.[45] She prefers knowledge to ignorance; she wants to know the difference between good and evil; she wants to choose knowingly; she refuses to follow blindly; and she is willing to pay a high price in order to live a life fitting for a being with intelligence as well as with freedom. How could God create beings with intelligence and curiosity, and then forbid them to pursue knowledge? Is that just a lack of insight on His part or is it malevolence? Karen Armstrong thinks it is lack of insight.[46] But the Gnostics thought it was malevolence.

The Gnostics interpreted the story of Genesis in a way that made Eve and Satan heroic. They surmised that the God of Genesis must be an imposter. What kind of God would criminalize knowledge and promote ignorance? The Church condemned the Gnostic reading, and burned their books.[47] Instead, it regarded humanity as unfit for knowledge, and understood goodness in terms of obedience without understanding. Jesus does not improve on this situation; on the contrary, he makes it worse.

The relationship between man and God in Christianity is more subservient and more uncomprehending than we find in Judaism. Moses and Job challenge God and censure his conduct from a moral point of view. When the Israelites made a molten calf of gold to worship, God was furious. He said to Moses, "let me alone, that my wrath may wax hot against them, and that I may consume them" (Exodus 32:10). But Moses

> besought the Lord his God, and said, Lord, why doth thy wrath wax hot
> against thy people, which thou hast brought forth out of the land of

Egypt with great power, and with a mighty hand? Wherefore should the
Egyptians speak, and say, for mischief did he bring them out, to slay
them in the mountains, and to consume them from the face of the earth?
Turn from thy fierce wrath, and repent of this evil against thy people.
Remember Abraham, Isaac, and Israel, thy servants, to whom thy swear-
est by thine own self, and saidst unto them, I will multiply your seed as
the stars of heaven . . . . (Exodus 32:11–13)

When Moses admonishes God, he reminds him of his promise, he
appeals to his sense of decency, and finally, he appeals to his pride and
sense of shame—what would the Egyptians say? As a result, "the Lord
repented of the evil which he thought to do unto his people" (Exodus
32:14). Moses therefore succeeds in changing God's conduct for the
better. Job also questioned the goodness and moral rectitude of God.
And he concluded that God was not always good.[48] But in Christianity,
God's goodness is beyond reproach, no matter what He does or says.
The very idea of questioning God's goodness is deemed to be the unforgivable sin against the Holy Ghost; as we have seen earlier, it is the sin
that merits eternal damnation.[49] Jesus undermines the more enlightened
elements in the Old Testament by affirming unquestioning obedience as
the hallmark of goodness. As we have seen, he is no friend of reason or
knowledge. Faith and belief without understanding is what he demands.
Of course, he promises that the mysteries will all be cleared up at the
end of the world, which he expected to happen very soon. But the end
has not come and nothing has been cleared up. And faith without
understanding remains the ideal of his Church.

When morality is reduced to mindless, uncomprehending, obedience, the dictates of morality seem like arbitrary dictates of power and
domination. Not surprisingly, immorality, which is to say, the purposeful flouting of the dictates of morality, becomes heroic. In this way,
Christianity invites the sort of Promethean revolt that Nietzsche and his
postmodern admirers represent. It is not revolt against oppression, injustice, or exploitation, but a revolt against morality; because in the context
of Christianity, morality is presented as the supreme oppressor: the
destroyer of life, nature, spontaneity, exuberance, pleasure, and any
dreams of happiness in the only world we know.

If the good is foreign to our nature, and if there is nothing in our
nature that inclines us to the good, then goodness is not constitutive of
human nature, happiness, or fulfillment, but quite the reverse. The
good is subversive of our being. In other words, wickedness is according
to nature, and goodness is a subversion of nature. This deprecation of
morality incites transgression—from Eve to Nietzsche. It invites a

Promethean revolt that romanticizes evil because it is supposedly natural.

The deprecation of morality is intimately connected to the conception of morality as an inner state of siege—an internalization of terror that makes man his own worst enemy. So understood, the triumph of morality is the defeat of man, and the undoing of his vital powers. And what self-respecting creature wishes to have his nature subverted and mutilated? Every fiber of one's being rebels at such a prospect.

6. Romanticizing Evil

It is one thing to say that evil is natural, and quite another thing to say that nature is evil. Christianity blurs this distinction; its overarching emphasis on the Fall suggests that everything natural is evil. The result is a wholesale demonization of nature, which in turn leads to a merciless effort to repress her.

The influential ideas of Paul, Augustine, and Luther have contributed to the Christian demonization of nature. If human nature is in "bondage to sin," then the good is foreign to our nature. This means that all acts of righteousness are supernatural gifts of God—for there is nothing in our nature that inclines us to the good. The upshot of the matter is that wickedness is according to nature and goodness is a subversion of nature. Goodness is not constitutive of human happiness or fulfillment, but quite the reverse. The good is allied with self-sacrifice and self-abnegation, at least in this world. The result is that the good is severed from nature and its pleasures. All natural delight in living is debased as carnal, and must be rooted out like Satan. And more often than not, woman becomes the symbol of nature, life, joy—and the devil.

So understood, morality is a triumph over nature; it is the triumph of the Spirit in its struggle against the flesh. But the Spirit is no part of man—it is an alien imposition. One could say that it is a gift, or that it is the divine within. But if the divine is harsh, arbitrary, and domineering, then the gift of grace is more like a curse, and the "light of thy countenance, O Lord" (to use Aquinas's description of the moral law), is something we would rather live without.

It is a testimony to the potency of Christian assumptions that they pervade the philosophy of Christianity's greatest critic. Nietzsche's revolt against Christianity is a puerile revolt of the child against the parent. It is not a reasoned dissent. The transvaluation of values is not a reevaluation of the values of Christianity. It is a *transgression* that leaves the original authority intact. Nietzsche does not succeed in challenging the

Christian conceptions of good and evil; he merely celebrates whatever Christianity deems to be evil.

Nietzsche's Promethean revolt has its source in his inclination to take the Christian point of view too seriously. Christian assumptions are so deeply ingrained in his thought, and weigh so heavily upon him that he had to rebel in order to gain an ounce of sanity and self-esteem. His revolt made sense only within the horizon of Christianity. It was the sort of revolt that Christianity inspires and incites. In other words, Nietzsche's revolt against Christianity is part of the logic of Christianity itself. It is no accident that his father and grandfather were both Lutheran ministers.

Instead of challenging the Christian view of nature and human nature, Nietzsche adopts it. For Nietzsche, human beings are violent, fierce, rapacious, savage, selfish, cruel, and carnal. They revel in violence and take pleasure in witnessing the suffering of others.[50] They are creatures of nature—and nature and injustice are one. In his revolt against the Christian demonization of nature, Nietzsche sets out to valorize nature and champion her cause. He understood the polarities in Christian terms—morality versus nature. And he declared himself to be a champion of the natural, wild, and untamed. He pretended that nature is beyond good and evil; but this ploy did not fool anyone. In valorizing nature, Nietzsche championed evil.[51]

Nietzsche accepted the antagonism between human nature and civilization. And he sided with the underdog. He posed as a champion of nature and the instincts against civilization and its repressions. He lamented the fact that the history of Western civilization has been the history of the sublimation of cruelty and the domestication of man. He thought that Christianity has tamed man and robbed him of his vital energies; it has crippled his savage instincts; it has made him a placid animal. Man is no longer to be feared; he has been broken, crushed, despoiled, and domesticated. His savage instincts have been outlawed. Nietzsche poses as the spokesman for the savage instincts against the so-called progress of civilization.[52] In *The Genealogy of Morals*, Nietzsche questions the worth of morality itself.

Nietzsche is the architect of the view of conscience as the internalization of terror. And as the liberator of the instincts, he inspires his admirers to revolt against conscience. He anticipates Freud by claiming that when the natural instincts are dammed up, when they have no outlets, they turn inward against the self in the form of bad conscience:

Hostility, cruelty, the delight in persecution, raids, excitement, destruction all turned against their begetter . . . . man began rending, persecuting, terrifying himself, like a wild beast hurling itself against the bars of its cage.[53]

According to Nietzsche, man declared war on his instincts and severed himself violently from his animal past. How did this happen? Why did the instincts not rebel or explode? Why did they succumb to the repressions of civilization? Nietzsche thinks the answer lies in the feeling of a debt. Primitive men believed that they had a debt to their ancestors; they believed that all their blessings had their source in the sacrifices of the ancestors. This debt could only be discharged by obedience to the will of the ancestors, and by sacrifices. Accordingly, they sacrificed their crops, their animals, and their firstborn. The more they prospered the more glorious the ancestors seemed, until they were deified. But then, a very astonishing god appeared on the scene—the god of Christianity. The image of the crucified God was utterly ingenious—it presented the spectacle of a debt that could not be repaid. When one has sacrificed everything, and there is nothing left to sacrifice, then one is forced to sacrifice one's instincts in an endless life of penance. Nietzsche longs for the healthy gods of the Greeks, the gods who could be blamed for all our transgressions, and whose function was to absolve man of guilt. It is not innocence that Nietzsche longs for, but merely the absence of guilt.[54]

Nietzsche poses as a liberator of the savage instincts in their war against conscience and morality. But Nietzsche himself is not capable of carrying out this revolt. Instead of affirming life and pleasure, he courts suffering. In *Thus Spoke Zarathustra*, the sage refuses to alleviate pain and suffering as Jesus did. On the contrary, he tells the hunchback to love his deformity and to affirm life even in the face of suffering. Nietzsche thought that happiness and misfortune are brother and sister, twins who grow tall together. He celebrated the value of suffering and admonished those whose compassion led them to relieve the suffering of others. He chided Christians for their eagerness to relieve suffering, and he accused them of secretly being the devotees to a religion of "smug ease."[55]

What can explain Nietzsche's desire to suffer? What is the point of all this suffering? Could it be anything other than a need for expiation? Does Nietzsche feel remorse over his blasphemies and transgressions? What else could explain his need to suffer? Perhaps Nietzsche was not the free spirit he longed to be. He seems to be filled with remorse, guilt, and the symptoms of a bad conscience. He seems to be writing about himself when he describes man as a creature that has been tamed and domesticated. Clearly, he did not have the constitution to carry out the Promethean revolt that he inspired. He shrank from his own conception of the overman when he described him as a Caesar with the heart of Christ. But Nietzsche's followers succeeded beyond his wildest dreams.

No one has portrayed the impressionable readers of Nietzsche better than Dostoevsky's Raskolnikov in *Crime and Punishment*. At the heart of the matter is the conviction that crime is heroic—that it raises the individual above the ordinary level of humanity. The key is not just the ability to carry it out, but also the ability to triumph over all pangs of conscience. This is the real triumph—it is a triumph over the inner state of siege, a triumph over the garrison within, and a triumph over the psychological tyranny of civilization. André Gide's *Lafcadio's Adventures* deals with the same theme. But there is no need to resort to examples from fiction. The famous Leopold–Loeb case of Chicago, 1924, was a real-life example of the sort of depravity that Nietzsche can inspire. Two young men read Nietzsche, and decided that the proof of their superiority, the proof of their victory over the herd, is the ability to commit a crime (to abduct and kill a young boy and bury his body), without feeling any pangs of guilt or remorse. Meyer Levin's novel *Compulsion* dramatizes this case.

The same disposition can be found among Nietzsche's existential and postmodern admirers—Jean Paul Sartre, Michel Foucault, Georges Bataille, and others. Sartre liked to boast about growing up without a superego, because his father died when he was a child. And he wrote an admiring book about a criminal.[56] He dubbed him a saint, and claimed that his treacheries were a sign of his freedom and superiority. Bataille provided an equally flattering portrait of Gilles de Rais, the real-life version of the mythical Bluebeard. In *The Trial of Gilles de Rais*, Bataille rails against a feminized world that cannot provide such a great warrior with an outlet. Foucault echoes the same complaints about our feminized world in his book, *I, Pierre Rivière*, which is an account of the saga of a young man who killed his mother, brother, and sister with an axe. As Foucault's commentary makes clear, what is truly intolerable is not the brutality of Rivière's crime, but the world in which his mother tyrannizes over his father—a domestic condition that is supposedly symbolic of modernity. It is not Rivière's crime that is truly terrible, but the world that robs him of his protest by declaring him insane instead of condemning him to death.[57]

Contrary to popular belief, postmodernism is not just one more chapter in the history of liberalism; it is part of the legacy of revolt against biblical morality. As I have argued elsewhere, transgression (not freedom) is the central theme of postmodernism.[58] But if transgression is to be heroic, then the demands of the established order must be absolute and unyielding; and the consequences of disobedience must be crushing. In other words, to make transgression significant, an arbitrary and capricious power capable of inflicting a dreadful punishment is necessary. And these are not the conditions of a permissive, open, disputatious, or liberal society. It is my contention that postmodernism is not necessarily liberating. It is part of Nietzsche's legacy of revolt. But in a world without the executioner, the convent, and the strap, Nietzsche's postmodern followers find that revolt lacks luster.

Postmodern revolt from Nietzsche to Foucault is an indication that the voice of conscience has become a sign of weakness, a symbol of defeat and demise. A Promethean revolt against conscience has become fashionable. Scoffing at the rules of morality and silencing the voice of conscience have become a special triumph indicating liberation from the psychological oppressions of the civilizing process. Conscience has lost its status as something separate from political power. It is now merely an internalization of conventional authority. Conscience is therefore the symbol of the unnatural process by which man has been robbed of his wild and original self. And even when they doubt (as Foucault did) that there ever was a natural or true self that is capable of freedom, they nevertheless embark on an endless struggle to attain the unattainable.

Even the rational and hardheaded Freud, succumbed to the seduction of a Promethean revolt. Like Nietzsche, he regarded the civilizing process as "comparable to the domestication of certain species of animals."[59] And he considered this domestication to be "positively unhealthy."[60] But it is necessary if man is to survive. In *Civilization and Its Discontents* where he sets out to defend civilization against its romantic and pastoral detractors, Freud ends by admonishing civilization for its excessive demands on the instincts.[61] He warns that too much repression will trigger an insurrection. He saw World War I as a case in point. He surmised that the war broke out because the instincts were so dammed up that they finally exploded.[62] And in his exchange with Einstein about war in general, he wondered why people such as Einstein are so opposed to war.[63] Why not accept it as a necessary outlet for the beleaguered instincts? All this can be understood as a dispassionate description of the human condition. But in truth, Freud was deeply ambivalent—about civilization, conscience, and morality. And no less than his postmodern followers, he also romanticized evil as the wild and natural.

The "ambivalence of feeling," which is central to Freudian psychology—feelings of love and hate simultaneously toward the same person, especially persons close to us, such as mothers, fathers, or lovers—characterizes Freud's attitude toward civilization (and morality). He can't quite decide if he is a friend or foe of civilization. On one hand, he is confident that civilization cannot eradicate the naturally aggressive instincts; nothing that civilization does can eliminate the savage impulses of man; civilization can repress, sublimate (i.e. redirect and rechannel) the instincts, but it cannot eradicate them. So understood, civilization is merely a thin veneer behind which lurks primeval man— a savage beast with a lust for killing. The best thing that civilization can do to prevent the instincts from erupting is to provide them with legitimate opportunities for self-expression—war, sports, and procreation, are necessary outlets.

On the other hand, Freud worried that the process of domestication may totally succeed—and "the displacement of instinctual aims and the restriction of instinctual impulses" and the impairment of sexual function that they involve, may lead to the "extinction of the human race."[64] But what exactly was he afraid of losing, if the original humanity is savage and murderous? I surmise that it is the savage that he cherishes as the natural, original, and unspoiled. And this brings him perilously close to romanticizing evil.

The clearest illustration of Freud's valorization of evil is manifest in his discussion of the hero or the "great man." Unlike the ordinary man, the great man does not become the victim of the civilizing process. He retains his original nature, unspoiled by civilization. The difference between him and the ordinary man is stark. So much so that we are led to conclude that strictly speaking, there is no universal Freudian psychology. There is the psychology of the masses, and the psychology of the heroes or great men.

There is a fundamental puzzle at the heart of Freudian psychology that can only be solved by making a radical distinction between the great man and ordinary folk. The puzzle is this. How can a creature so filled with guilt, a creature that longs for suffering as a means of expiation, be governed first and foremost by the "pleasure principle"? The answer to this puzzle puts into question the role of the pleasure principle in the Freudian economy of the mind. Freud observed that the masses long for great men as a substitute for the primeval father. And they usually find what they need in the great man—the strong autocratic leader who tyrannizes over them, abuses them, and ill-treats them.[65] All this talk makes sense only if Freud renounces the pleasure principle as the supreme explanatory tool. His own observations reveal that the masses are masochistic; they long for strong abusive leaders; they readily embrace the instinctual renunciations required by civilization; they readily internalize the terror of civilization; they readily identify with the garrison within. At the same time, they look longingly and with admiration at those who dare to defy the taboos, trample on the prohibitions, gratify their instincts, and affirm nature. Therein lies Freud's ambivalence about the civilizing process. In valorizing the great man, Freud romanticizes nature understood in Christian terms as evil. Within the Christian horizon, the good is insipid. It is not an achievement. But clinging stubbornly to the savage self, defying the crippling powers of the domesticating forces, is a heroic accomplishment.

I would like to suggest that the inversion of the Freudian thesis might provide greater insight into human psychology. In *Totem and Taboo*, Freud maintained that the observance of a taboo is a "renunciation of something really wished for."[66] This led him to conclude that the severity of the prohibition of incest is an indication of the intensity of the original impulse. But instead of thinking that desires and impulses precede the creation of prohibitions, I am inclined to think that the reverse is often the case. Prohibitions give rise to desires. There is a desire for the prohibited just because it is prohibited. It is the appeal of the forbidden fruit. On one hand, the appeal of the forbidden is understandable if the prohibition is totally arbitrary and incomprehensible. Under such circumstances, the appeal of the forbidden has its source in the pleasure of defying the arbitrary and irrational command. But when the command is neither arbitrary nor irrational, the appeal of the forbidden just because it is forbidden, is puerile. This is the sort of puerility that fuels the thinking of postmodern writers such as Georges Bataille and Michel Foucault.

Postmodern thought is trapped within the Christian horizon of thought. And not surprisingly, it continues the Christian fixation on sex. But in the absence of Christian prohibitions—in the context of a secular and sexually permissive society—writers such as Foucault and Bataille worry that sex might become dreary. As a result, they long for the sexual repressions of the Middle Ages. Bataille's literary work is peppered with orgiastic debaucheries (including rapes and murders), which are committed in a convent, a holy sepulcher, or some other religious sanctuary. When they are not forced to witness steamy sexuality, celibate priests are likely to be victims of sexual crimes—like the priest who was raped, murdered, and mutilated by Simone—Bataille's rapacious female heroine.[67] The religious sanctity of the settings and the self-abnegation of the priests are intended to heighten the erotic quality of the transgressions. Bataille considers sex to be natural, but not interesting or erotic. Eroticism is possible only in the context of the most severe taboos and prohibitions of civilization; in the absence of the latter, sex has no appeal. What makes sex appealing is its transgressive quality.

The importance of Bataille's concept of transgression for understanding Foucault cannot be overstated. Foucault bluntly states that sexuality knew its "greatest felicity of expression" in the Christian world of sin.[68] In *The History of Sexuality*, Foucault complains that the medicalization of sex exposes it to the light of day and robs it of its secret and transgressive qualities.

Supposedly, modern scientism has ruined sexuality. Only the medieval world of sin can lend sexuality the support or enhancement on which it can thrive. In *Hurculine Barbin*, the supposed memoirs of a hermaphrodite, Foucault presents a Gothic story of forbidden sexuality in a convent setting that mimics the literary works of Bataille.[69] There is no doubt that Foucault relished the appeal of the forbidden.

What is interesting is that Bataille and Foucault affirm the repressions of civilization—not because they are necessary for survival, as Freud believed, but because they are necessary for the erotic experience itself. They are convinced that the erotic experience is the product of the repression of the natural impulses—and repression is the work of civilization.

In the minds of these writers, the pleasure of sex has become parasitic on the severity of its prohibition within the Christian tradition. In this way, what was a natural instinct has become pathological. This pathology makes the prohibition a necessary condition for pleasure. The result is a lust for the prohibited that knows no bounds. This explains the appeal of sadomasochism for Foucault.[70] That is one form of sexual gratification that is still taboo in a sexually permissive society. The same pathology explains Bataille's preoccupation with the forbidden in novels such as *My Mother*, in which a young man has sexual relations with his mother and her lesbian lover. The affair takes place after the death of the young man's father, which is no doubt a reference to the death of conscience or the superego. In all these examples, the assumption is that transgression liberates whatever it is that has been mercilessly repressed by the prohibitions of civilization.

In conclusion, biblical morality unwittingly leads to a Promethean revolt and its attendant valorization of evil. When the moral life is reduced to submissive, blind, uncomprehending obedience, evil becomes a heroic defiance. And for all its talk about liberating humanity from the yoke of the Mosaic Law, Christianity has imposed an even harsher law that is not satisfied with restraining the hand, but insists on commanding the mind. The result is that the moral life came to be understood as an inner state of siege, the war of the Spirit against the flesh, the aggressive instincts turned inward, and a garrison in a conquered city. This understanding of morality invites a Promethean revolt against God, morality, and conscience—a revolt against the forces of oppression. This triumph over conscience is naturally understood as a heroic revolt in the name of the natural, wild, original self, which has been domesticated and despoiled by civilization. This is not a romanticization of nature; this is not a rejection of the assumption that human nature is depraved. On the contrary, it is a valorization of nature in all its depravity.

I am not criticizing this view of the moral life simply because it has deleterious consequences, but because it cannot account for salient aspects of human experience. It leaves those who are in the grip of this vision marveling at the success of civilization, bewildered at its ability to demand and receive greater and greater triumphs of instinctual renunciations. It turns philosophers into detectives struggling to uncover the tricks by which civilization achieves its conquest over humanity. But there is no mystery in the success of civilization, because human nature is not as depraved as Christianity would have it, and civilization is not as oppressive as Freud and his cohorts believe. Far from thwarting our nature, civilization offers us just what we long for—but that is precisely the trouble.

PART V
TERROR, IDEALS, AND CIVILIZATION

The relation between terror and civilization has been seriously misconstrued in the history of the West. Two contradictory theories have flourished side by side—the naïve and the cynical. Interestingly, both have their roots in biblical religion. The naïve view is simpleminded and dualistic. It assumes that terror and civilization are opposites. It assumes that the function of civilization is to impose order on chaos, to conquer the bestial and barbaric, to civilize the savage races, to bring the wicked to their knees, and to smoke the terrorists out of their caves. On this simplistic view, terror and civilization are deadly enemies that stand in stark opposition to one another.

This naïve view of the relation between terror and civilization presupposes a profoundly singular understanding of the good; it defines itself as the civilized, the right, and the good, while regarding skeptics, opponents, and detractors as allies of the forces of evil. The singularity of the good fosters a dualistic vision—the world is divided into good and evil, God and Satan, formed consciousness and deformed consciousness, the defenders of civilization and the enemies of civilization. When it succeeds in penetrating the realm of politics, this dualistic vision is militant, violent, and extreme. Bringing the struggle against evil into the political domain destroys politics because the latter is not primarily a conflict between good and evil; more often than not, it is a competition between a plurality of competing and incommensurable goods.

Side by side with this naïve and dualistic view of the relation between terror and civilization, is a more sophisticated, but deeply cynical view that has informed Western thought. And like the naïve view, the cynical view also has its roots in the biblical tradition. In particular, the Christian assumption that human nature has been profoundly corrupted by the mythical Fall, has led to the view that repression, terror, and tyranny are necessary to civilize a fallen and thoroughly wicked humanity. Human beings are so depraved that civilizing them is not an easy affair; they must be terrorized if they are to be improved. Far from being opposites, terror and civilization are intimately linked. Civilization cannot succeed without terror. Terror is integral to the civilizing process. Without the imminent threat of violent death, social order would collapse into violence and chaos; terror keeps our animality at bay. Terror is the secret of civilization. Terror is the silent force behind the apparent geniality of social life. It makes it possible for us to live with one another; it makes it possible to live at all. This view of civilization has dominated Western thought from Augustine to Nietzsche.

The assumption is that fear of violence and death—fear of the executioner, the pedagogue, and the strap—keeps man's brutality in check. Civilization fights brutality with even greater brutality, petty thugs with a Leviathan. It is not simply the case that Alexander the Great must crush all the little pirates. Physical terror must be perpetually on display to tame the ambitions of ordinary men—because ordinary men are pirates, killers, hooligans, savages, and thugs at heart. But, as society becomes stronger, it manages to turn man's savage instincts inward against the self. In this way, its grip on the instincts becomes more complete. As a result, it is able to relax and dispense with its more gruesome punishments— drawing and quartering, boiling in oil, pouring molten lead down the throat, and the like. Power becomes less terrible until it becomes almost invisible. But one should not be fooled by appearances. Terror has not disappeared; it has merely been internalized and transfigured into a spiritual and psychological terror. The result is the creation of an inner state of siege—a garrison in a conquered city.

Even though civilization is intended to stamp out terror and barbarism, it must use the very methods that it seeks to stamp out in order to sustain itself—not only from internal chaos, but also from external conquest. This is what led Reinhold Niebuhr to say that as people become more civilized, they lose those qualities that allowed them to thrive, succeed, and dominate in the first place—they become soft, slack, and vulnerable.[1] No longer able to conquer, they become victims of conquest. The assumption is that in this world, one must either dominate or be dominated. And this is what led Freud to admire the "great man" whose savage instincts and vital powers have not been domesticated or despoiled. Only "great men" who have escaped the debilitating effects of civilization can lead others, because only they can do the brutal sorts of things that are necessary to sustain civilization.

The cynical view of the relation between terror and civilization is quite compatible with the naïve view, and that explains why they often appear side by side. Both excuse, justify, and conceal the atrocities done in the name of civilization. However, the heightened awareness of the internalization of terror eventually backfires and leads to a wholesale rejection of all civilized morality.

1. Beyond Naïveté and Cynicism

It is time to transcend both the naïveté and the cynicism of the biblical horizon of thought. It is time to overcome the simplemindedness of Christian dualism and the political militancy of the *realpolitik* that it promotes and justifies. As I have indicated, I have no intention of replacing the belief in the evil of human nature with faith in its inherent goodness. Nor do I have any intention of denying the close alliance between terror and civilization. In so far as civilization is almost invariably accompanied by a certain political organization of life, terror is always a component of civilization. The political is primarily a monopoly over force and the instruments of violence. This fact of social life is often forgotten in the prevalence of the democratic myth according to which government is rule of the people, by the people, in the interest of the people. But the fact is that democracy cannot extinguish the fundamental political reality of sovereign and subject, and that is not a relation of equality, but the reverse. It is a relation of such profound inequality of power that it cannot but inspire terror. So, while it is useless to deny that terror and civilization are intimately linked, the manner in which the relationship has been conceived in Western thought needs to be reconsidered, if not dramatically revised. Terror is indeed a pervasive element of social life, but it is not the secret of society; it is not the pivotal explanation of civilization.

Those who make too much of evil in human nature are led to believe that terror in some form or other—spiritual, political, or psychological— is the key to civilization. The intellectual dominance of the Christian tradition, with its emphasis on human depravity, has obscured the fact that evil is not at the heart of the human drama. Human beings are not, as a rule, attracted by ignorance and brutality. Instead, they hunger for something noble enough to inspire action, something grandiose enough to camouflage the drudgery of life, and something beautiful enough to give comfort. What appeals to human beings is something good or something that appears in the guise of the good.

Human beings are rarely content to live and die like beasts. They are determined to invest their lives with profound dignity, if not cosmic significance. They yearn to be part of something much greater than themselves—they long for some grand ideal that is magnificent and majestic, splendid and sublime. And they are willing to risk or sacrifice their lives in order to invest them with meaning. Nothing moves people as much as lofty ideals—they demand much and receive even more.

Ideals enchant the world; they give it shape, order, beauty, and meaning. They make sense of a world of discord and dissonance. They make sense of our struggles, our triumphs, our losses, and our sacrifices. Ideals give us something higher to live by and for, so that we do not become hopelessly entangled in the petty details of daily life. Ideals cannot rescue human life from the banality of everydayness, but they can give the mundanity of existence a measure of grandeur. Ideals make us imagine that we are part of something greater than ourselves—something even greater than our society. From that perspective, our pains and our losses are somewhat easier to bear, because we imagine ourselves to be upholding an ideal that is loftier than ourselves.

Ideals appeal to us as individuals in our all too human projects of self-making. Ideals focus on a cluster of related goods, which are intended to inspire the self-formative project that is integral to human development and maturity. Ideals serve as models for the human project of self-development. They tell us what sort of people we should be. Ideals are closely connected with morality, but they are nevertheless distinct from morality and should not be confused with it. Strictly speaking, morality is about duty; it is about the minimum that is owed to others. But ideals are the farthest thing from moral minimalism. They set a heroic standard that is supposedly higher than morality. And while they often overlap with morality, they also come into conflict with it.

Existentialists and liberals may denounce ideals (so understood) as a snare. They would prefer to bid us cultivate our unique individuality. They are inclined to think that living according to the ideals of an inherited tradition is cowardly because it consists of following the crowd instead of being true to oneself. But what is this self to whom we should be true? How do we go about cultivating our unique individuality? We must decide who we are before we can be true to ourselves. Ideals provide us with models according to which we can shape the self to whom we can be true.

Ideals provide only the abstract patterns; it is up to us to provide the cloth. Ideals are abstractions akin to Plato's forms; it is up to us to bring them to life. This is not merely a question of following, it is a creative activity—and this is the case even when we are not the authors of the ideals to which we aspire. The process of self-fashioning is at least as creative as the activity of Plato's Demiurge, or master craftsman, who does not create the world out of nothing, but fashions the pre-existing primordial stuff according to the forms or ideals before him.[2] Like the

Demiurge, we are neither the authors of the ideals nor of the material at hand. And like the Demiurge, the materials at hand—our personal limitations, our opportunities, and our circumstances, restrict us. And even though we are not the authors of ourselves or of the ideals to which we aspire, we are nevertheless instrumental in bringing these ideals to life.

For example, the triumph of the Christian ideal over the pagan ideal was the triumph of an ideal that preached meekness over an ideal that espoused self-assertion. The pagan ideal bid one fight when one's honor was at stake, but the Christian ideal recommended forgiveness. The pagan ideal praised proper pride, but the Christian ideal counselled humility. The pagan ideal was defiant in the face of insurmountable odds, but the Christian ideal counselled surrender to the will of God. The Christian ideal was passive, whereas the pagan ideal was active. The Christian ideal was feminine (in the best sense of the term), whereas the pagan ideal was masculine (in the best sense of the term). The Virgin Mary is the personification of the Christian ideal, while Achilles is the embodiment of the pagan one.

There is no doubt that as individuals or as groups, we may have a preference for one ideal over another. But all ideals must have some share in goodness; and it is this goodness that is the source of their appeal. To say that some ideals emerge full-blown in all their decadence is to confuse taste with judgment. Nietzsche's criticism of Christianity, like the rest of his philosophy, suffers from this confusion. He did not like the ideal that Christianity had to offer, so he concluded that it was no ideal at all. He saw it as the triumph of the weak and decadent over the strong and noble. He thought that Christianity was a retrogression from the high to the low, from the master morality to the slave morality, from the warrior aristocracy to the priestly aristocracy, from physical prowess to purity of heart, from an emphasis on performance to a concern with intentions, from a masculine morality to a feminine morality, and from a healthy sensuality to a sickly asceticism. Nietzsche thought that such a triumph could only be accomplished by deceit, chicanery, and subterfuge. I would certainly not deny the role of deceit and subterfuge in the victory of Christianity.[3] But no amount of trickery can account for its stunning success. Although I am hardly inclined to sing the praises of Christianity, I am not convinced by the denunciations of its most vocal critic. The view that Christian ideals emerged full-blown in all their decadence is implausible. Christianity could not have succeeded as well as it did if it were merely retrogression—it must have contained something of genuine beauty; only the latter could explain its success.

The triumph of Christianity over Greek and Roman civilizations cannot be explained in terms of the triumph of the decadent, the inferior, and the rancorous. This description does not fit the Christian martyrs. The martyrs did not inspire awe and admiration because they were weak and decadent. Nor can the success of Christianity be explained by terror—spiritual or otherwise. The Church is the decrepit manifestation of something that must have been free and beautiful.

The success of Christianity cannot be explained by presenting it as a process by which weakness and mediocrity supplanted strength and magnificence, because only the latter can attract. And even the Church, which is admittedly despicable, could not have succeeded as well as it has, if it contained only hypocrites.

Every ideal has its distinctive beauty; but every ideal is also flawed. Sometimes it is admirable to be passive, but at other times, it is contemptible. Being passive in the face of evil, injustice, and tyranny is not appropriate, especially when there is an opportunity to make a difference. As we have seen, Augustine's "godly ruler" reveals how obscene resignation can be. In some circumstances it is more commendable to act, to fight, to take a stand, but at other times it is despicable—as when Achilles has a tantrum because Agamemnon took his favorite slave girl.

In our postcolonial generation, the Christian ideal is often regarded as little more than a façade that conceals and supports an ideology of domination—the domination of women as well as the domination of the peoples of Asia and Africa. First you teach them the beauty of surrender, and then you conquer and exploit them. The passive ideal needs to be balanced by the active pagan ideal of defiance and self-assertion. The two ideals are not mutually exclusive. On the contrary, I think that ideals are strongest when they are cross-fertilized.[4] When ideals are insular or resistant to outside influences, they become ridiculous caricatures without charm or humanity. The two ideals—Christian and pagan, surrender and defiance, passivity and activity, can be combined in ways that make each one more enduring and more attractive. Neither ideal can serve as the single guiding light of life.

Every ideal is inclined to insist that it alone is true and real—that it is imbedded in the nature of the world. For example, despite the harsh vision of God and of nature, the Christian ideal tried to root itself in the nature of reality. The Virgin Mary played a significant role. As the mother of God, she softened God's image. According to a famous story, there were all sorts of people in heaven who were not supposed to be there. Noticing this, Jesus rebuked Saint Peter for not being as vigilant as he should be in manning the gates of heaven. In his own self-defense,

Peter replies that he has been very careful to shut all the gates, but Mary came along and opened all the windows.[5] In other words, Mary allows people to get into heaven, who strictly speaking don't belong there. She makes it easier to get into heaven than the likes of Augustine, Luther, Calvin, or Bunyan, thought it would be. In short, she softens the world. And this feminized universe serves to support the Christian ideal of surrender to the will of God.

Those who prefer masculine ideals will denounce the feminized universe of Christianity as based on lies, falsehoods, and illusions that conceal the harsh reality. They will maintain that only masculine ideals are rooted in nature and in truth. Nietzsche is the supreme representative of this position. But to insist that only the harsh and the austere are real is to be arbitrarily selective. Nature drowns us with her floods and starves us with her famines, but she also consoles us with her sunshine and delights us with her rainbows. Besides, the claim that only the harsh has a foundation in nature flies in the face of the nearly universal experience of maternal love. In a sense, the Christian understanding of reality is intended to balance the scales.

I am inclined to think that the resilience of Christianity is inseparable from the enduring appeal of the feminine ideal personified by Mary. But in the final analysis, she failed to soften the world. The Christian paean to resignation became aggressive when Christianity managed to co-opt the coercive power of the state for its own ends.

Ideals have a collective as well as an individual dimension. The collective dimension of ideals is more problematic. It is one thing to aspire to be a Christian; but it is quite another thing to aspire to live in a totally Christian culture. It is one thing to aspire to the ideal of self-rule or self-determination; but it is quite another thing to aspire to live in a democratic society.

Once an ideal manages to win the hearts and minds of men and women, once its appeal becomes irresistible, then visionaries cannot help but imagine the beauty that would overwhelm the world if only everyone would conform to the ideal in question. The more powerful an ideal gets, the more it is likely to insist on being sovereign. Once an ideal is widely accepted by society, it can begin to put pressure on the state to use its coercive power to support the ideal in question. The moral authority of society is necessary before an ideal can be successfully imposed by fiat.

Properly understood, the state seeks peace, order, and a modicum of justice. But these goals are not glamorous enough; society insists on something more. The goals of the state are too minimalist for her liking.

She aspires to a higher standard. Invariably, she is in the grip of some ideal or another. And she aims to make the state the instrument for the realization of her ideal. But when the state succumbs to the pressure of society, it loses its objectivity, its impartiality, and its ability to perform its function well—to secure a modest peace, order, and justice.

Conservatives tend to underestimate the power of society. They mistake it for a fragile flower, which needs the protection of the coercive machinery of the state if she is to survive. And like an opportunistic woman, society basks in her assumed fragility. She is the great pretender. She exaggerates her weakness; all the while she harbors a ferocity that is all too often beyond the comprehension of the state. She flatters the state that he alone can secure her well-being; she assures him that without him she is doomed. Conservatives are gullible enough to believe in the fragility of society, just as men are gullible enough to believe in the equally dubious fragility of women.

Far from thinking, as Edmund Burke did, that society is a priceless and fragile fabric that takes many generations to weave and is instantly torn asunder in a rash moment of revolt, I am inclined to think that society is a formidable force. Far from requiring the protection of the state, she is the *éminence grise* or the power behind the throne. All its monopoly over force notwithstanding, the state would collapse like a house of cards without the support of society. Without the latter, the state could not elicit the voluntary compliance needed for its survival. Indeed, I would go even further and maintain that the state, properly understood, needs to be protected from the corrosive and corruptive power of society.

The distinction between the state and society mirrors the relationship between morality and ideals. The distinction is akin to the distinction between the right and the good. The right refers to what is morally right and just, while the good refers to a desirable state of affairs. The proper relation between the right and the good is a subject of much debate among moral philosophers.[6] Consequentialists in general and utilitarians in particular, maintain that the good is primary and the right is subordinate or instrumental to the good. Crudely expressed, the right is whatever succeeds in bringing about the desired state of affairs, which is defined as the good.[7] If limiting our population were necessary to attaining the good life, then abortion and infanticide would be right. If our conception of the good were defined as a society that is united by a single set of values, then censorship of literature and education would be justified. If the good in view were understood as minimizing pain and maximizing pleasure, as Jeremy Bentham maintained, then slavery would have to be abolished. If John Rawls is right in thinking that automation makes it possible to enslave only a very small portion of the population, while the rest have a pleasant life of leisure, then the greatest happiness would be better served by an institution of slavery.[8]

The subordination of the right to the good mirrors the subordination of the state to the ideals of society. Invariably, society attempts to subordinate the state to its own conception of the good. But the right cannot be subordinated to the good without defiling the good in question, because the means are integral to the end in view. The right is constitutive of any good that is worthy of pursuit.[9] The effort to resist the subordination of the right to the good (as defined by society) belongs to the state. And that is a monumental task that is more often than not doomed to failure because society is a passionate advocate for the good, understood as the collective quest for a particular ideal. The neutrality, impartiality, and rationality of the state are always threatened by the zeal and bigotry of society.

When an ideal gains ascendancy in a society, when it becomes widely accepted as the supreme good that cannot be surpassed, then both individuals and the state are co-opted into its orbit. Conscience is the mechanism by which society co-opts individuals, and justice is the means by which society co-opts the state. I will discuss each in turn.

If its ideal is to succeed, society must internalize it; it must make it the stuff of conscience. In so doing, it is not internalizing terror; it is internalizing its values, and that is a very different matter. By co-opting us into its schemes, society is able to blind us to the unjust and dastardly means that are often used to pursue its ideals and destroy its rivals. In this way, society poses a special danger to our natural moral sensibilities. It has the uncanny ability to internalize its values, and to turn its demands into the authoritative moral voice of conscience. But it does not follow that conscience is just a construct of power. To declare that conscience is a natural human phenomenon that exists independent of society, and to maintain that it speaks with an authoritative moral voice is not to deny the influence of society or its capacity to internalize its norms, no matter how perverse. There are plenty of examples of how civilizations can silence or pervert conscience. Only then, can human beings do hideous things with a clear conscience.

Hannah Arendt's *Eichmann in Jerusalem* illustrates this point—it is a decisive refutation of the inclination to rely on the infallibility of conscience. Arendt was convinced that Eichmann was not a diabolical monster who suffered from a murderous hatred of Jews. Nor was he a tormented man suffering from pangs of guilt inflicted by his conscience.

On the contrary, as minister of transportation who delivered millions of Jews to a horrible death, he felt that he was doing his duty, and acting in accordance with the dictates of his conscience.[10]

In *The Adventures of Huckleberry Finn* we also get a glimpse of how society can corrupt conscience. When Aunt Sally hears a boiler explosion, she asks if anyone is hurt, and Huck replies "No'm: killed a nigger." Aunt Sally is relieved, because "sometimes people do get hurt."[11] The exchange reveals the extent to which society can anesthetize its members to its injustices. It can dehumanize a whole class of people without much difficulty.

We do the same thing to our native population. The effect is not just to make us oblivious to the injustices of our society, but also to make us ardent believers in its moral rectitude. A society that convinces its citizens of its justice can more easily elicit their support. On one hand, Huck thinks it is his duty as dictated by his conscience to report on Jim because he is a runaway slave. He is convinced that he will go to hell if he does not listen to his conscience. But his own sentiments and his friendship with Jim make him unable to betray Jim, and so, he resigns himself to going to hell. Huck is not a sophisticated person; and such unsophisticated people generally identify the authoritative moral voice of conscience with their social duties.

Society thrives on this spurious identity. Freud wrongly assumed that there is nothing more to conscience but this spurious identity. But instead of following Freud in thinking of conscience as a garrison in a conquered city, we should consider it the voice of justice—a voice that must often rail against the authority and terror of civilization. Huck did not understand that his inability to act as his society demanded was not a failure, but a triumph of conscience. He did not understand that his moral sentiments, which were at odds with his social duty, are also part of his conscience.[12] Jonathan Bennett has argued that Huck's sentiments won out over his conscience. But there is no reason for excluding sentiments from conscience—conscience has often been understood as the capacity to empathize with others—David Hume and Adam Smith have defended this view.[13] Unlike Eichmann, Himmler is believed to have had empathy for his victims. His physician reports that he suffered from dreadful nausea and vomiting on account of his work. Yet, he was a true believer in the Nazi vision of the ideal world order. What made him ill was the means necessary to achieve it. Himmler triumphed over his sentiments and fulfilled his social duty; but this was a failure of conscience.[14]

The nature of conscience is a subject of complex dispute among philosophers.[15] Relativists see it merely as the internalization of social norms.[16] Objectivists consider conscience as an authoritative moral voice independent of society. Some consider it the voice of God within. Aquinas described it as "the light of Thy countenance, O Lord, signed upon us."[17] Bishop Butler (1692–1752) expressed a similar view.[18] Some regard conscience as a function of reason, but others join David Hume and Adam Smith in allying it with sentiment. In my view, there is no reason to choose between these views. They are all true. Conscience is an independent moral voice *and* the voice of society; distinguishing between them is a function of reason *and* sentiment. We are naturally endowed with empathy for fellow creatures that suffer. But our society can create conditions that destroy or enlarge our sympathies. We must always be on guard against the perversions of society, and we need both our reason and our sympathy to guide the way.

Just as it co-opts individuals to its goals by means of conscience, society co-opts the state by identifying its ideals with justice. Once this identity is accomplished, the rationality, neutrality, and impartiality of the state are doomed. The cool sagacity of the state is overpowered by the fiery passions of society. The ascendancy of the Christian ideal within Roman society led the emperors to confuse the goals, interests, and aspirations of the Church with the right and the just. In this way, the state lost its neutrality and its capacity to maintain order among diverse citizens who did not share the same beliefs about the nature of metaphysical reality. Once it was co-opted by the Church, the Roman state became the instrument of the Christian persecution of rival sects. If the state is to provide peace and order in a climate of freedom, it must be shielded from the zealous fanaticism of society. But the task is doomed to fail in the long run. The state is not the only loser; the ideal is also tarnished and compromised by it collusion with power.

Ironically, the success of an ideal sows the seeds of its demise. The capitulation of the state to the demand of society—the demand to give its ideal special protection—sets the stage for the decay of the ideal. Once coercion is used to sustain and uphold an ideal, it loses the spirit of freedom and spontaneity that made it attractive in the first place. What it gains in security, it loses in loveliness. Instead of being the inspiration behind the creative project of self-fashioning, it becomes the stuff of conformity, the betrayal of the self, an empty shell, and a false posture that may be necessary to avoid persecution at the hands of a society that is well armed and dangerous. In this way, the ideal is infected with hypocrisy and parody. Success is therefore the undoing of ideals. When they become successful, ideals inevitably become mired in power and politics, deceit and dissembling. In this way, a thing of beauty becomes contemptible.

In a greedy quest for sovereignty, ideals collude with the powers that be. But far from inspiring the latter with the spirit of justice and moderation, they convince the powers that be that the ideal is worthy of every sacrifice, iniquity, and abomination. Whether the ideal is Christianity or democracy, its complicity with power makes the ideal more strident; and this taints the ideal, unless the iniquities committed in its name are kept secret. But secrecy cannot be maintained indefinitely; and in the end, the hypocrisy is exposed and the ideal is tarnished. But ideals do not decay just because they are corrupted by power; that is only part of the story. Power has a way of revealing the inner shortcomings of ideals—and they all have their shortcomings.

When an ideal decays, the vacuum left behind gives a new ideal a chance to conquer the hearts and minds of those in search of a principle by which to order their lives. Christianity was the triumph of an oriental and Semitic religion over the civilizations of Greece and Rome.[19] This success cannot be explained by maintaining that the Christian ideal was inherently superior to the pagan one. Christianity triumphed in an atmosphere in which pagan ideals suffered from an existential atrophy to which all ideals are vulnerable. In late Roman civilization, pagan ideals were decayed, and were therefore no longer attractive, exemplary, or inspiring. Proper pride had given way to boastfulness; self-assertion had been replaced by domination, and fighting for honor had given way to vengeance and cruelty. And the *Pax Romana* had become merely the name of Roman conquest and cruelty. In other words, Nietzsche's beloved master morality had become nothing more than the brutality of Rome. It was precisely in light of this decayed ideal of valor, that the Christian emphasis on humility, surrender, and love, managed to conquer the heart and mind of a decaying empire. In this way, the triumph of Christianity can be seen as the triumph of a more powerful and enchanting ideal. After all, as Nietzsche himself was forced to admit, mercy and forgiveness (as opposed to revenge) are the prerogative of the strong.

When an ideal is tarnished by its close alliance with political power, the powerful may be denounced as frauds that are not fit to represent the ideal in the world. In a letter to Pope Leo X, Martin Luther denounced the Roman Catholic Church as a "licentious den of thieves," a "shameless brothel," and a kingdom so filled with "sin, death, and hell" that even the antichrist could add nothing more to its wickedness.[20] But far from giving up on Christianity, Luther dismissed the evils committed by the Church as the work of bad men who are neither informed nor inspired by the true ideal of Christianity. The intention is to insulate the ideal from its historical manifestations. Contemporary apologists use the same tactic. Eventually, the effort to insulate ideals from their manifestations in the world fails, and the ideal itself comes under attack and the weakness inherent in it is exposed. I have no way of telling when this will happen to Christianity. The latter has been exceptional among ideals in its capacity to survive its own atrocities. This is true of the transcendental monotheistic religions in general. They are not only more zealous than polytheistic religions, but also more resilient.

The disenchantment with the Christian ideal took a long time to materialize. The corruption of the Catholic Church led to the Reformation. The latter unleashed the hellish and bloody conflicts of Catholics and Protestants, which gave way to the Enlightenment rejection of Christianity and the emergence of the modern secular state. Modernity was an all-out assault not only on the prejudices and superstitions of Christianity, but also on the ideal of surrender itself. John Stuart Mill was critical of the passive ethos and was in favor of the active one.[21] He argued that moralists and religious types may prefer the passive personality; but all of the progress of mankind has its source in the active personality. The latter is not content to be acquiescent and submissive; it is not content to endure the evils of existence, instead it struggles against them no matter what the odds. Instead of bending to circumstances, the active personality bends circumstances to itself. Instead of resigning itself to the hardships of life, the active personality sets out to improve human life by intellectual and practical ingenuity. The passive type is not as pious as we are likely to assume; on the contrary, the passive type is filled with envy, rancor, and malice toward the successful, energetic, and fortunate—witness the Orientals. Mill did not mention the fact that the Oriental personality type that he dismissed is also the Christian ideal.

It is often believed that modern liberal society is devoid of all ideals. It is part of liberal propaganda to declare that liberalism is neutral *vis à vis* the good, and that it allows a hundred flowers to bloom. But the liberal aspiration to a totally neutral public space is both impossible and disingenuous. It is impossible because no society can resist the allure of ideals, and disingenuous because liberal society espouses particular ideals. In truth, liberal society has its own dominant ideal—that of the active, strong, free, rational, independent, iconoclastic, and eccentric individual. In a liberal society, where individuality and independence are venerated, contributions to communal and mutually dependent groups struggle for recognition and respect. The family is one mutually dependent unit that has suffered in the context of liberal society. It is not surprising that women have left their homes in an effort to find worth as individuals, even if it means doing menial work outside the realm of mutually dependent relations. But in defense of liberal society, it must be pointed out that antithetical ideals are not repressed or persecuted, even if they are not necessarily admired. But human beings are inclined to seek admiration.

Modernity has defeated Christianity; and the active ideal has once again replaced the submissive one. But the active ideal has also come on hard times. Its activity is inseparable from the modern conquest of nature, the rapacity of capitalism, and its resulting environmental degradation. And for all its hostility to Christianity, the singular understanding of the world infects modern rationalism. No less than Christianity, modernity rejects the plurality of the right and the good. It is determined to export its ideals to a recalcitrant world—not in the name of salvation, but in the name of reason, prosperity, and progress. So, whether active or passive, secular or religious, the West remains profoundly singular in its understanding of the good. When the state takes upon itself the task of enlightening the world, we can be sure that the ruthless fanaticism of the biblical horizon has not been transcended. Now, the West conquers in the name of reason *and* God at the same time. But to conquer in the name of reason is to betray the cold pragmatism of enlightenment rationality. The cool neutrality of the liberal state is the true legacy of the Enlightenment. A state that is totally in the grip of the partiality of society is likely to be oppressive to its citizens, and dangerous to its neighbors. This is not to say that the state cannot be dangerous even when it is *not* in the grip of some ideal or other. But in the absence of some lofty ideal, the state may seek to amass territory for its own self-aggrandizement. But then again, it is unlikely to pursue this territorial imperative if it is not easily attainable. In other words, its neighbors must be weak, disorganized, and easy to conquer; otherwise, it would not be worth the trouble. But a state that is fighting the infidels for the sake of the kingdom of heaven, or a state that is conquering the globe in the name of freedom and democracy, is unlikely to be cognizant of the obstacles in view. It will embark on its mission regardless of how hopeless the task may be; it is oblivious to danger, unmindful of the most formidable foes, and contemptuous of prudence. It is willing to embark on large-scale massacres not for territory or for any other tangible good, but just because it cannot bear the thought that the world contains heathens who are oblivious to the singular magnificence of its ideal. Nor is the endless nature of the task a deterrent. On the contrary, it regards endless war, continual self-sacrifice, and ceaseless struggle, to be hallmarks of a noble and genuinely human existence.

In such a world, there is utter disdain for the minimalist state—the state that serves life, pleasure, and happiness—that is to say, the state that is not consecrated to the service of a grand and noble ideal, which demands endless sacrifice. The liberal state is intended to be a minimalist state. It insists on its neutrality *vis à vis* the good. It makes a valiant effort to be neutral with regard to the plurality of goods vying for its attention and protection. But even a liberal state that is conscious of the task at hand is often swamped by the enthusiasm of society. For example, in Canada, the reigning Liberal Party could not resist the pressure from the neoconservative opposition (the Alliance Party) to provide a definition of the family. Instead of demurring, and refusing to define what is not in its power to define, instead of recognizing that it is not necessary to define the family in order to give tax benefits to those who support dependent children, the Liberal Party was bamboozled by the opposition into defining the family in very strict and rigorous terms that corresponded with the ideal of the neoconservatives.

A liberal state is an achievement that has a long history—a history that allowed the West to transcend the murderous grip of warring Christian factions. But the achievement is not all that secure. It is always vulnerable to the premodern forces that are disenchanted with its secular minimalism. They long to make the state the handmaid of a grand ideal, which they imagine is identical with cosmic truth and justice. The neoconservative administration of George W. Bush is a classic case in point. It rejects the minimalist goals of a secular liberal state in favor of the fervor and intensity of a state devoted to a grand and noble ideal. It is bent on turning the American state into a military machine consecrated to the dissemination of the democratic ideal around the globe. Members of the administration imagine that by bringing democracy to the world, they are giving the less fortunate nations the gift of truth, freedom, and justice. And how can the world refuse such a gift? Those who are inclined to refuse it must be demonic; in which case, it is legitimate to crush them. This picture of the world rests on the spurious identity of democracy with justice and good government. It never occurs to those who are in the grip of an ideal that it is just one ideal among others. Nor does it occur to them that their ideal is seriously flawed. Instead, they echo the singularity and dualism that animates the biblical tradition. Unhappily, the political problems of the modern world are thoroughly biblical.

In the politics of the twenty-first century, we are confronted by two civilizations, each claiming to be privy to the one true revelation; each claiming to be the representative of the one true God; each is convinced that it is on the side of truth and justice, while its enemy is allied with Satan, wickedness, and barbarism. These shared assumptions make both civilizations averse to diplomacy and compromise. This is another way of saying that they are incapable of politics understood as a domain of dialogue, concession, compromise, and cooperation. When our enemies are defined as the incarnation of evil, there is nothing that we can do to them that is off-limits. No amount of pain and suffering that we inflict is illegitimate. The ultimate goal is the total annihilation of the enemy, which amounts to the eradication of evil from the world. The language of George W. Bush clearly reflects this dualistic biblical sensibility—and so does the language of Osama bin Laden. The result is that the world loses all complexity; it is polarized into two camps: good and evil, God and Satan, civilization and barbarism, *us* and *them*.

2. A Clash of Civilizations?

We are living in an age that can be described as a clash of civilizations. But contrary to Samuel Huntington and others, the conflict between Islam and the West has its source in the sameness and not the difference between these two worlds.[22] It is not a conflict between a secular liberal society and a religious, biblically inspired culture. Far from being opposites, both parties are informed by the same biblical morality and the same biblical self-understanding—and that is what accounts for the deadly nature of the conflict.

Bush has declared a war on terrorism. He is convinced that terror and civilization are opposites. He considers himself a *defender of civilization*, while considering his enemies to be the enemies of civilization. And being a defender of civilization, he is determined to eradicate the enemies of civilization in every corner of the globe. Again and again, he echoes Jesus (Luke 11:23) in declaring that those who are not with him are against him; those who are not with him are with the terrorists. Every country that is not an ally in the war on terrorism, every country that is not an ally of the United States, every country that is resentful of America's global dominance, is an enemy. Needless to say, God is on America's side; she is the representative of justice, truth, and civilization. Meanwhile, her enemies are the incarnation of evil, barbarism, and terror.

Government officials never cease to remind Americans that this is not an ordinary war; this is a war against evil; the foe has no right to be treated according to the ordinary rules of war; the fighters are not soldiers but "unlawful combatants." The United States has denied the status of POWs to young men found fighting on the side of the Taliban government of Afghanistan. Nor has the American government denied reports of the inhumane treatment that these prisoners have received. In the war against evil there are no rules. Nothing that can be done to vanquish evil is out of bound.

After bombing Afghanistan, the Bush administration proceeded to identify "the axis of evil" that will direct its military strategy. It has warned its citizens that the war on terror will be a long war. It would have been more honest to tell the American people that it will be an endless war, because the fight against evil is infinite. And it must be pointed out that nothing could gladden the heart of a neoconservative government more than the prospect of endless war. Being political realists, American neoconservatives assume that only the looming threat of a common enemy can unite a people into a cohesive social order. If no such enemy exists, it must be invented.[23]

When the Soviet Union collapsed, the American Right despaired. Luckily, Osama bin Laden came to the rescue. The trouble is that the new enemy has no army, no air force, no tanks, and no nuclear weapons. It is a challenge to keep such an enemy looking menacing, relative to the only superpower in the world—the only nation whose military might is unmatched. However, the enemy is wily and unpredictable, and it has penetrated deep into Canadian, if not also into American territory; so, it is poised to strike at any time.

From the point of view of political realists and neoconservatives, the situation could not be more advantageous.[24] The presence of a constant threat is believed to be the best way to unite people behind their government; it also allows government to amass powers that a free people would not normally tolerate.

It must be kept in mind that fear is the greatest ally of tyranny. And as long as Americans are kept in a state of trepidation and apprehension, they will not worry about losing their freedom. In short, by insuring the endless nature of the struggle against evil, biblical dualism lends support to neoconservative assumptions. As we have seen, Christianity has a tendency to exaggerate the evil of human nature, and this explains why it is generally the enemy of freedom and the ally of repression where politics is concerned. The alliance between the Christian Coalition and the American Right is therefore no coincidence.

The rhetoric of Osama bin Laden and his al Qaeda network are no less dualistic, bombastic, absolutistic, immoderate, or polarizing. The views of Islamic fundamentalists do not differ from the views of the Christian Coalition. Both are heirs of the same biblical dualism.

This dualistic posture polarizes the world, radicalizes politics, denies plurality, and precludes self-criticism and self-understanding.

Understanding the world in dualistic terms has the effect of substituting politics with religion. The language of diplomacy and compromise is replaced by the language of *jihad* or the struggle against the cosmic forces of evil. Life is radicalized; and all choices are polarized. Politics properly understood is eclipsed; it is disabled; it is removed from the equation; it cannot diffuse the conflict.

In my view, political conflicts are not necessarily, or even primarily, conflicts between good and evil. More often than not, they are conflicts between competing and incompatible goods. The function of politics is to create order in the midst of plurality and diversity. Politics is the art of devising means by which people can live peacefully even when their conceptions of the good come into conflict. Politics presupposes the recognition that there are many roads to righteousness. This is not a relativistic posture. This is not a denial of truth and justice. This is not a postmodern claim that all truth is someone's truth, and all justice is someone's justice. The distinction between good and evil, justice and injustice is fundamental to politics. But the self-righteous attitude that leads one to imagine that our own interests are identical with the cosmic good has the effect of blinding us to the injustices we inflict in the pursuit of that single good. Recognition that there is a plurality of goods, and that there is more than one righteous way of life, is a prerequisite to the cultivation of the moderation that is critical to the art of politics.

3. Terrorism: From Samson to Atta

There is an uncanny resemblance between Samson's attack on the temple of the Philistines as described in the Bible (Judges 16:26–31) and the terrorist attack on the World Trade Center in New York on September 11, 2001. The Bible tells us that on a busy holiday when about three thousand Philistines were celebrating in the temple, Samson decided to use his superhuman strength to push away the pillars that held up the temple so that the whole edifice came crumbling down, crushing him and hundreds of innocent people in the rubble.

On September 11, 2001, Mohamed Atta hijacked a plane and crashed it into one of the towers of the World Trade Center. Atta's crime was more technically sophisticated, but morally speaking the two crimes were identical. In both cases innocent victims were buried alive in the rubble—innocent people met a gruesome death that they could not

TERROR, IDEALS, AND CIVILIZATION / 149

have anticipated or deserved. It is difficult not to conclude that Samson was as much of a terrorist as Atta. Yet, we regard Atta as a criminal—the incarnation of evil—but we go along with the Bible in portraying Samson as a hero. Is there any difference between them that would justify such radically different assessments?

It may be argued that Samson was merely an instrument of God's will. And God wished to punish the Philistines for their idolatry and their iniquity. They deserved what they got. Besides, Samson sacrificed his own life in order to carry out the justice of God. But if we accept this excuse for Samson, we must also accept it for Atta. It can be argued equally well that Atta was an instrument of God's will; and that God wanted to punish the Americans for their arrogance and iniquities. So, Atta gave up his life to carry out the will of God. But what is all this talk about God's will? Is that not a way of concealing our own iniquities by attributing them to God? Of course it is. The trouble is that this biblical way of thinking and speaking remains prevalent, not only among the Islamic fundamentalists, but also among the Christian fundamentalists who dominate the Republican Party—and that includes President George W. Bush.

After September 11, the leader of the Moral Majority, Jerry Falwell, and the founder of the Christian Coalition, Pat Robertson, declared that the terrorist attack was a deserved punishment from God for America's sins. In particular, they suggested that the sins of feminists, gays, and lesbians are the reason that God has inflicted this terrible suffering on America. Many Americans were shocked and dismayed at the vulgarity of this public statement at a time of national grief and hardship. This candid expression of their true sentiments turned out to be a public relations nightmare. Falwell and Robertson had to apologize publicly to limit the damages. But in truth, Falwell and Robertson's interpretation of the events of September 11 are perfectly compatible with the Christian tradition of divine Providence, from Augustine to Luther, Calvin, and Voegelin.

Unlike tyrants, terrorists are a double-edged sword. They can be understood as the instruments of God to punish the people, but they can also be understood as "public avengers" (to use Calvin's term) who deliver a people from unrighteous domination.[25] The Christian fundamentalists see Atta as a manifestation of the wrath of God against America, and the Islamic fundamentalists agree. But from the Islamic perspective, Atta is also an avenger who will deliver them from the domination of a global tyrant. It is important to note that one does not have to believe in the inherent goodness or morality of the avengers to see the effects of their actions as a manifestation of divine will. The belief that Samson or Atta are God's "public avengers" is compatible with regarding them as evil. God is an artist, and he knows how to use black to enhance his canvas.

The Islamic and Christian traditions are intimately linked; everything depends on the will of God; everywhere the hand of God is at work. So, if we accept the view that Samson was an instrument of God, then we must accept the view that Atta was also an instrument of God. We must remember that the God of the Jews, Christians, and Muslims is the same biblical God. To skeptics, this God appears wrathful and cruel, but to believers, He is just. That may be. But what is disturbing is the nature of His justice and its heroes.

In the biblical story of Samson, we cannot help noticing that the biblical author assumes that there are no innocent Philistines. The Philistines are evil by virtue of being Philistines. The biblical God is indifferent to the innocence of individuals. He punishes the Philistines as a people. The whole community is punished for the iniquities of some. Nor does God deny that this is indeed His brand of justice, as we have seen.[26] The Puritans were acutely aware of this aspect of divine justice, and it accounts for their meddlesome politics, which is to say, their preoccupation with the private vices of their neighbors. It is understandable to worry about the private vice of one's neighbors and fellow citizens if we are convinced that we will pay a collective price for their vices.[27] This is the thinking behind the statements made by Pat Robertson and Jerry Falwell.

The same biblical logic is used by the Islamic enemies of America. Just as there are no innocent Philistines, so there are no innocent Americans. All Americans deserve to suffer for the greed and injustice of their government's social policies. And this means that the terrorist attack was morally justified. Islamic apologists regard the incident as a politically motivated crime that has nothing to do with Islam. But clearly, this is disingenuous.

The logic of biblical dualism has the effect of polarizing the world. We are on the side of God, and our enemies are allied with Satan. The world is organized into two tidy categories—us and them, good and evil, God and Satan. The political struggle against our enemies is therefore part and parcel of the cosmic struggle between the forces of good and evil. Once the world is understood in these terms, it becomes clear why Samson is a hero and Atta is a villain. Samson is on our side. That is all.

Is there any hope of escaping from this impasse? It seems to me that our only hope is to cultivate the self-criticism and self-understanding that transcends the simplistic biblical dualism—"we good" and "they bad." We are civilized, and they are terrorists.

No one has tackled the story of Samson more honestly or more boldly than Maurice Yacowar in his delightful novel, *The Bold Testament*.[28] The novel is a postmodern retelling of the story of Samson as told from Delila's point of view—which is to say, from the Philistine point of view. This has the effect of revealing truths that are glossed over in the Bible. For example, Delila makes it clear that the Promised Land was heavily populated, and that the Philistines were eventually wiped out by the Hebrews. These facts are acknowledged in the Bible.

In the postmodern view, as represented by Michel Foucault and others, every group has its own truth and its own knowledge. The victors have their truth and the vanquished have theirs. It is also a fact that the victors generally write the histories. The Bible is therefore written from the Hebrew point of view—the point of view of the victors. The postmodern project consists in the liberation of the "subjugated knowledges," which is to say, the vanquished perspectives.[29] However, postmodernism is skeptical about truth. It denies that there is such a thing as truth independent of perspective. And that is precisely its problem. If there is no such thing as truth, if all of life and especially politics, is a war of mutually conflicting propagandas, then there is no sense telling the story from the point of view of the subjugated—the Philistine point of view. The new story simply replaces one set of lies with another.

But clearly, this is not the case. Telling the story from more than one perspective brings us closer to the truth, even if we cannot have the whole truth and nothing but the truth. Yacowar's retelling of the story accomplishes just that. It gets us closer to the truth not just by inverting the Bible, but by allowing us to see in the canonical text what is never denied, but is quickly glossed over. The biblical propaganda does not deny the fact that the Promised Land was heavily populated, but it brushes it aside as if to say it was an insignificant fact. The biblical propaganda portrays Samson as a hero who was responsible for "liberating" his people from their oppressors. But the Bible does not deny that Samson was also a brute whose superhuman strength was criminally out of control (Judges 14:19). For the sake of basic law and order, Samson had to be put behind bars to make the community—any community—safe. This is the side of the story that Delila (i.e. Yacowar) brings out. It is not a matter of replacing one set of lies with another. The story that Delila tells is totally recognizable. It is not an inversion of the tale as we know it. It brings us closer to the truth because it highlights aspects of the canonical story that are glossed over, and therefore allows us to see the Bible, that sacred text, as a text like any other—a flawed and one-sided account of historical events as told by the victors. This is a necessary step in the project of self-criticism and self-understanding.[30]

4. Transcending the Biblical Horizon

The biblical horizon accounts for both the naïveté and cynicism of the current approach to politics. On one hand, it fosters a naïve dualism—God is on our side and our enemies are the allies of Satan. This self-righteous naïveté radicalizes and polarizes the world, while making self-criticism and self-understanding impossible. On the other hand, the biblical horizon encourages and justifies a cynical *realpolitik*. The two postures are theoretically distinct, but in practice they are both inclined to belligerence rather than diplomacy. The result is that politics is eclipsed by religion on one hand, and militarism on the other. To transcend the biblical horizon, it is necessary to get beyond both biblical dualism and *realpolitik*.

The first step in transcending biblical dualism is to acknowledge the plurality of the good. At the very least, it is necessary to acknowledge that there is truth on both sides, and that the enemy often has a legitimate case. This is the first step in the project of self-criticism and self-understanding.

The next step is for the protagonists to see themselves through the eyes of the enemy. In other words, something like Yacowar's experiment must be attempted. In what follows, I will describe the current conflict from two perspectives: an American liberal perspective and an Islamic fundamentalist perspective. Each perspective represents half the truth. And together they expand our capacity for self-criticism and mutual understanding. My experiment is intended to reveal that the adversaries are not only moved by mutual fear and revulsion, but also by mutual envy and attraction.

From the Islamic fundamentalist perspective, America is the incarnation of Satan. No. She is even more interesting and seductive than Satan. She is more akin to the Whore of Babylon. She has invented a new and more insidious form of colonialism. She is not satisfied with amassing wealth and power. Her goal is to conquer the hearts and minds of Muslim men and women around the globe. She will settle for nothing short of global spiritual dominance. She aims to create a global culture. Global capitalism is the instrument of American imperialism. Her goal is not just to sell Coke or Nikes; she aims to sell a particular way of life—a hedonistic way of life devoted to the pursuit of wealth and pleasure.

The new colonialism subjugates the soul; it conquers not with the sword, but with seductive, sexy advertising. Muslim souls are more at risk than they have ever been before.

The new world order is armed with a powerful new religion and new gods. It is devoted to the worship of Mammon and Dionysus—the god of wine, sex, and revelry. The new global culture thrives on vice. The endless pursuit of pleasure, luxury, and self-indulgence, churns the wheels of the capitalist economy and augments its profits. This satanic religion has conquered the globe in the name of universal prosperity. But Satan lies; no universal prosperity is at hand.[31] Global capitalism will make America richer, while leaving the poorest of the poor more impoverished than they ever were before, not only materially, but also spiritually.

We can imagine that Islamic rhetoric continues as follows. Islam is in greater danger than it has ever been before. It is the duty of all Muslims to defend the faith against the infidels. It is true that the Koran talks of *jihad* as an inner struggle, a spiritual struggle against the forces of evil within. But it also condones another kind of *jihad*—taking up arms to defend the faith. And the faith is clearly threatened, as it has never been before. No doubt the Christians will point to the militancy of Islam with self-congratulation. They will proudly invoke the name of God the Son—a God of love and self-sacrifice. But as soon as they are in positions of power, they behave in the cruel and vengeful ways of God the Father. However, Muslims do not have two or three deities, but only one God. And the only authority available to interpret his word is the sacred text. There is no clergy, no Church hierarchy, and no official interpretation of the Koran.[32] And those who think that it is acceptable to use every means to defend the faith when it is threatened are not simply fringe lunatics.

From the American liberal perspective, it is clear that Islamic hatred of America is born of envy. Islamic societies are so repressive that the Whore of Babylon is bound to have unmistakable appeal. Societies that deprive their citizens of freedom destroy the capacity for self-restraint. The *hijab* is the ultimate symbol of Islamic repression. It is no longer an expression of piety or the love of God. With the defeat of the Taliban, Afghani women are now allowed to walk the streets of Kabul, unveiled. But most of them do not dare, because they fear that their men are too wild and unrestrained. At least, that is what they said on television when interviewed by Western journalists. What Islamic societies fear most is themselves. They fear their own incapacity to deal with freedom; they fear the seductive appeal of American liberty. Even the terrorists, who sacrificed their lives in the attack on the World Trade Center, were seduced by the Whore of Babylon. We hear that they frequented nightclubs, went drinking, whoring, and spent the rest of their leisure time watching American television—"Bay Watch" was a favorite.

The American liberal perspective continues as follows. Islamic culture must confess that its populace is not educated for freedom. That is why it is so easily seduced by the trashiest aspects of American culture. That is why it trembles before the Whore of Babylon. It is time for Islamic culture to stop blaming the evil empire for all its troubles; it is time to look inward for the source of its difficulties.

Assuming my own voice once again, I am inclined to conclude that both sides have legitimate claims. There is no doubt that Arab hatred of the United States has its source in envy and resentment of America's success and prosperity as well as its enviable capacity to sustain social order under conditions of relative freedom. In contrast, internal division, economic collapse, turmoil, confusion, tyranny, repression, and helplessness riddle the Islamic world. But there is also envy on the other side.

It may sound surprising to suggest that Americans also suffer from envy of the Arab world. This is especially true in the most powerful circles, which is to say, among American neoconservatives and the Christian Right. The American Right believes that the Islamic view of America is not off the mark. The irony is that the Whore of Babylon has a fundamentalist heart. On some estimates, as many as forty-eight percent of Americans claim to be born-again Christians—including President George W. Bush, and former President Jimmy Carter. As a result, America suffers from a profound self-loathing.

On the surface, American society appears to be the model of liberal modernity gone mad. Pornography is her biggest export. She cannot sell chewing gum or cars without relying on sex appeal. There was a time when the Islamic world could look to the West to satisfy its hunger for scientific knowledge. But now it sees the West as providing mainly pornography and gadgets such as computers, which make the pornography even more accessible. America hates the Islamic world because it speaks with the voice of its own conscience. The enemy is a reminder that America is Faustian— that she has sold her soul to the devil for wealth and power.

American self-contempt and envy of the Islamic world is particularly evident in the writings of neoconservatives. Samuel Huntington's *Clash of Civilizations* is a case in point. At first blush, the book appears to be a diatribe against the Muslim enemy. But on closer examination, the denunciation of the Islamic enemy is laced with envy. In particular, Huntington envies them their unliberated women, their high birth rate, their youthful population, their religiosity, and their close-knit communitarianism. In short, he envies their illiberality. Like other American neoconservatives, Huntington regards liberalism as the greatest threat to American well-being and success. Liberalism has given birth to feminism, and the latter has turned American women against childbearing. They are no longer busy making soldiers. Meanwhile, the population continues to age. How long can they keep the Islamic menace at bay? That is the gist of his *realpolitik* thinking. And that is the source of his envy.

In my view, political realism is seriously flawed. It is based on the distinction between hard power and soft power. Hard power is military might—tanks, planes, nuclear warheads, submarines, and soldiers—lots of soldiers. Soft power is culture, communication, films, books, music, and entertainment. Political realists, such as Huntington, assume that hard power is critical for achieving hegemony and dominance in the world. They tend to overlook the force of soft power. But this flies in the face of historical experience. One of Nietzsche's greatest insights is the recognition that those who win the wars rarely succeed in imposing the yoke of their own culture on the defeated. The Greeks are a classic case in point. They lost militarily to the Macedonians and the Romans, yet Greek culture continued to dominate.

By the same token, America has not acquired its current world dominance through military conquest. It did not defeat the Soviets. The Soviet Union collapsed of its own accord. American hegemony has its source in its economic and cultural supremacy. Ironically it has decided to rely more and more on its military might—and this may be its undoing. But it is also a result of the *realpolitik* mentality that characterizes the current administration. But its enemies know better. They know that the formidable strength of the United States has been cultural. The World Trade Towers were clear symbols of that economic and cultural supremacy. It is the latter that the Islamic enemies of the United States fear more than its military might.

The conflict between America and the Islamic world is primarily a war of propaganda—a cultural war in which each of the antagonists is determined to win the sympathy, admiration, and moral approval of the world. Each is claiming to be the victim; each is claiming to be on the side of God, truth, and justice. Each is relying on the same biblical dualism that makes the antagonists equally intransigent, immoderate, and intolerant. It is unlikely that they will abandon this biblical rhetoric and move in the direction of a more moderate and pluralistic politics.

One question remains: which one is likely to win the contest for world opinion? Which one is likely to be more persuasive or credible?

I dare say that for all its power and resources, the United States is at a serious disadvantage. The biblical imagery of good and evil (on which both parties rely) does not favor a superpower. The biblical narrative favors the oppressed and persecuted and not the powerful—the enslaved Hebrews, not their Egyptian overlords, David not Goliath, the Christians not their Roman tormentors. The world's only superpower does not fit the biblical imagery; it cannot play the role of the persecuted for long. It may have gotten away with it briefly after September 11, but it cannot continue to do this after the bombing of Afghanistan, the war with Iraq, and its indiscriminate support of Israel's war on the Palestinians. The more it flexes its military muscle, the more it looks like the oppressor, the more it risks losing the war of propaganda—even among its own citizens. Witness the young man from California who converted to Islam and fought on the side of the Taliban.

The statistics that indicate that more people in America and around the world have converted to Islam since September 11 are troubling. It reveals that Islam has some of the resilience of Christianity: it refuses to be tarnished by its crimes. If Muslims succeed in adopting the posture of victims, if they succeed in presenting themselves as the oppressed people of God, rather than the aggressors, then the United States may emerge as the world tyrant and global bully. By utilizing the powerful biblical imagery, Muslims may win the war of propaganda.

One does not have to succumb to the appeal of biblical imagery to find the prospect of a single superpower pushing its weight around the globe reprehensible. Unless the United States starts to use its power wisely, it will lose the cultural war. But it will not be the only loser. Israel will also be a loser—and so will Jews around the world. As long as American foreign policy remains unchanged, as long as its corporate institutions remain rapacious, the anti-globalization forces will unite with the anti-Semitic forces to elect more and more immoderate politicians in Europe and elsewhere. The United States can turn the tide only if it is willing to abandon the biblical rhetoric of good and evil in favor of a secular rhetoric of diplomacy and compromise. But this is not likely as long as the current administration is in power.

In conclusion, the perspectival approach makes it possible to transcend the biblical horizon. It makes it possible to abandon the naïveté of dualism as well as the cynicism of *realpolitik*. The perspectival approach reveals that each of the protagonists has a legitimate case to make against the other. Neither is without fault; and neither has the whole truth on its side. Each is in quest of a distinctive ideal, which is not compatible with the ideal of the other. And even though I have little sympathy for the Islamic way of life, I believe that a world in which only one flower is allowed to bloom—the liberal flower—is pitiful. But worst of all, the current globalizing forces promote nihilism, despondency, and despair—and these are the breeding ground of senseless terror.

When people believe that their ideals are the only ones of any merit, and when they are determined to use the power of the state to inflict their ideals on others, they become fanatical killers. It is highly ironic that the ideal of surrender, the feminine and passive ideal, has been the source of so much aggression. Unhappily for the world, we can expect more of its self-righteous brutality—in its Christian, Muslim, and Judaic manifestations. The so-called war on terrorism has all the fanaticism of a religious war, coupled with the deadly weapons of a technological age. Those who believe that civilization is barbarism with technical skill are not far off the mark. More often than not, it is barbarism with technical skill *and* a clear conscience.

NOTES

Part I Metaphysics of Terror

1. See e.g., Hiram Cato "Explaining the Nazis," *Quadrant* (October 1986), pp. 61–68. Cato associates liberalism with the Weimar Republic and the subsequent terrors of Nazi Germany. This association of freedom with terror is at the heart of conservative and right-wing fears. And while these fears are not unfounded, a return to biblical religion is no solution.

2. Garry Wills, *Papal Sin* (New York: Doubleday, 2000).

3. Garry Wills, *Saint Augustine* (New York: Viking Penguin, 1999). A biography that can only be described as an apology to his Christian hero. See also the defense and tribute to Augustine in *Papal Sin*.

4. I will not pretend to uncover the historical Jesus. Since Jesus did not leave a written legacy, it is difficult to know with any accuracy what he actually taught and said. All we have is secondhand reports. Any claims to have discovered the "historical Jesus" are conjecture.

5. Friedrich Nietzsche, *Genealogy of Morals*, Essay I, Francis Golffing, trans. (New York: Doubleday & Co., 1956). It may be argued that Jesus shared Nietzsche's antipathy to the rule of priests.

6. Friedrich Nietzsche, *The Anti-Christ* (1895), R. J. Hollingdale, trans. (London: Penguin Books, 1968), Sec. 39: "There has been only one Christian, and he died on the Cross." Nietzsche rejects the idea that Christianity is a set of beliefs and doctrines. Instead, he thinks that it is a doing or a not doing of many things. I think that Nietzsche is wrong. Even Jesus made belief, especially in himself as the Son of God, fundamental to being Christian and being saved.

7. Edward Westermarck, *Christianity and Morals* (New York: Macmillan, 1939).

8. The authenticity of the Gospel of John has varied through the ages. On the whole, scholars thought of the synoptic Gospels (the first three Gospels: Matthew, Mark, and Luke) as a fairly accurate account of the historical Jesus with some embellishments. But the Gospel of John was regarded as a theological interpretation that may not reflect Jesus's own self-understanding. But the discovery of the Dead Sea Scrolls in 1947 has led scholars to think that the Gospel of John may be an accurate reflection of how Jesus talked. The manuscripts discovered there are dated at the time that Jesus lived and their language and imagery is very close to the language and imagery of the Fourth Gospel. See C. H. Dodd, *Historical Tradition in the Fourth Gospel* (Cambridge, England: Cambridge University Press, 1963).

9. Martin Luther (1483–1546), "Preface to the New Testament," in *Martin Luther: Selections from His Writings*, John Dillenberger, ed. (New York: Doubleday, 1961), p. 18.

10. This concern with self-salvation at the heart of Christian ethics led Machiavelli to maintain that the ideal prince, someone who was truly devoted to his fatherland, had better not be a Christian. And if he was, he had better love his country more than his soul, because he may have to do things to save his country that may damn his soul. In my view, Machiavelli's political tactics are neither wise nor effective, as the example of his hero, Cesare Borgia, illustrates. Borgia was a political failure, not just because he was unlucky as Machiavelli maintained but because he was a scoundrel. Nevertheless, Machiavelli has a legitimate point to make against Christianity. Anyone who is so focused on self-salvation cannot attend to the collective good of a nation, a tribe, or a family.

11. See "The Infancy Gospels," in *The Other Bible*, Willis Barnstone, ed. (New York: Harper & Row, 1984). The story of the children who were turned into goats is part of the *Arabic Infancy Gospels* that were first translated by Henry Sike in 1697. This Christian apocrypha was available in the times of Mohammed and has made its way into the Koran.

12. Matthew 22:23 and Luke 20:27: The Sadducees "deny that there is any resurrection." They questioned Jesus and ridiculed him saying when a woman who has married seven different men dies, whose wife will she be in heaven? But the Pharisees, who did not reject the idea of immortality, had different objections to Jesus's creed.

13. Scholars attribute the emphasis on faith to the Gospel of John, which they used to discount, but since the discovery of the Dead Sea Scrolls at Qumran in 1947, scholars are inclined to consider the Gospel of John to be authentic. See Hugo Meynell, *Is Christianity True?* (London: Geoffrey Chapman, 1994), pp. 72 ff.

14. Saint Thomas Aquinas, *Summa Theologica* [*ST*], translated by the Fathers of the English Dominican Province (Westminster, Maryland: Christian Classics, 1911), Pt. II-II, Q. 151, Art. 1. Aquinas is here quoting Augustine approvingly.

15. Aquinas, *ST*, Pt. II-II, Q. 13, Art. 3. My italics.

16. Ibid., Pt. II-II, Q. 14, Art. 1.

17. Ibid., Pt. II-II, Q. 13, Art. 3.

18. It seems that Christian virtue consists above all in sheepish conformity and unquestioning obedience. It is no wonder that Jesus was eager to amass mindless, devoted, zealous, and unquestioning disciples. The analogy of the shepherd (himself) and his sheep (the believers) is appropriate (John 10:11). Equally appropriate is the analogy likening believers to little children: "except ye be converted, and become as little children, ye shall not enter into the kingdom of heaven" (Matthew 18:3; Mark 10:15).

19. J. Wilhelm, "Heresy," *Catholic Encyclopedia* (New York: The Encyclopedia Press, 1910), pp. 256–62. Wilhelm writes, "toleration came in only when faith went out; lenient measures were resorted to only where the power to apply more severe measures was wanting" (p. 262).

20. Ibid., p. 260.

21. His reason for tolerating Jews was extremely vain and self-congratulatory—namely because their religion bears witness to the truth—i.e. our religion. It is a testimony to the greatness of our faith that even our "enemies" (as he calls the Jews) cannot help but bear witness to our faith. Aquinas thought this situation very advantageous and it was the reason he thought the Jews should be left unmolested. In contrast to Judaism, Aquinas thought that pagan religion is "neither truthful nor profitable" and is "by no means to be tolerated" except to avoid "scandal" or some greater evil, especially when pagans and unbelievers are very numerous, Aquinas, *ST*, Pt. II-II, Q. 10, Art. 11, "Ought the Rites of Unbelievers to be Tolerated?"

22. Aquinas, *ST*, Pt. II-II, Q. 11, Art. 3, "Ought Heretics to be Tolerated?" Aquinas thought that heretics who repent should be forgiven and taken back into the fold. Indeed, they can be forgiven a second time. If they transgress a third time and then repent, they should be forgiven, but killed anyway, and left to God to decide if their repentance was sincere, Aquinas, *ST*, Pt. II-II, Q. 11, Art. 4.

23. Ibid., Q. 11, Art. 4.

24. Saint Jerome as quoted by Aquinas, Ibid., Q. 11, Art. 4.

25. Aquinas, *ST*, Pt. II-II, Q. 11, reply to objection 3.

26. I am indebted to my former colleague Jack MacIntosh for this insight.

27. At the First Council of Nicaea (325), the assembled bishops agreed that the Son of God is "consubstantial" with the Father. This was intended to establish the equal divinity of Jesus with God. The bishops who refused to accept this were banished along with Arius.

28. Martin Luther, "A Treatise on Christian Liberty," (1520), in Martin Luther, *Three Treatises* (Philadelphia, Pa.: The Muhlenberg Press, 1943), p. 267.

29. Martin Luther, "Preface to the Epistle of St. Paul to the Romans," in John Dillenberger, ed., *Martin Luther: Selections from His Writings* (New York: Doubleday & Co., 1961), p. 22.

30. Ibid., p. 25.

31. Martin Luther, "A Treatise on Christian Liberty," p. 262.

32. Ibid., p. 271.

33. Ibid., pp. 271–72.

34. Ibid., p. 272.

35. Ibid., p. 274.

36. Ibid., p. 274.

37. The Ranters flourished in the late 1640s and early 1650s. See Jerome Friedman, *Blasphemy, Immorality and Anarchy: The Ranters and the English Revolution* (Athens, Ohio: Ohio University Press, 1987).

38. Luther, "A Treatise on Christian Liberty," p. 268.

39. For a fictional account of the amoral logic of this theology, see James Hogg, *The Private Memoirs and Confessions of a Justified Sinner*, 1824 (Toronto: Oxford University Press, 1981).

40. See further discussion in "Hell and Damnation" and "The Angst of Salvation" in this chapter.

41. John Bunyan, *Grace Abounding to the Chief of Sinners*, 1666 (London: Penguin Books, 1987).

42. Ibid., p. 73.
43. Ibid., p. 27.
44. Ibid., pp. 28, 31, 39, 43, 46, 47, 57, 73.
45. Ibid., p. 84.
46. See R. H. Charles, *A Critical History of the Doctrine of a Future Life: In Israel, in Judaism, and in Christianity* (London: Adam and Charles Black, 1899). See bibliography for more details.
47. Friedrich Nietzsche (1844–1900) was particularly skillful in describing the maliciousness of the priestly morality. But Nietzsche shared with the priests, the belief in the active malevolence of human nature. He was convinced that public executions and other forms of exquisite torture were cultivated, not to improve or rehabilitate the criminal but for the purpose of pleasure and entertainment derived from witnessing excruciating pain. The difference between Nietzsche and Christianity is his veracity, his love of nature with all its depravity, and his eagerness to provide malice with an outlet. See Nietzsche, *Genealogy of Morals*, Essay I. See bibliography for more details.
48. This dualistic vision also makes it impossible to entertain the idea that there can be more than one good way or right path.
49. Augustine conveniently interprets this "figuratively." Apparently, the coals of fire are the burning sighs of penitence, which heal the pride of those who have done wrong. See *On Christian Doctrine*, D. W. Robertson, Jr., trans. (New York: Macmillan Publishing Company, 1958), Sec. XVI, p. 93.
50. His full name was Origines Adamantius. He was born in Egypt, probably Alexandria. He was famous for his three-level interpretation of the Scripture—literal, moral, and allegorical. See his *On First Principles* (New York: Harper & Row, 1966). See bibliography for more details.
51. Origen, *Spirit and Fire: A Thematic Anthology of his Writings*, 1938, Hans Urs von Balthasar, ed., Robert J. Daly, trans. (Washington D.C.: Catholic University of America, 1984), p. 346.
52. Ibid., p. 348.
53. Ibid., p. 129.
54. Ibid., p. 333.
55. More recently, the Church of England expressed a similar view. See *Doctrine in the Church of England: The Report of the Commission on Christian Doctrine appointed by the Archbishops of Canterbury and York in 1922* (London: Society for Promoting Christian Knowledge, rep. 1962, ca. 1938), pp. 218–19. The bishops explain that heaven is life in the company of God, and that Hell is the reverse. Therefore, hell is for those who, of their own volition fail to "respond to the call of Divine love." But they also add that some believe that these souls will be "lost" forever, while others believe that the "Love of God will at last win penitence and answering love from every soul." And they maintain "there is room in the Church for both views."
56. Origen, *Spirit and Fire*, p. 358.
57. Augustine, *City of God*, Henry Bettenson, trans. (London: Penguin Books, 1972), Bk. XXI, ch. 17.
58. Joseph Hontheim, "Hell," in *The Catholic Encyclopedia* (New York: The Encyclopedia Press, Inc., 1910), Vol. 7, pp. 207–11.

59. See e.g., Charles, *A Critical History of the Doctrine of a Future Life*. Charles thinks that the Christian conceptions of heaven and hell are purely spiritual, and any references to the body, to burning, and to fire are to be understood figuratively. See also *Doctrine in the Church of England*, p. 219. Hell is described merely as "exclusion from the fellowship of God."

60. The theologians who busy themselves in reinterpreting Jesus's words to suit the ideas of the day do not agree with what Jesus actually says, so they reinterpret it to mean something totally different, which they and their age find palatable. This exercise of making Jesus's words compatible with current moral sentiments may give the illusion that the teaching of Jesus is timeless because no matter how much moral ideas change, he seems to be saying the right things. But this theological exercise does much damage to the instinct for truth. This argument has been presented most eloquently by Walter Kaufmann in *The Faith of a Heretic* (New York: Doubleday & Co. Inc., 1961), see esp. ch. 5, "Against Theology." See also Westermarck, *Christianity and Morals*. It seems to me that something more than the instinct for truth is lost. This self-defensive posture also destroys any possibility of self-criticism.

61. Augustine, *City of God*, Bk. XXI, ch. 9, p. 984; see also Bk. XX, ch. 22, p. 944.

62. Ibid., Bk. XX, chs. 10, 12, 14; Bk. XXI, chs. 1, 5. See also, Augustine, *On Christian Doctrine*, Sec. XXI, where he states that neither the human soul nor the body will suffer complete annihilation.

63. Augustine, *City of God*, Bk. XXI, chs. 4–5.

64. Ibid., Bk. XXII, ch. 25.

65. Aquinas, *ST*, Suppl. Q. 93, Art. 1.

66. Ibid., Suppl. Q. 97, Arts. 4, 5, 6.

67. Ibid., Suppl. Q. 97, Art. 4.

68. Ibid., Suppl. Q. 98, Art. 4. On one hand, the damned must be deprived of light because darkness is their lot but on the other hand, they must witness the joy of the blessed so that they can be tormented by envy and regret as well as by the fire. But how can they witness the joys of the blessed if they are totally enveloped in darkness? This is the sort of scholastic puzzle that Aquinas generally excels at, but he fails to deal with this one.

69. Ibid., Suppl. Q. 99, Art. 1.

70. Baptism allows infants to partake in the Passion of Christ, by which Jesus paid the penalty for original sin. Unbaptized babies are damned. See *ST*, Pt. III, Q. 46, Art. 4, and Pt. III, Q. 69, Art. 2.

71. Ibid., Appendix I, Q. 1, Art.1.

72. Underneath this view is usually the cynical conviction that there is absolutely no rational or persuasive reason to be moral; and that morality is a necessary sacrifice by the individual for the sake of society. In other words, the question that Glaucon asks Socrates in the *Republic*: "Why should I be moral?" has no persuasive answer unless we resort to the fiction of the afterlife. Without belief in hell, there is no personal motive for morality. Hugo Meynell makes this case in "Glaucon's Question," *New Black Friars* (February, 1972), pp. 73–82. An even more cynical writer, Leo Strauss, who poses as a devotee of Plato, denies that Plato has given any persuasive answers to that question, because there are no persuasive answers to be had.

See Strauss's essay on Plato's *Republic* in *City and Man* (Chicago, Ill.: University of Chicago Press, 1964). See also my exposé of Strauss's cynical religiosity in *The Political Ideas of Leo Strauss* (New York: St. Martin's Press, 1988), and *Leo Strauss and the American Right* (New York: St. Martin's Press, 1997). One need not despair of human nature to believe that the threat of damnation is a motivation to avoid sin. Saint Thomas Aquinas was not at all cynical about human nature; nevertheless, he believed that the threat of hell was salutary. See *ST*, Suppl. Q. 99, Art. 1, Reply to Objection 3.

73. Jonathan Edwards, "Sinners in the Hands of an Angry God," in *Jonathan Edwards: Representative Selections*, C. H. Faust and T. H. Johnson, eds. (New York: Hill and Wang, 1935), pp. 163–65.

74. Edwards, "The Future Punishment of the Wicked: Unavoidable and Intolerable," in *Jonathan Edwards*, p. 148. In my view, the real sermons of Edwards are even more fantastic and surreal than the sermon in James Joyce's *A Portrait of the Artist as a Young Man* (London: Penguin Books, 1914, 1992).

75. John Bunyan, *Grace Abounding to the Chief of Sinners*, p. 8.

76. Ibid., p. 19.

77. Ibid., p. 29.

78. Ibid., pp. 27, 73.

79. Ibid., p. 11. This logic is dramatized in the fiction by Hogg, *The Private Memoirs and Confessions*.

80. Bunyan, *Grace Abounding*, pp. 44, 84.

81. Ibid., p. 25.

82. Ibid., p. 66.

83. Augustine, *Confessions*, R. S. Pine-Coffin, trans. (London: Penguin Books, 1961).

84. *The Holy Qur'an*, Maulana Muhammad Ali, trans. (Chicago, Ill.: Specialty Promotions Co. Inc., 1973), ch. 35, verse 33.

85. *Qur'an*, ch. 55:46–78.

86. Marcion thought that only men will be saved. He thought that women were like beasts and did not have immortal souls. He also denied that Christ was born of woman. He made a great contrast between the God of the Old Testament and the God of the New Testament. The former was evil while the latter was good. Jesus was the incarnation of the new God, who existed from the foundation of the world. But the disciples did not understand him because they were still thinking in Old Testament terms. That was why it was necessary for Paul to be inspired by a special revelation; otherwise Jesus's entire teachings would have been lost. The work of Marcion was destroyed by the Church and he was denounced as the worst of heretics. What we know of his ideas we have only through the criticism of Tertullian. See Adolph Harnack, *History of Dogma*, Vol. I, Neil Buchanan, trans. (London: Williams & Norgate, 1905).

87. See Deuteronomy 25:5–10.

88. Contrary to those who believed that only men will be saved, Augustine pointed to this passage as evidence that there will be both sexes in heaven—but not to

worry, because the female organs "will be part of a new beauty, which will not excite the lust of the beholder," *City of God*, Bk. XXII, ch. 17.

89. *Doctrine in the Church of England*, p. 219.

90. William Blake noted that in *Paradise Lost*, things generally get exciting only when Satan comes on the scene and that Milton was of "the party of the devil" without knowing it. See Blake, *The Marriage of Heaven and Hell*, in G. E. Bentley, Jr., ed., *William Blake's Writings*, Vol. I (Oxford: The Clarendon Press, 1978), p. 80. See also C. S. Lewis, *Preface to Paradise Lost* (London: Oxford University Press, 1942), p. 94 ff. See bibliography for details.

91. *Doctrine in the Church of England*, p. 219.

92. Jonathan Edwards, "The Eternity of Hell Torments," in *The Works of President Edwards* (Worcester: Isaiah Thomas, 1808), Vol. 7, p. 415.

93. Aquinas, *ST*, Suppl. Q. 94.

94. Ibid., Art.1.

95. Ibid., Art. 2.

96. Ibid., Art. 3. Realizing the sadistic implications of all this pleasure, Aquinas argues that the direct source of the pleasures of the blessed will be their own deliverance as well as the manifestation of Divine justice. Even though they will be clearly visible to the blessed, the actual tortures of the damned will be only the "indirect" source of their pleasure. He makes the same argument about God, saying that God also rejoices in these punishments, but only in so far as they are required by His justice. But he does not explain what kind of justice requires *eternal* torment. Clearly, this argument is forced.

97. Augustine, *City of God*, Bk. XX, ch. 22.

98. See Jonathan Bennett, "The Conscience of Huckleberry Finn," *Philosophy*, Vol. 49 (April, 1974), rep. in John Arther, ed., *Morality and Moral Controversies* (New Jersey: Prentice-Hall, 1981), pp. 13–20.

99. Roger Manwell and Heinrich Fraenkel, *Heinrich Himmler*, pp. 132, 197, 184, 187, as quoted by Jonathan Bennett.

100. This is the standard view among Christian writers. See the excellent essay by Jonathan Edwards, "The Doctrine of Original Sin Defended," in *Representative Selections* where Edwards argues that original sin not only refers to the sin of Adam and Eve but also to human depravity in general.

101. See Kaufmann's excellent essay on Job, "Suffering and the Bible," in *The Faith of a Heretic*.

102. Sigmund Freud, *The Future of an Illusion* (New York: Doubleday & Co., 1927).

103. John Bunyan, *The Pilgrim's Progress*, 1678 (London: Penguin Books, 1965).

104. Ibid., p. 200.

105. Saint Paul invites this reading. Compare *Romans* 7:23 with *Romans* 8:2.

106. Bunyan, *The Pilgrim's Progress*, p. 216.

107. Ibid., p. 199.

108. John Bunyan, *Grace Abounding to the Chief of Sinners*, p. 14.

109. Jonathan Edwards, *The Works of President Edwards* (Worcester: Isaiah Thomas, 1808), Vol. IV, pp. 260–61. Edwards thinks that the legal spirit is insidious and that it lingers even in the souls of those who decry it.

110. Ibid., Vol. IV, p. 261.

111. Jonathan Edwards, "The Eternity of Hell Torments," in *The Works of President Edwards*, p. 415.
112. Origen, *Commentary on the Epistle to the Romans: Books 1–5*, Thomas P. Scheck, trans. (Washington, D.C.: The Catholic University of America Press, 2001), p. 161.
113. Harnack, *History of Dogma*, Vol. II, p. 367.
114. C. S. Lewis uses the same motif in his story *The Lion, the Witch and the Wardrobe*. The Lion (Christ) tricks the witch by offering to suffer instead of the sons of Adam. The witch agrees, but is tricked. See bibliography for more details.
115. For a very interesting work on the atonement, see Gustaf Aulén, *Christus Victor: An Historical Study of the Three Main Types of the Idea of the Atonement*, A. G. Herbert, trans. (New York: Macmillan Co., 1969). Aulén is a champion of Luther, and he argues that Luther revives the ideas of the Greek fathers regarding the Atonement. But he is not willing to say that the ransom was paid to the devil to buy us back. Instead, he says that God was both the reconciler and the reconciled. Even if this idea makes sense, which I am not sure it does, it defeats the case he wants to make. Aulén's best idea in his interpretation of Luther is that the latter's view of the Atonement is a Hegelian *aufgehoben* whereby God's love and mercy transcend His wrath. See bibliography for more details.
116. The concept of "satisfaction" also plays a large role in the view of the Atonement as presented by Saint Anselm of Canterbury, *Why God Became Man*, Edward S. Prout, trans. (London: Religious Tract Society, 1887). See bibliography for details.
117. Aquinas, *ST*, Pt. III, Q. 46, Art. 2.
118. Ibid., Pt. III, Q. 47, Art. 3.
119. Ibid., Art. 4. According to Aquinas, the Passion of Christ accomplishes several things. It pays the penalty for original sin, which is eternal damnation. And since it is more than sufficient to pay the penalty for all humanity, it reconciles man to God. By the disobedience of one man, the whole human race was alienated from God, so, it is fitting that by the obedience of one man, the whole human race is reconciled to God. Through the Passion, Christ triumphs over death of body and soul. He shows us that we will rise as he did, and neither our body nor our soul will be condemned to death. The Passion absolves humanity of original sin and makes the forgiveness of sin possible. Through the Passion we are dead to sin and alive to God. Christ has rescued us from "bondage to sin"; he has loosened the power of the devil over us. All this is very standard, but it poses serious difficulties for Aquinas's philosophy. So much rests on the Passion that it makes all of life previous to the Passion incomprehensible. Was there no possibility of forgiveness before the Passion? Was humanity "in bondage to sin" or in the devil's power? Were the temptations of the devil totally irresistible prior to the Passion? What happened to our freedom to choose between good and evil—the freedom that Aquinas has always maintained was not obliterated by the fall? The Passion does not fit well with the rationalist model that Aquinas has tried to impose on

Christianity. In the final analysis, Aquinas's rationality is compromised and the doctrines of Christianity are watered down and made benign, if not insipid.

120. Aquinas, *ST*, Pt. III, Q. 48, Art. 2.

121. Ibid., Art. 2.

122. Ibid., Pt. III, Q. 49, Art. 4. The same view was held by Origen of Alexandria, see his *Commentary*, p. 161.

123. See Geoffrey May, *Social Control of Sex Expression* (New York: William Morrow & Co., 1930), p. 79.

124. W. H. Kent, "Indulgences," *Catholic Encyclopedia* (New York: Encyclopedia Press, 1910), Vol. 7, pp. 783–88. Not surprisingly, the sale of indulgences was one of the reasons for Luther's censure of the Catholic Church—not just because of the corruption it involved but also because Luther thought that life had to be one continuous penance.

125. Rufus M. Jones, "Flagellants" in James Hastings, *Encyclopedia of Ethics and Religion*, Vol. 6, pp. 49–51.

126. Pope Clement VI and Emperor Charles IV prohibited flagellation pilgrimages.

127. The efforts on the part of the Church to suppress it were largely due to the Brotherhood's belief that salvation can be achieved through penance and without the mediation of the Church. The Church objected to the practice primarily because it made the Church superfluous.

128. Some defenders of Christianity acknowledge that our God is indeed savage, but they believe in obeying Him nevertheless. See R. C. Zaehner, *Our Savage God* (London: Collins, 1974), see esp. ch. 6: "God: Mad or Bad?" He tells us that we should consider it an honor to enter the gas-chambers of such a God and to meet our death and destruction at his hands.

129. This logical conclusion is suggested by William Empson in *Milton's God* (London: Chatto & Windus, 1961).

130. One of the peculiar aspects of Aquinas's formulation is that it seems to forget about the Incarnation. Jesus is treated as the new man who replaces Adam, and whose obedience cancels out the disobedience of Adam. But if we take the Incarnation seriously and keep in mind that Jesus was supposed to be the incarnation of God, then what we have is God obeying Himself. And it is not clear how *that* could succeed in canceling man's original disobedience. The whole formulation makes God terribly unperceptive. He mistakes the obedience of Christ for the obedience of mankind. He is fooled into thinking that Christ's obedience unto death is an indication of some grand *human* transformation that warrants the removal of the eternal punishment that is due to Adam's sin.

131. One of the earliest efforts to defend the goodness of the Christian God was by Marcion. According to Marcion, Jesus offered his life as the ransom to save us from the bloodthirsty God of the Old Testament and win us to the loving God of the New Testament. This is an ingenious way to defend the goodness of the Christian God. But the Church denounced Marcion as the first son of Satan, and destroyed his work. We know it only through the critical account of Tertullian. See Harnack, *History of Dogma*, Vol. 1, ch. 5.

132. Empson makes this important point in *Milton's God*.
133. Garry Wills, *Papal Sin*.

Part II   Politics of Terror

1. Augustine, *City of God*, Henry Bettenson, trans. (London: Penguin Books, 1980), Bk. XI, ch. 1, Bk. XV, chs. 1–6.
2. Henry Paolucci, ed., *The Political Writings of St. Augustine* (Indiana: Gateway Publishing Co., 1962), pp. 135–36. See also Augustine, *City of God*, Bk. XIX, ch. 6.
3. Gotthold Ephraim Lessing, *Nathan the Wise*, Bayard Quincy Morgan, trans. (New York: Frederick Ungar Publishing Co., 1955). Fyodor Dostoevsky, *The Grand Inquisitor*, Constance Garnett, trans. (New York: Liberal Arts Press, 1948).
4. Eric Voegelin, "On Hegel: A Study in Sorcery," *The Collected Works of Eric Voegelin*, Vol. 12, Ellis Sandos, ed. (Baton Rouge, Louisiana: Louisiana State University Press, 1990), p. 217. See also "The Eclipse of Reality," *The Collected Works of Eric Voegelin*, Vol. 28, and *Science, Politics and Gnosticism* (Chicago: Henry Regnery 1968), pp. 99 ff.
5. This is the gist of the first three volumes of Voegelin's *Order and History* (Baton Rouge, Louisiana: Louisiana State University, 1956). But in the jacket cover of the fourth volume, *The Ecumenic Age* (Baton Rouge, Louisiana: Louisiana State University Press, 1974), Voegelin is said to "break with the course originally charted." But it is important not to overestimate this "break." It is merely a strategic move that allows Voegelin to deal with history in a nonlinear fashion and to identify those who have the true consciousness of reality from those who do not. He maintains, as he did at the end of *Science, Politics and Gnosticism*, that Christianity does not have a monopoly on the true understanding of reality. Otherwise, Voegelin's intellectual position remains unchanged—what constitutes "spiritual clarity" and "spiritual deformity" remains the same.
6. Elaine Pagels, *The Gnostic Gospels* (New York: Random House, 1979); Elaine Pagels, *Adam, Eve, and the Serpent* (New York: Random House, 1988); Hans Jonas, *The Gnostic Religion: The Message of the Alien God and the Beginnings of Christianity* (Boston: Beacon Press, 1958).
7. See Augustine, *Two Books on Genesis Against the Manichees*, Ronald J. Teske, trans. (Washington D.C.: The Catholic University of America Press, 1991), p. 111. See also Elaine Pagels, *Adam, Eve, and the Serpent*, esp. ch. 3.
8. See Pagels, *The Gnostic Gospels*, and *Adam, Eve, and the Serpent*; see also Jonas, *The Gnostic Religion*.
9. Voegelin, *Science, Politics and Gnosticism*, p. 114. Voegelin makes it clear that this vision of God as inscrutable is a sign of "high spiritual clarity" even when it takes an Islamic rather than a Christian manifestation.
10. Voegelin, *New Science of Politics*, p. 57. See also *Science, Politics and Gnosticism*, pp. 102–04.
11. Voegelin, *Science, Politics and Gnosticism*, p. 109.

12. This incoherence may have its roots in Voegelin's effort to reconcile the pagan philosophy of Plato with the Christian philosophy of Augustine. But the Platonic vision of life as participation in the divine ground is difficult to reconcile with the radical transcendence of Voegelin's Augustinian heritage. But it is also the case, as I shall argue, that radical transcendence is a posture that is difficult to sustain.

13. Voegelin, *New Science of Politics*, p. 57. See also *Science, Politics and Gnosticism*, pp. 102–04.

14. Voegelin, *Science, Politics and Gnosticism*, p. 105.

15. Voegelin, *New Science of Politics*, p. 109.

16. Contemporary apologists such as Karen Armstrong blame "modernity" for the extremism of fundamentalism. See Karen Armstrong, *The Battle For God* (New York: Alfred A. Knopf, 2000). Armstrong denies that any of these religions are radical by nature; she claims that it is modernity that drives them mad and incites them to radicalism. She regards fundamentalism as a strictly modern phenomenon. I count her among the plethora of religious apologists of our time.

17. In support of this view, it is worth noting that the rise of the postmodern version of moral skepticism has given political realism a fashionable new lease on life. See James Keeley, "Toward a Foucauldian Analysis of International Regimes," *International Organization*, Vol. 44, No. 1 (Winter, 1990), pp. 83–105.

18. It must be noted that a pessimistic assessment of human nature is the foundation of political realism. For example, Machiavelli thought that human beings were too selfish to be good citizens. Unless they are united by a common enemy and their self-preservation is threatened, people are not likely to be willing to sacrifice their own interests for those of the state. So, if you want political health, you need a formidable enemy, and if you don't have one, then you had better invent one. Freud thought that war is necessary to give the aggressive instincts a legitimate outlet, without which human beings would be neurotic and self-destructive. Hobbes thought that the human striving for power after power ending only in death can be kept in check only by an overarching force great enough to keep all others in check. Whatever their differences, political realists consider terror, not justice, to be the foundation of political order.

19. Augustine, *City of God*, Bk. IV, ch. 4.

20. For peculiar reasons of his own, Kojève could not celebrate this state of affairs. See Shadia Drury, *Alexandre Kojève: The Roots of Postmodern Politics* (New York: St. Martin's Press, 1994).

21. Fukuyama's book was understood as a celebration of the triumph of American democracy and capitalism—its ambivalence was totally missed. See Drury, *Alexandre Kojève*, ch. 12.

22. Augustine, *Confessions*, Vernon J. Bourke, trans. (Washington: Catholic University of America Press, 1953), Bk. IX, Sec. 9.

23. See Eric Voegelin's review of Leo Strauss, *On Tyranny* in the *Review of Politics*, Vol. 11, No. 2 (1949), pp. 241–44. In response to Voegelin, Leo Strauss rightly observed that the doctrine of Caesarism is merely a justification

of tyranny. But having justified the tyranny of the wise, Strauss is not in a particularly strong position to censure others for justifying tyranny. See Shadia Drury, *The Political Ideas of Leo Strauss* (New York: St. Martin's Press, 1988), ch. 5, and Drury, *Alexandre Kojève*, ch. 10.

24. Joseph DeMaistre, "The Pope," in *The Works of Joseph DeMaistre*, ed. and trans. Jack Lively, with a Forward by Robert Nisbet (New York: Schocken Books, 1971), pp. 141, 144–45.

25. Joseph DeMaistre, *The Saint Petersburg Dialogues*, 9th Dialogue, in *The Works of Joseph DeMaistre*, p. 270.

26. Maistre, "The Pope," p. 249.

27. Maistre was puzzled by the high esteem in which the soldier is held in comparison to the horror that surrounds the executioner. The latter is the pillar of the social order; he brings death only to convicted criminals; he acts rarely; and he acts with restraint and skill. Nor is there need for more than one executioner in every province. In contrast, we can never have enough soldiers, and they continually slaughter thousands of innocent men without a modicum of restraint. Yet we heap honor and respect on the soldier, but regard the executioner with dread and loathing. Maistre surmised that there can be only one explanation—the need for expiation through the suffering of the innocent.

28. Maistre, *The Saint Petersburg Dialogues*, 9th Dialogue, p. 270.

29. Ibid., 7th Dialogue, p. 253.

30. Joseph DeMaistre, *Enlightenment on Sacrifices*, in *The Works of Joseph DeMaistre*, p. 291, italics in original.

31. Albert Camus, *The Rebel*, Anthony Bower, trans. (New York: Vintage Books, 1956). This was the basis of Camus's critique of Nietzsche. The latter worshiped the absurd; he made it the standard of human conduct. But as I have argued, Christianity made the same mistake. It turned the harsh doctrines of Jesus into a full-fledged metaphysics of terror, and then it made the latter the standard of human life and conduct. The result is not the raising of moral standards as Jesus hoped, but the very reverse.

32. Augustine, *City of God*, Bk. XII, ch. 6. John Calvin echoes Augustine in *Institutes of the Christian Religion*, 2 vols., John Allen, trans. (Philadelphia: Presbyterian Board of Christian Education, 1936), Bk. II, ch. 4.

33. Augustine, *City of God*, Bk. XIV, ch. 1. See also Augustine, *The Enchiridion on Faith, Hope, and Love*, edited with and Introduction by Henry Paolucci (Chicago: Regnery Gateway, 1961), ch. XXX, p. 37.

34. Martin Luther, "Bondage of the Will," in John Dillenberger, ed., *Martin Luther: Selections from His Writings* (New York: Doubleday & Co., Inc., 1961).

35. John Calvin, *Institutes of the Christian Religion*, Bk. II, chs. 1–5.

36. Pelagius was a British monk who argued against the Augustinian doctrine of bondage of the will, original sin, and native depravity. He traveled through Rome, North Africa, Palestine, and Asia Minor. With the help of his Irish associate Coelestius, Pelagius was very influential until he and his associates were condemned by an imperial edict and by the pope—largely thanks to the tireless efforts of Augustine and the Council of Carthage. See Augustine's response to the Pelagians in his, *Against Julian*, Mathew A.

Schumacher, trans. (New York: Fathers of the Church, Inc., 1957). See also J. Pohle, "Pelagius and Pelagianism," *Catholic Encyclopedia* (New York: Encyclopedia Press, 1913), Vol. 11, pp. 607–08.

37. Augustine, *The Enchiridion*, ch. LXV, p. 77.

38. C. S. Lewis, *Mere Christianity* (New York: Macmillan Publishing Co., 1943), pp. 38–39, 59.

39. See my discussion of "Sin as Unbelief," Part I, section 3.

40. Saint Augustine, *On Christian Doctrine*, D. W. Robertson, Jr., trans. (New York: Library of the Liberal Arts, Macmillan Publishing Company, 1958), Prologue, p. 4.

41. Augustine mentions hearing that a pagan rebuttal of his views has been written, but the authors are unable to publish it without danger to themselves. And Augustine warns them not to publish it if they know what is good for them. *City of God*, Bk. V, ch. 26.

42. Augustine, *City of God*, Bk. VI, "Preface."

43. Martin Luther, "Bondage of the Will," pp. 178, 181.

44. See e.g. Sheldon Wolin, *Politics and Vision* (Boston: Little, Brown and Co., 1960); see also Larry Arnhart, *Political Questions* (New York: Macmillan Publishing Co., 1987).

45. It follows that successful revolutionaries are also from God. But this is a conclusion that Augustine was not willing to draw, but his Puritan followers did.

46. *The Political Writings of St. Augustine*, p. 164, and Matthew 22:21.

47. Ibid., p. 165.

48. Ibid., pp. 177, 166.

49. Ibid., p. 178.

50. Ibid., pp. 179–80.

51. Ibid. and Luke 3:14.

52. Ibid., p. 164.

53. Ibid., pp. 193 ff.

54. Augustine, *Against Julian*, Introduction.

55. Reported in Uta Ranke-Heinemann, *Eunuchs for Heaven: The Catholic Church and Sexuality*, 1988, John Brownjohn, trans. (London: André Deutsch Ltd., 1990), p. 63. As we have seen, the Church is capable of inventing doctrines to improve on the Scriptures, and avoid the embarrassment of publicly defending the theology of Jesus. The doctrine of purgatory is one example. But in the case of original sin, the Church stuck to the Gospels and denounced those who made efforts to improve them.

56. The "conversion" of Constantine is a matter of debate among historians. It is not clear if his conversion was due to faith or to political opportunism.

57. Edward Gibbon, *The Decline and Fall of The Roman Empire* (New York: Random House, Inc., 1932), ch. XXI, p. 671.

58. *Theodosian Code*, Clyde Pharr, trans. (Princeton, New Jersey: Princeton University Press, 1952), see "Novels of the Sainted Theodosius," Title 3.8.

59. Ibid., "Novels of the Sainted Theodosius," Title 3.3.

60. Ibid., Bk. IX, Title 7.5.

61. Ibid., "Sirmondian Constitution," Title 6.

62. Ibid.
63. Ibid., Bk. IX, Title 7.3; see also "Novels of the Sainted Majorian Augustus," Title 9. It is worth mentioning that Constantine's son Crispus and his wife Fausta were executed on charges of adultery.
64. Ibid., Bk. IX, Title 7.4.
65. Ibid., Bk. IX, Title 24.2.
66. Ibid., Bk. IX, Title 24.1.
67. Ibid., Bk. IX, Title 24.4.
68. Ibid., Bk. XVI, Title 5.15 ff.
69. Ibid., "Novels of the Sainted Theodosius," Titles, 3.1 and 3.4.
70. Augustine, *City of God*, Bk. V., ch. 26.
71. John Calvin, *Institutes*, Vol. II, ch. XX.
72. Reinhold Niebuhr, *Christianity and Power Politics* (New York: Charles Scribner's Sons, 1940), p. 51.
73. Ngũgĩ Wa Thiong' O, *The River Between* (Oxford: Heinemann Educational Publishers, 1965). The novel is much more complex, and I have not done justice to it.
74. See e.g., Norman Podhoretz, *The Prophets: Who they Were, What they Are* (New York: Simon & Schuster, 2002). Podhoretz rails against Reform Jews, liberals, and Christians who interpret the prophets as people concerned with oppression and social justice; instead, Podhoretz paints a picture of the Bible emphasizing Jewish exceptionalism, ritual sacrifices, gender inequality, and everything abhorrent to the liberal-minded.

Part III   Ethic of Love

1. See e.g., Edward Westermarck, *Christianity and Morals* (New York: Macmillan, 1939).
2. The world did not come to an end as Jesus led his listeners to believe—he said it would happen in their own lifetime (Luke 21:32). One would think that the failure of this prophecy would have seriously damaged his reputation, but it has not. Instead, Christianity has postponed the end indefinitely.
3. *Sacred Books of the East*, quoted in Westermarck, *Christianity and Morals*, p. 44.
4. Ibid., p. 44.
5. As it turned out, Socrates suffered no harm for his disobedience. Historians suggest that the reason was that Critias was one of his former students, and had a soft spot in his heart for his old teacher. This also raises the question: why did Socrates have pupils like Critias and Alcibiades? Was that an accident or did he corrupt them? In my view, Hegel has the best answers to these questions. See his *Lectures on the History of Philosophy*, 1840, 3 vols., E. S. Haldane, trans. (London: Routledge and Kegan Paul Ltd., 1892, 1955), Vol. 1.
6. See Garry Wills, *Papal Sin* (New York: Doubleday, 2000), p. 40.
7. Aquinas, *ST*, I–II, Q. 91 ("Of the Various Kinds of Law"), Art. 5. Aquinas rightly observes that the old law restrains the hand whereas the new law controls the mind.

8. Just how widespread the practice of polygamy was among the Jews in Jesus's time is a subject of some debate. See e.g., Michael Satlow, *Jewish Marriage in Antiquity* (Princeton: Princeton University Press, 2001).
9. Aristotle, *Nicomachean Ethics*, Bk. III, ch. 5.
10. For simple fornication (i.e., consensual sex between two unmarried adults), the penance recommended was one year on bread and water. See Geoffrey May, *Social Control of Sex Expression* (New York: William Morrow & Co., 1930).
11. I am indebted to Walter Kaufmann for this distinction. See his outstanding work, The *Faith of a Heretic* (New York: Doubleday & Co., 1961), p. 214. Kaufmann argues that the distinction between impulse and act is critical to morality. In its absence, morality becomes a matter of luck.
12. May, *Social Control of Sex Expression*.
13. Edmund Morgan, *The Puritan Family* (New York: Harper & Row, 1944), the quotation within the quotation was from Thomas Hooker, *The Christians Two Chiefe Lessons* (London, 1640), p. 213.
14. Quoted in William H. Lazareth, *Luther on the Christian Home: An Application of the Social Ethics of the Reformation* (Philadelphia: Muhlenberg Press, 1960), p. 207.
15. Helmut Gätje, *The Qur'an and Its Exegesis: Selected Texts with Classical and Modern Muslim Interpretations*, Alford T. Welch, trans. (Berkeley, Ca.: University of California Press, 1976), ch. xii, "Polygamy," a commentary on Sura 4:3 of the *Qur'an* by Muhammad Abduh, p. 249. See also Geraldine Brooks, *Nine Parts of Desire: The Hidden World of Islamic Women* (New York: Doubleday, 1994).
16. See Richard Robinson, *An Atheist's Values* (Oxford, England: Basil Blackwell, 1964); see also Westermarck, *Christianity and Morals* and Kaufmann, *The Faith of a Heretic*.
17. It is something of a mystery why those who refuse to do any harm will be persecuted. Will they be too good for a sinful world? Will they be hated because their pacifism threatens national security? Or will they be hated because their conception of loving their enemies is so perverse—like kidnapping Jewish children and bringing them up as Christians so that they will be saved?
18. Martin Luther, "A Treatise on Christian Liberty," in *Three Treatises* (Philadelphia, Pa.: Muhlenberg Press, 1943). See bibliography for more details.
19. Martin Luther, "Preface to the Complete Edition of Luther's Latin Writings," in John Dillenberger, ed., *Martin Luther: Selections from His Writings* (New York: Doubleday & Co., 1961).
20. Luther, "Preface to the Epistle of St. Paul to the Romans," in *Selections*, p. 20.
21. Ibid., p. 21.
22. Luther, "Bondage of the Will," in *Selections*. As we have seen, Jesus also distinguishes between the children of God and the children of the devil. See bibliography for more details.
23. Luther, "Preface to the Epistle of St. Paul to the Romans," in *Selections*, p. 21.
24. Uta Ranke-Heinemann, *Eunuchs for Heaven: The Catholic Church and Sexuality*, 1988, John Brownjohn, trans. (London: André Deutsch Ltd., 1990). See bibliography for more details.

25. Ranke-Heinemann claims that Jesus was just being ironic, that this passage should not be taken literally. I think she is quite right in saying that the passage need not be taken literally.
26. Augustine, *Desancta virginitate* (Holy Virginity), John McQuade, trans., in *Writings of St. Augustine*, Roy J. Deferrari, ed. (New York: Fathers of the Church, Inc., 1955), Vol. 15, ch. 23, p. 168.
27. Aquinas, *ST*, Pt. II-II, Q. 152, "Of Virginity," Art. 1.
28. Ibid., Pt. II-II, Q. 154, "Of the Parts of Lust," Art. 3.
29. Ibid., Pt. II-II, Q. 151, "Of Chastity," Art. 4.
30. Saint Gregory of Nyssa, "On Virginity," in *Ascetic Works*, Virginia Woods Callahan, trans. (Washington D.C.: The Catholic University of America Press, 1967), p. 47.
31. Ibid., p. 51.
32. Aquinas, *ST*, Pt. II-II, Q. 151, "Of Chastity", Art. 3.
33. Heinrich Krämer and Jacob Sprenger, *Malleus Maleficarum* (New York: Dover, 1971).
34. As reported by Luther and quoted in William Lazareth, *Luther on the Christian Home*, p. 9.
35. Ibid., p. 74.

PART IV Psychology of Terror

1. Sigmund Freud, *Five Lectures on Psycho-Analysis*, James Strachey, trans. (New York: W. W. Norton & Co., 1977), pp. 24–25.
2. Sigmund Freud, *Dora: An Analysis of a Case of Hysteria* (New York: Macmillan, 1963). The book reads like a detective novel. Freud was convinced that Dora's neurotic symptoms had their source in her refusal to admit the truth about her sexual attraction to her father's friend. His strategy was to get her to admit her guilt. Clearly, he was convinced that the confession of guilt was the key to her cure.
3. Sigmund Freud, *Moses and Monotheism*, Kathrine Jones, trans. (New York: Vintage Books, 1939), p. 174. See bibliography for more details.
4. Ibid., pp. 102–03.
5. Ibid., pp. 105–06.
6. Ibid., p. 152.
7. Ibid., p. 106. This is one of the reasons that anthropologists such as James Frazer believe that Christianity introduces pagan rituals into Judaism.
8. Sigmund Freud, *The Future of an Illusion*, 1927, James Strachey, trans. (New York: Anchor Books, 1964).
9. Freud, *Moses and Monotheism*, p. 129.
10. Ibid., p. 156.
11. Ibid., p. 173.
12. Ibid., p. 174.
13. Sometimes Freud refers to the killing of the primeval father as a myth that represents our own resentment and hostility toward our real father for enforcing the repressions and prohibitions of civilization, which frustrate

our instinctual gratifications. But in this work, he deals with the myth as a historical reality.

14. Sigmund Freud, *Interpretation of Dreams*, 1900, James Strachey, trans. (London: The Hogarth Press, 1953), p. 264, my italics.
15. Sigmund Freud, "Our Attitude Towards Death," in *Civilization, Society and Religion*, Penguin Freud Library, Vol. 12, Albert Dickson, ed. (London: Penguin Books, 1991), p. 86.
16. Carlo Collodi, *Pinocchio*, Joseph Walker, trans. (Santa Rosa, Ca.: 1968).
17. This was suggested in a cryptic footnote without explanation or elaboration by Nomi Maya Stolzenberg, "Jiminy Cricket: A Commentary on Professor Hill's Four Conceptions of Conscience," in Ian Shapiro and Robert Adams, eds., *Integrity and Conscience*, Nomos, XL (New York: New York University Press, 1998).
18. Freud, *Moses and Monotheism*, p. 173.
19. Freud, "The Disillusionment of the War" (1915) in *Civilization*, Albert Dickson, ed., p. 69. See bibliography for more details.
20. Friedrich Nietzsche, *The Genealogy of Morals*, 1887, Francis Golffing, trans. (New York: Doubleday Anchor Books, 1957), Essay II, Secs. xiv and xv. See bibliography for more details.
21. Sigmund Freud, *Civilization and Its Discontents*, James Strachey, trans. (New York: W. W. Norton & Co., 1961), pp. 70–71, my italics. How did it happen? Again the story is about dependence and fear. Just as primitive men felt a debt and a dependence on their ancestors, and just as they were afraid of the consequences of losing the goodwill of their ancestral spirits, so as children, we are dependent on the love of our parents and are afraid of the consequences of losing that love.
22. Ibid., p. 72.
23. It may be argued that Freud is simply dealing with conscience as shaped by a Christian civilization. There is some truth to this. But as I will show, Freud also thinks that this understanding of conscience is universally applicable; he thinks that Christianity is a profound repository of psychic truth.
24. Sigmund Freud, "The Moses of Michelangelo," in *Collected Papers*, Vol. IV, Joan Rivière, trans. (London: Hogarth Press, 1925). See bibliography for more details.
25. Exodus xxxii:19. In Exodus xxxiv:29, we are told that after the forty days and nights that Moses spent on the mountain with God, writing the tables of the covenant, the divine luster was reflected in his face. The beams of light that emanated from Moses's face were translated as horns of light in the Latin translation of the Bible. This is the simple reason that medieval artists and Michelangelo portray Moses with horns. See *The Pentateuch and Haftorahs*, Hebrew Text, English translation and commentary, J. H. Hertz, ed. (London: Soncino Press, 1964), p. 368. I am indebted to my colleague, Eldon Soifer of the University of Regina, for this reference.
26. Only if the betrothed damsel is lying with a man in the city, and does not cry out for help, does she merit stoning. But if the betrothed damsel is forced to lie with a man in the field, and does not cry out, then she is innocent, because crying out would have been useless; and only the man is put to death.

27. When Judah was told that his daughter-in-law Tamar had played the harlot (after the death of her husband), he said, "Bring her forth and let her be burnt" (Genesis 38:24). But it was casually reported that on his way to Timnath, Judah made use of a prostitute (Genesis 38:15).
28. It is unfortunate that this Victorian morality has been granted scientific legitimacy not only by psychoanalysis, but also by the new Darwinism. See Robert Wright, *The Moral Animal* (New York: Random House, 1994).
29. See Freud, "The Taboo on Virginity," discussed in the bibliography.
30. The only contentious aspect of the biblical formulation is the reference to one's neighbor. Does that include all humanity or only one's fellow citizens?
31. Sigmund Freud, *Totem and Taboo*, A. A. Brill, trans. (New York: Random House, 1918). See bibliography for more details. In his account of exogamy, Claude Lévi-Strauss makes the same assumptions as Freud about the innateness of incestuous desire and the necessity of repressing it. In *The Elementary Structures of Kinship*, Lévi-Strauss suggests that exogamy is a momentous achievement that is the key to the transition from nature to culture. Following Freud, he rejects the thesis that the prohibition indicates a natural or instinctive repugnance: if there is such a natural repugnance, why bother with the prohibition? Instead, Lévi-Strauss proposed his famous theory of "the gift." He surmised that exogamy requires a renunciation of a coveted object, and that marriage is part of an economic system of exchange intended to contribute to the circuit of generosity in the community. The prohibition of incest is the foundation of social life because the latter is premised on an outer movement rather than a withdrawal into the self. This is a key to uncovering the structure that is hidden at the heart of all civilized life— namely the renunciation of instinct. In his critique of Lévi-Strauss, Georges Bataille does not question this fundamental assumption. Bataille agrees with Lévi-Strauss that far from reflecting a natural repugnance, the prohibition of incest indicates an unnatural renunciation that is demanded by culture. Bataille thinks that the man who marries his own daughter is comparable to the man who drinks up his entire stock of champagne by himself without inviting friends to drink with him. The analogy sounds bizarre, because girls are not like champagne. The man who invites friends over to drink also drinks himself, and this is hardly comparable to the plight of the father who offers his daughter's hand in marriage. The father does not enjoy his daughter sexually before marrying her off to another. But there is a sense in which women are like champagne in the primitive societies described by Lévi-Strauss and Bataille—they are coveted objects that are "pledged to communication." By giving away your champagne, you are likely to get more. By giving away your daughter, you are likely to get a wife for your son.
32. Freud, *Totem and Taboo*, p. 41.
33. Ibid., p. 43.
34. See Randall Baldwin Clark, "Platonic Love in a Colorado Courtroom: Martha Nussbaum, John Finnis, and Plato's *Laws* in Evans v. Romer," in *Yale Journal of Law and Humanities*, Vol. 12, No. 1 (Winter 2000), pp. 1–38.
35. Edward Westermarck, *The Origin and Development of Moral Ideas*, Vol. II (London: Macmillan and Co., 1917), ch. XL, "Marriage." See also more

recent anthropological support for Westermarck's thesis in Arthur P. Wolf, *Sexual Attraction and Childhood Association: A Chinese Brief for Edward Westermarck* (Stanford, Ca.: Stanford University Press, 1995). See Freud's refutation of Westermarck in *Totem and Taboo*, pp. 158 ff.

36. Wolf, *Sexual Attraction and Childhood Association*.
37. Havelock Ellis, *Studies in the Psychology of Sex*, 2 vols. (New York: Random House, 1906). See Freud's discussion of Ellis in *Totem and Taboo*, p. 159.
38. Michel Foucault, *Power/Knowledge*, ch. 6, "Truth and Power," p. 119.
39. Ibid., ch. 3, "Body/Power," p. 58.
40. Ibid., p. 56.
41. Freud, "Our Attitude Towards Death," in *Civilization*, Albert Dickson, ed., p. 80.
42. Ibid., p. 81.
43. Ibid., p. 81.
44. Ibid., p. 84.
45. Nietzsche complains that the Bible confers no dignity on crime, and contains no idea of "active sin." He contrasts the biblical myth of the Fall with the Promethean myth and finds the former wanting because it makes the act of hubris feminine in an effort to undermine it. Nietzsche is partially right, but the biblical myth does not succeed. See Friedrich Nietzsche, *The Birth of Tragedy*, Francis Golfing, trans. (New York: Doubleday Anchor Books, 1956), p. 64.
46. Karen Armstrong, *In the Beginning: A New Interpretation of Genesis* (New York: Ballantine Books, 1996).
47. Elaine Pagels, *Adam, Eve, and the Serpent* (New York: Random House, 1988).
48. For the most profound reflections on Job, see C. G. Jung, *Answer to Job*, R. F. C. Hull, trans. (Princeton, N.J.: Princeton University Press, 1958). See also Kaufmann, *The Faith of a Heretic*.
49. See my discussion in Part I, Sec. 3, "Sin as Unbelief."
50. Nietzsche, *Genealogy of Morals*, Essay II, Sec. vi, p. 197. In his account of the origin of punishment, we get a glimpse of his conception of human nature. Nietzsche suggests that punishment was originally compensation for harm done. But how can inflicting pain constitute a repayment of a debt or compensation for harm suffered? Nietzsche's answer is that beholding suffering gives pleasure and causing suffering gives even greater pleasure. So, the debt is repaid in the form of the extraordinary pleasures of cruelty. See bibliography for more details.
51. For the best argument to that effect, see Philippa Foot, "Nietzsche's Immoralism," in Richard Schacht, ed., *Nietzsche, Genealogy, Morality: Essays on Nietzsche's Genealogy of Morals* (Los Angeles, Ca.: University of California Press, 1994).
52. Nietzsche, *Genealogy of Morals*, Essay I, Sec. xi, p. 176.
53. Ibid., Essay II, Sec. xvi, p. 218.
54. Ibid., Essay II, Sec. xxiii, p. 228.
55. Friedrich Nietzsche, *Joyful Wisdom*, Thomas Common, trans. (New York: Unger Publishing Co., 1960), Aphorism # 338.

56. Jean-Paul Sartre, *Saint Genet* (Paris: Gallimard, 1952).

57. For more detailed discussions of these works, see Shadia B. Drury, *Alexandre Kojève: The Roots of Postmodern Politics* (New York: St. Martin's Press, 1994).

58. Ibid., chs. 8 and 9.

59. Einstein and Freud, "Why War?" in *Civilization*, Albert Dickson, ed., p. 361.

60. Ibid., p. 358. Supposedly, when the aggressive instincts are directed to the external world, the "organism is relieved and the effect must be beneficial."

61. Freud, *Civilization and Its Discontents*.

62. Freud, "The Disillusionment of the War," in *Civilization*, Albert Dickson (ed.), p. 361.

63. Einstein and Freud, "Why War?" See bibliography for more details.

64. Ibid., p. 361.

65. Freud, *Moses and Monotheism*, p. 140.

66. Freud, *Totem and Taboo*, p. 47. Freud explains that when a taboo is violated, the violation can be expiated through penance, which is to say, the renunciation of a possession or a liberty. He thinks that this is "the proof" that a taboo is a renunciation of what is wished for.

67. Georges Bataille, *Histoire de l'oeil*, 1928, translated as *The Story of the Eye*, by Joachim Neugroschel (San Francisco: City Lights Books, 1987).

68. Michel Foucault, "A Preface to Transgression," in Foucault, *Language, Countermemory, Practice* (Ithaca, N.Y.: Cornell University Press, 1977), pp. 29–52. This is a translation of Foucault's "Hommage à Georges Bataille," which originally appeared in *Critique*, Nos. 195–96 (1963), pp. 751–70. In this tribute to Bataille, Foucault finds no need to distinguish between writing in his own name, and giving an account of Bataille's thought.

69. Michel Foucault, *Hurculine Barbin: Being the Recently Discovered Memoirs of a Nineteenth-Century Hermaphrodite*, Richard McDougal, trans. (New York: Pantheon, 1980).

70. See James Miller, *The Passion of Michel Foucault* (New York: Simon and Schuster, 1993).

Part V   Terror, Ideals, and Civilization

1. Reinhold Niebuhr, *Christianity and Power Politics* (New York: Archon Books, 1940).

2. Plato, *Timaeus*.

3. The Catholic Church has been instrumental in concealing the dark aspects of the religion of Jesus. It has replaced the inscrutable God of Christianity with a more palatable and more rational deity. It has presented the world with a God that human beings can understand—a God who is concerned about conduct—a God who demands goodness and righteousness and prohibits wickedness—a God who is willing to back His commands with eternal rewards and punishments. Protestant critics from Luther to Hegel have denounced the Church for judaizing Christianity, which is to say, making it into a prudential ethic. By the same token, it must be admitted

that judaizing Christianity has had the effect of making it more palatable and enduring, though not necessarily more humane.

4. Mathew Arnold, "Hellenism and Hebraism," in *Culture and Anarchy*, J. Dover Wilson, ed. (Cambridge, England: University of Cambridge Press, 1957). See bibliography for details.

5. See Jaroslav Pelikan, *Mary Through the Centuries: Her Place in the History of Culture* (New Haven: Yale University Press, 1996).

6. See the debate over this in John Stuart Mill, *Utilitarianism, with Critical Essays*, Samuel Gorovitz, ed. (New York: The Bobbs-Merrill Co., Inc., 1971).

7. John Rawls, *A Theory of Justice* (Cambridge, Mass.: Harvard University Press, 1971), Secs. 5, 6, and 84.

8. John Rawls, "Two Concepts of Rules," in *The Philosophical Review*, Vol. 64 (January, 1955), pp. 3–32.

9. J. J. C. Smart and Bernard Williams, *Utilitarianism For and Against* (London: Cambridge University Press, 1973). This is an excellent example of the debate.

10. Hannah Arendt, *Eichmann in Jerusalem: A Report on the Banality of Evil* (New York: Viking Press, 1963). Arendt's picture of Eichmann is meant to refute the infallibility of conscience, and highlight the banality of evil. In recognizing the connection of evil with stupidity, Arendt sides with the Greeks (with Plato and Aristotle as well as Aquinas in so far as he was an admirer of Aristotle). But it is important to point out that this view of evil as banality is decidedly un-Christian because Christianity insists on the human love of evil as the conscious, knowing, and willful defiance of God.

11. Mark Twain, *Adventures of Huckleberry Finn*, 1884 (New York: Random House, 1996).

12. For a different interpretation of Huck's predicament, see Jonathan Bennett, "The Conscience of Huckleberry Finn," *Philosophy*, Vol. 49 (April, 1974), rep. John Arthur, ed., *Morality and Moral Controversies* (New Jersey: Prentice Hall, 1981, 1996), pp. 13–20.

13. See David Hume, *A Treatise of Human Nature*, 2nd ed. (Oxford: Oxford University Press, 1978); Adam Smith, *The Theory of Moral Sentiments* (Oxford: Oxford University Press, 1976). For modern examples of this view, see Annette Baier, *A Progress of Sentiments* (Cambridge, Mass.: Harvard University Press, 1991); and Lawrence A. Blum, *Moral Perception and Particularity* (Cambridge: Cambridge University Press, 1994). Jean Jacques Rousseau also appeals to sentiment. But his view is ambiguous. See Margaret Ogrodnick, *Instinct and Intimacy: Political Philosophy and Autobiography in Rousseau* (Toronto: University of Toronto Press, 1999), esp. "Conscience and Instinct," pp. 151–61. Ogrodnick finds evidence that Rousseau thinks that natural human empathy is destroyed by civilized society. She also thinks that for Rousseau conscience is the product of society. But instead of harnessing natural human empathy, it destroys it. Conscience makes people feel guilty, and this in turn leads them to rationalize and justify their conduct in a desperate effort to find inner peace. Ogrodnick

shows how Rousseau silenced his own conscience by providing a rational justification for abandoning his children to the orphanage.

14. Bennett thinks it was a triumph of conscience—the conscience created by a "bad morality," "The Conscience of Huckleberry Finn."

15. Thomas E. Hill Jr., "Four Conceptions of Conscience," in Ian Shapiro and Robert Adams, eds., *Integrity and Conscience, Nomos*, XL (New York: New York University Press, 1998). See also essays by Nomi Maya Stolzenberg, Elizabeth Kiss, and George Kateb, in the same volume.

16. For an account of relativist theories, see William Frankena, *Ethics* (Englewood Cliffs, N.J.: Prentice-Hall, 1973).

17. Aquinas, *ST*, Pt. II-II, Q. 91, Art. 2. This is not to say that society cannot act on conscience, Aquinas recognized that conscience can be silenced or perverted by a bad society. Aquinas defines sin as acting contrary to the dictates of conscience. If conscience is right, then acting contrary to conscience is both sin and wrongdoing. But if your conscience is in error, then in acting contrary to your conscience you sin while doing the right thing. That is the way that Huck's actions can be understood within this tradition. Huck sinned, but he did the right thing. But if you act according to an erroneous conscience, then you will do wrong, but you will not sin or incur any blame.

18. Joseph Butler, *Five Sermons* (Indianapolis, Ind.: Hackett Publishing Co., 1983).

19. Some philosophers and historians regard Western civilization as containing a homogeneous set of values that have their origins in ancient Greece and were further enriched and developed by Christianity. See e.g., Alaisdair MacIntyre, *Whose Justice? Which Rationality?* (Notre Dame, Ind.: University of Notre Dame Press, 1988).

20. Martin Luther, "The Freedom of a Christian," 1520, in *Martin Luther: Selections From His Writings*, John Dillenberg, ed. (New York: Doubleday Anchor Book, 1961), p. 46.

21. John Stuart Mill, *Considerations on Representative Government, 1861*, ch. III, in *Collected Works of John Stuart Mill* (Toronto: University of Toronto Press, 1963), Vol. xix, pp. 406 ff.

22. Samuel Huntington, *The Clash of Civilizations and the Remaking of World Order* (New York: Simon & Schuster, 1996).

23. For a more complete analysis and criticism of neoconservatism, see Shadia B. Drury, *Leo Strauss and the American Right* (New York: St. Martin's Press, 1997).

24. It is important to recognize that Samuel Huntington is one of the leading neoconservative intellectuals. And from the neoconservative point of view, declaring that America still has formidable enemies is good news. This is especially the case after the dark tidings of Francis Fukuyama in his *The End of History and the Last Man* (New York: Free Press, 1992). Fukuyama declared that America has won the Cold War and has defeated all her enemies. The book was received as a manifestation of American triumphalism. But nothing could be further from the truth. Fukuyama was a student of Huntington and had imbibed neoconservative values. He could not

reasonably gloat in the absence of enemies. A civilization that has defeated all its enemies can look forward only to cultural decay and decline. The title of Fukuyama's book alone indicates this. The concept of the "last man" is borrowed from Nietzsche's prognostications of the decay of Western civilization.

25. John Calvin, *Institutes of the Christian Religion*, Vol. II, ch. XX, Sec. xxx.

26. See my discussion in Part I, "How Glad are the Glad Tidings?"

27. See Edmund Morgan, *The Puritan Family* (New York: Harper and Row, 1944).

28. Maurice Yacowar, *The Bold Testament* (Calgary, Alberta: Bayeux Arts Incorporated, 1999). See bibliography for more details.

29. Michel Foucault, *Power/Knowledge: Selected Interviews and Other Writings 1972–1977*, Colin Gordon, trans. (New York: Pantheon Books, 1980).

30. Like Maurice Yacowar, Rick Salutin of *The Globe and Mail* has recognized the importance of self-criticism; with brilliance and courage, he has provided an unflagging critique of the United States and Israel. It is to the credit of both these men that they are Jewish.

31. For the best and most penetrating critique of global capitalism, see Linda Mcquaig, *All You Can Eat: Greed, Lust and the New Capitalism* (Toronto, Ontario: Penguin Books, 2001).

32. Ernest Gellner, *Muslim Society* (New York: Cambridge University Press, 1981). Gellner argues that Islam is more suited to the modern world because it is more democratic and more egalitarian than Christianity. Any man who is willing to apply himself and study the Koran can become one of the *ulamas* or scholars who interpret the Koran. But it must also be admitted that the situation can be anarchic—with one scholar claiming that certain tactics and practices are permissible and another denying that they are. Moreover, the fact that there is no clerical hierarchy means that there is nothing to rebel against, and the prospect of a revolutionary transformation of the faith by a rebel reformer such as Martin Luther, is highly unlikely.

ANNOTATED BIBLIOGRAPHY

Anselm, Archbishop of Canterbury (1033–1109). *Why God Became Man.* Edward S. Prout, trans. London: Religious Tract Society, 1887.
Saint Thomas Aquinas's view of the atonement follows that of Saint Anselm. See my discussion of this Latin theory in Part I, "Ransom for Sin." For Anselm man cannot be saved without God's "satisfaction" when it comes to paying for our sins. However, "satisfaction" that is proportional to sin is beyond human power. Therefore, Jesus offers to pay the price on our behalf. The ransom for sin is due to God (not the devil), and is required by His justice. Nothing is due to the devil but punishment. God gave his Son to pay the price for sin. This was an example to inspire human beings never to abandon justice despite the hardships entailed. But this argument is not convincing. A sentence that is impossible for the convicted to satisfy, even by death and eternal torment, is a poor model of justice.

Aquinas, Saint Thomas. *Summa Theologica.* Fathers of the English Dominican Province, trans. Westminster, Maryland: Christian Classics, 1911.
I rely on Aquinas throughout. See especially my discussion of his justification of the Inquisition in Part I, "Sin as Unbelief," his view of heaven, in Part I, "Is Heaven for Sadists?" and his understanding of the Passion of Christ in Part I, "Ransom for sin."

Armstrong, Karen. *In the Beginning: A New Interpretation of Genesis.* New York: Ballantine Books, 1996.
This is a brilliant and insightful work. Her interpretation of the Bible challenges orthodox views in significant ways. For example, she challenges the Christian orthodoxy that God is omnipotent and all-knowing. Instead, she reveals Him to be rather baffled by His own creation. As Armstrong rightly points out, a God who parades all the animals before Adam so that he can choose a companion does not understand his own creature. And how can he create creatures in his own image without anticipating that they will desire knowledge? She suggests that the story is about a creator whose creation proves too much for Him, and spins out of control. Armstrong challenges the view that history is the providence of God. Armstrong denies that the God of Genesis is benevolent—he is as much a destroyer as a creator; He is vengeful and cruel as well as benevolent. His cruelty and callousness is revealed in the story of the flood. In Armstrong's eyes, Noah does not appear to be all that righteous. He is passive, asks no questions, and does not plead with God, or rebuke Him for killing the innocent along with the guilty. In the end, Armstrong sees Noah as the victim of God's holocaust; he is damaged by his

184 / ANNOTATED BIBLIOGRAPHY

experience—the devastation and the bloated dead bodies everywhere are too much for him, and he purposely induces a drunken stupor to survive it—and this is when his youngest son finds him naked in his tent. On another matter, Armstrong regrets that the Israelites did not bless their daughters. But it seems to me that these blessings that went from father to favored son were often more of a curse. And it must be noted that some who were refused blessings were successful nevertheless.

Arnold, Mathew. "Hellenism and Hebraism." In *Culture and Anarchy*, J. Dover Wilson, ed. Cambridge, England: University of Cambridge Press, 1957.

Arnold argues that Hellenism emerged before its time. It can only come to its own after the perfection of the soul that Hebraism accomplishes. His efforts at reconciling the two ideals are not very successful.

Augustine of Hippo. *The City of God*. Henry Bettenson, trans. London: Penguin Books, 1972.

I regard Augustine as the most influential of all Church fathers, much to the detriment of Christianity. See especially my discussion of his views on heaven in Part I "Is Heaven for Sadists?" and his political views in Part II, "Treachery with a Clear Conscience," "Christian Arrogance," and "Christian Militancy."

Aulén, Gustaf. *Christus Victor: An Historical Study of the Three Main Types of the Idea of the Atonement*. A. G. Herbert, trans. New York: Macmillan Co., 1969.

Aulén distinguishes between the juridical Latin view of the Atonement and the Patristic view. He regards Anselm as a model of the Latin view. The latter is narrow and juridical. According to Aulén, the Patristic view is superior and much more dramatic than the Latin view, because it understands the Atonement as the victory of Christ over the forces of evil. Aulén argues staunchly that this view need not be dualistic because God does everything, including letting the evil powers have dominion. The change that takes place as a result is not a subjective change in man, but a change in the whole relation of God to His creation. This understanding of the Atonement was eclipsed by the narrow juridical approach of medieval scholastics, but was supposedly revived by Luther, who is totally misunderstood by Protestant theologians. The thesis is grand, but the attempt to attribute the sunny doctrines of Irenaeus to Luther are not convincing. I agree with Aulén that the interpretation of the Greek fathers is superior to the narrow juridical interpretation of the medieval Church for reasons that I give in my discussion of Aquinas's view in Part I, "Ransom for Sin." I also agree that Luther is more Catholic than the pope, and that his views have their source in the New Testament. But the latter is not as cheery as Irenaeus and other Greek fathers make it out to be. Aulén has some good insights, but he misrepresents Luther by ignoring the dark side of his Christianity. See my discussion of Luther in Part III, "Inner State of Siege."

Bailie, Gil. *Violence and the Sacred: Humanity at the Crossroads*. New York: Crossroad Publishing Co., 1995.

This is an engaging work of anthropology that relies heavily on the work of René Girard, *Things Hidden Since the Foundation of the World*. The fundamental idea of Girard and Bailie is that human culture has its source in scapegoating. The latter is represented as sacred violence and distinguished from profane violence. Sacred violence serves to keep ordinary or profane violence at bay.

Bailie and Girard believe that we live in a world in which the distinction between sacred and profane violence is collapsing, and this threatens the foundation of culture. They also think that Christianity is at the heart of this collapse because it opens our eyes to the whole phenomenon of scapegoating violence. Christianity supposedly reveals what has been hidden since the beginning of time—namely, the violent basis of civilized life. Girard and Bailie are critical of anthropologists such as Joseph Campbell and James Fraser who are struck by the similarity of Christianity to primitive religions—especially its similarity to the Dionysus–Orpheus–Bacchus myth of the dead and resurrected god (p. 128). Bailie argues that these similarities are superficial in comparison to the differences. According to Bailie, the Christian story is told from the point of view of the victim, and reveals the innocence of the victim, and the iniquity of scapegoating violence. Bailie thinks that the crisis of our time lies in the waning power of collective violence to generate social solidarity. The whole thesis is premised on the assumption that prior to Christianity no one had the ability to see the shortcomings of their own group think. The thesis is presented in a gripping style, but upon the slightest reflection, the thesis sounds silly, in view of the fact that Christianity has augmented sacred violence to global proportions.

Budziszewski, J. *The Revenge of Conscience: Politics and the Fall of Man.* Dallas: Spece Publishing, 1999.

This staunchly conservative Christian suggests that the torments of conscience are the revenge of God for the Fall. Having expelled Adam and Eve from the Garden for disobeying his commands, God implants His law into their hearts so that they will be forever tormented by inner conflict and at odds with themselves. Budziszewski resorts to the usual Christian tactics of argumentation; ideas are not refuted; instead, they are rejected as symptoms of vice. For example, nihilism is the result of pride—those who reject God just want to be God. And anyone who considers objecting to the dogmas espoused in this book, is accused in advance of being "in denial," which is to say, they know the truth, but refuse to acknowledge it. These are the sorts of tactics we have seen used by Augustine, Luther, and Voegelin. See Part II, "Christian Arrogance."

Bunyan, John. *Grace Abounding to the Chief of Sinners* (1666). London: Penguin Books, 1987.

I have gained more insight into Christianity from this book than from any other, except the Gospels. See my discussions in Part I, "Sin as Unbelief" and "Hell and Damnation."

Bunyan, John. *The Pilgrim's Progress* (1678). London: Penguin Books, 1965.

See my discussions in Part I, "The Angst of Salvation" and Part III, "Inner State of Siege."

Charles, R. H. *A Critical History of the Doctrine of a Future Life.* London: Adam and Charles Black, 1899.

It is remarkable how many Christian scholars find Jesus to be something of an embarrassment. They associate Christianity with the teaching of Saint Paul and the Church, but are reluctant to abandon Jesus altogether. As a result, they occupy themselves with endless scholastic acrobatics intended to show either that Jesus did not mean what he said or that much of what he said is not really an essential or "organic" component of the faith, but merely "primitive" or "Judaic" vestiges that have not been fully transcended despite the advent of the more "progressive" religion. In this book I have given plenty of reasons why Christianity might be considered a regress in comparison to Judaism. But according to these Christian scholars, the archaic elements that Jesus inherited from Judaism exist side by side with the new Christian ideas that he inaugurated. This tactic allows them to pick and choose whatever they like from what Jesus says, while dismissing what they dislike as mere vestiges of Judaism. For example, Charles thinks that a genuinely Christian understanding of heaven and hell is totally spiritual, and any suggestions by Jesus that the body plays a role in the experience of heaven and hell are merely relics of Judaism. When Jesus talks about eating and drinking in heaven, Charles insists that this must be understood figuratively. But he rightly points out that there will be no sexual relations in heaven—not even figuratively. Jesus says that in heaven men and women will have bodies like angels (Matthew 22:28). He does not say that men and women will have no bodies because heaven is a purely spiritual experience. But what Jesus says is irrelevant for Christian scholars such as Charles; they seem to know already what is and what is not genuinely Christian, and are not inclined to pay any attention to what Jesus says as authoritative or definitive. Following a long and venerable Christian tradition that includes Jesus, Augustine, and Aquinas, I have argued that a transfigured body plays a significant role in the experience of the torments of hell.

Elias, Norbert. *The Civilizing Process: The History of Manners* (1939). Edmund Jephcott, trans. Oxford: Basil Blackwell, 1978.

The book is dedicated to the memory of his parents who died in Breslau and Auschwitz. In this work, which is a fascinating history of manners, Elias argues that the civilizing process is a gradual advance of the threshold of shame regarding bodily functions, instinctual gratifications, libidinal drives and pleasures, and even the body itself. The process is not linear, but is characterized by advances and setbacks. But on the whole, the process has advanced the threshold of shame to the point where it has become almost "natural." And while the author denies that there ever were human beings who had no restraints of instinctual gratification, he thinks that the process reached its zenith in the nineteenth century. In the twentieth century, there has been a certain relaxation, but only in speech. The book focuses mainly on table manners, bedroom manners, bodily functions, and sexual relations. Although Freud is not mentioned, the argument is based on the Freudian assumption that civilization is at war with the instincts.

Empson, William. *Milton's God*. London: Chatto & Windus, 1961.

This book is much more than a commentary on Milton's *Paradise Lost*. It contains deep insights into the dark side of Christianity. This is particularly true of the doctrine of the Atonement as understood by Augustine, Aquinas, Anselm, and others. See my discussion in Part I, "Ransom for Sin."

Frazer, James George. *The Golden Bough* (1890). New York: Oxford University Press, 1994.

This famous and fascinating study of religion and magic has a tendency to deflate civilization in general and Christian civilization in particular. In discussing the rituals, beliefs, and barbarous practices of primitive people,

Frazer intends to show us the similarity between the beliefs and practices of savages and those of supposedly civilized people. Christian beliefs in particular have their origin in older religions and superstitions—e.g. the virgin birth, the killing and resurrection of the man-god, the transfer of sin, the representation of god as a convicted criminal, etc. In short, Christianity is the heir of barbarous superstitions that have not been swept away by science. But Frazer is not necessarily a champion of science as is often believed.

Freud, Sigmund. "The Disillusionment of the War" (1915). In Sigmund Freud, *Civilization, Society, and Religion*. Penguin Freud Library, Vol. 12, Albert Dickson, ed. London: Penguin Books, 1991.

Freud argues that the disillusionment that was so widely expressed upon the outbreak of World War I had its source in a mistaken idea about human nature. Freud shares the Christian view of human nature as thoroughly depraved. Morality is contrary to nature. Civilization cannot hope to transform man; it can only repress his brutish nature. See discussion of Freud in Part IV. My thesis is that Freud succeeds as well as he does because the culture is already predisposed to his ideas, which are thoroughly Christian, with a thin veneer of science.

Freud, Sigmund. "Our Attitude Toward Death." *Civilization, Society, and Religion*. Penguin Freud Library, Vol. 12, Albert Dickson, ed. London: Penguin Books, 1991.

Freud argues that primeval man survives in our unconscious, and is never annihilated by cultural advancement (p. 80). Primeval man took death seriously, and acknowledged it as annihilation. But he refused to believe in his own death. However, the death of a loved one made him taste death. But not willing to accept it, he invented spirits to deny the significance of his own death. From this came the belief in the after-life and in reincarnation. But primeval man had no scruples about killing—he was a remorseless killer and killed as a matter of course. This killer still survives in the unconscious of civilized man: "judged by our unconscious wishful impulses, we ourselves are, like primeval man, a gang of murderers" (p. 87). See my discussion in Part IV, "Guilt, Original Sin, and Expiation."

Freud, Sigmund. *Civilization and Its Discontents*. James Strachey, trans. New York: W. W. Norton & Co., 1961.

The central theme of the book is the irreconcilable conflict between the demands of the instincts and the restrictions of civilization. This is the view I argue against in Part IV, "A Garrison Within" and "The Moses of Freud: A Criticism."

Freud, Sigmund. *Moses and Monotheism*. Kathrine Jones, trans. New York: Vintage Books, 1939.

Freud maintains that Moses was an Egyptian who was converted to the monotheistic religion of Ikhnaton. The latter rejected the plurality of Egyptian gods in favor of one god, Aton. The latter was a gentle god who disdained ceremonies and sacrifices, demanded life in truth and justice, and was too sublime to be represented by any images whatsoever. But this religion was rejected and defeated by the powerful priests of Amon, who reclaimed power with all their ceremonies and their magic spells. But the religion of Ikhnaton did not disappear altogether; it simply went underground. Using his influential position, Moses led the Jewish people peacefully out of Egypt, and gave them his religion, including circumcision, which was an Egyptian custom. The Jews were therefore the "chosen people" of Moses. Later, they rejected his religion and killed him. Instead, they worshipped a more aggressive god who was more useful in their effort to conquer Canaan. The religion of Moses was again repressed, but not totally extinguished; it was kept alive by the prophets. After the destruction of the Temple, and the Babylonian exile, it was fully reinstated, or brought to full consciousness out of the unconscious. Freud compares the revival of the religion of Moses to the reawakened memory of something deeply traumatic, which is characteristic of a neurosis. That traumatic experience was the murder of Moses—the father, God the Father. Once murdered, the father is deified. In other words, God is really Moses in disguise. All the qualities of God in the Old Testament are in reality the qualities of Moses—he was jealous, hot-tempered, irascible, stern, and implacable. Judaism is a Father religion, and not surprisingly, it is fraught with guilt. And in Freud's estimation, this guilt has true historical or prehistorical foundations in the murder of the primeval father. Christianity emerges to expiate the sin, and relieve the guilt, through the sacrificial death of the son. Christianity is the religion of the Son, who seeks reconciliation with the Father. But unfortunately, Christianity continues the father/son rivalry because the son displaces the father and becomes himself the divine or the father incarnate. Freud thinks that Christianity is progressive, in so far as it admits the murder of the father. But Christianity is also regressive because it reintroduces the magic, the rituals, and the priests of Amon. The book presents itself as a daring scientific account of religion by a rational and scientific author. But his self-image notwithstanding, Freud is nevertheless a profoundly biblical thinker. His thought is deeply rooted in the Christian religion and its assumptions about human nature, guilt, original sin, sex, and the need for expiation. See my discussion of Freud in Part IV.

Freud, Sigmund (and Albert Einstein). "Why War?" (1933). *Civilization, Society, and Religion.* Penguin Freud Library, Vol. 12, Albert Dickson, ed. London: Penguin Books, 1991.

An exchange of letters initiated by Einstein, published in Paris in March, 1933. Circulation was forbidden in Germany. Einstein initiates the discussion by asking if there is any way to deliver man from the menace of war. Einstein thinks that this is a very urgent question in light of the advance of science and the deadly powers it places at man's disposal. He is also dismayed at the so-called intelligentsia, who are no better intellectually than the uncultured masses because they are just as likely to yield to collective hysteria. Although he does not put it so bluntly, Freud replies that it is both impossible and undesirable to eradicate the menace of war. War is natural, and has a basis in our instinctual life. In view of its solid biological foundation, why not accept war as part of life? Besides, it is very unlikely that we can eradicate it without causing serious psychic consequences in the form of nervous illness. We abhor war because it is the antithesis of civilization. To eradicate war, we would have to make civilization even stronger than it is. Freud claims that this is the only "solution." But one cannot suppose that Freud would be in favor of this "solution," even though he politely suggests it at the end of his letter, to avoid ending on a dismal note and shocking Einstein. But in the rest of the letter, he makes it clear that he thinks the psychological cost of this "solution" would be too great. The essay is an excellent summary of his thought. It also reveals Freud's ambivalence toward civilization. In Part IV, I suggest that the ambivalence has its source in the fallacious dichotomy he has created between civilization and the savage instincts. He wrongly places war on the side of the savage instincts while placing pacifism on the side of civilization. This is the sort of dualism that I argue against. In my view, there is nothing pacifistic about civilization. Only civilized men can be murderous savages.

Freud, Sigmund. "The Taboo on Virginity." *Collected Papers*, Vol. IV, Joan Rivière, trans. London: Hogarth Press, 1925.

    Freud suggests that it is possible to see virginity in women as a liability. He suspects that such an assumption can explain why the deflowering of the bride is often left to someone other than the bridegroom—e.g., prenuptial rights in the Middle Ages. Supposedly, the explanation is that being deflowered causes women to become hostile, and one does not want that hostility directed at the future husband. This essay is a testimony to Freud's colossal failure to comprehend female sexuality, let alone the feminine psyche.

Freud, Sigmund. "The Moses of Michelangelo." *Collected Papers*, Vol. IV, Joan Rivière, trans. London: Hogarth Press, 1925.

    Freud's interpretation of the sculpture highlights his conviction that there is a deadly conflict between civilization and the instincts. This is the thesis I argue against in Part IV, "The Moses of Freud: A Criticism."

Freud, Sigmund. *Totem and Taboo*. A. A. Brill, trans. New York: Random House, 1918.

    Freud understands taboo as a primitive prohibition imposed from without and directed at man's deepest desires and instincts. These desires do not disappear as a result of the prohibition; instead, they are repressed or forced into the unconscious. The dread of incest is the focus of the study. Primitive cultures are of special interest to Freud because he believes that they experience the original desire more keenly than civilized folk, who have repressed it deep in their subconscious. Freud maintains that the strength of the prohibition of incest is proof that it is a very powerful desire that is integral to the instinctual makeup of humanity. At the heart of the matter is Freud's fallacious dichotomy between civilization and the instincts. The same dichotomy informs Christianity. I think that the dichotomy is artificial and that Freud's argument on its behalf is fallacious. See discussion in Part IV.

Girard, René. *Things Hidden Since the Foundation of the World*. Stephen Bann and Michael Metteer, trans. Stanford, California: Stanford University Press, 1987.

    René is an interesting Christian anthropologist who thinks that religion is not something superfluous or based on fear and superstition, as rationalists tend to believe. Nor does he think that religion is invented by malicious and power-hungry priests, as Voltaire did. Instead, he thinks that religion is at the heart of culture in its effort to solve the chronic problem of violence. In other words, he begins with the Christian premise of the utter depravity of human nature, for which religion is the solution—and Christianity is the best solution. Religion solves the problem of violence by focusing all evil on a scapegoat who is regarded as guilty of iniquities that are the source of all the problems of the community. Once the scapegoat assumes the collective evil of the community, he is slain. The collective murder has a surprising result: it unites the community and gives it a temporary reprieve from violence. The victim is then deified as someone who invited his own death for the sake of the community. The victim is transformed into a divine savior, and human sacrifice is turned into a ritual that keeps profane violence at bay. Girard denies the apparent similarity between Christianity and these primitive sacrificial religions. He argues that Christianity reveals the secret foundation of all culture in scapegoating. Even though Jesus is a scapegoat, he is the scapegoat to end all scapegoats because he reveals the innocence of the scapegoat. In so doing, he reveals the lie on which culture depends for its order. Christianity destroys the primitive ground of order; it reveals that the scapegoat is innocent and that order can be had only if we renounce scapegoating altogether—but that is precisely what we are unable or unwilling to do. Girard's thesis is premised on taking the evil of human nature as fundamental and discovering that the scapegoat works to create a temporary peace. I think it is more plausible to think of religion as having its source in fear of hostile forces that manifest themselves in nature and need to be appeased by human sacrifices. It must be remembered that even in a technological age, man is defenseless in the face of nature—with her storms, earthquakes, volcanoes, tornadoes, floods, and famines. Girard's Christian preoccupation with the depravity of human nature leads him to suggest that it is the human love of violence and killing that is appeased by ritual sacrifice. But if it was so, it would follow that those sacrificed would be the deformed, the old, the crippled, the criminal, and the like. But instead, in cultures where human sacrifices prevailed, it was often the loveliest maiden, the handsomest youth, or the King's firstborn, who were sacrificed. In other words, human beings had to sacrifice or give up something of value to them in order to appease the hostile forces so that the harvest would not fail, the rain would come, and the sky would not fall. The same effort to appease hostile forces is also at the heart of the understanding of Jesus as a ransom for sin. There is little reason to think that Christianity has replaced the hostile gods of primitive religions with a God of love. See also Gil Bailie mentioned earlier.

Harnack, Adolph. *What is Christianity?* Thomas Bailey Saunders, trans. New York: Harper & Brothers, 1957.

This is a classic of liberal theology. Harnack believes that there are two concepts of the kingdom of God found in Jesus, one is old and Judaic and the other is new and spiritual. He thinks that the old Judaic one is the husk and the new spiritual one is the true kernel of Christianity that was introduced by Jesus in his attempt to "demythologize" the Jewish understanding of the kingdom of God. Clearly, Harnack is doing some of his own demythologizing.

Hiers, Richard H. *Jesus and Ethics*. Philadelphia: The Westminster press, 1968.

This is an excellent discussion of liberal Protestant theology and its efforts to reconcile the historical Jesus with the dogmas of the Church. Particularly troubling is the conflict between Jesus's historical pessimism and liberal optimism. Hiers reveals how different liberal Protestant theologians proceed to "demythologize" Jesus's eschatological and Messianic understanding of the kingdom of God. Accordingly, liberal theologians such as Adolph Harnack, Albert Schweitzer, and Rudolf Bultmann conceive of the kingdom of God, not as a cosmic world-transfiguring event, but as something that exists in our hearts. And they spend a great deal of effort and ingenuity trying to show that their modern interpretation of the kingdom of God is nevertheless true to the historical Jesus. What emerges is the extent to which liberal theologians consider Jesus "primitive" and "Judaic" in comparison to the kerygma (i.e. the Church's preaching). Hiers is not critical; he is informative and charitable.

Kramnick, Isaac and Moore, Laurence R. *The Godless Constitution: The Case Against Religious Correctness.* New York: W. W. Norton & Co., 1997.

This is a splendid case against the Religious Right in America. They argue that the Constitution was intended to be godless, but the American nation was not. When religion is mired in partisan politics, as it is in America today, it loses its ability to provide moral leadership. They argue that it is not politics that will make citizens moral; moral citizens are necessary to make democracy viable. While I agree with them, I have more doubts about the moral worth of Christian ethics, for reasons that I outlined in Part III.

Lewis, C. S. *The Lion, the Witch, and the Wardrobe.* New York: HarperCollins Publishers, 1950.

This is part of a series of children's stories called "The Chronicles of Narnia," which draw heavily on Christian theology. Narnia is a fantasy land ruled by the wicked White Witch. In Narnia it is always winter, but never Christmas. The adventures of the children in Narnia mimic the adventures of the human soul in its historic relation to God. Just as all of Narnia is held captive by the White Witch, so the human soul is held captive by the devil. It is our own sins that keep us hostages of the devil, just as Edmund's pride and greed made him the prisoner of the White Witch. Like the devil, the Witch tricks the children by making terrible things appear wonderful—like death by Turkish delight! Anyone who opposes her will or is caught enjoying plum pudding is instantly turned into stone. Man is in need of salvation from the forces of evil, just as Narnia needs to be liberated from the tyranny of the White Witch. Aslan, the lion, represents Christ: he is a powerful creature who dies an ignoble death as a sacrifice for the sins of others. His death liberates Narnia from the grip of the White Witch. Suddenly, the snow melts and the flowers bloom. Like Christ, the lion triumphs not only over evil, but over death itself. All those who have been turned into stone by the Witch come back to life, and every trace of the wicked White Witch and her supporters are hunted down and destroyed by Peter, who leads the army of Aslan against the forces of evil. Lewis's story reveals the extent to which Christianity lends itself to militant fairy tales. Like Christianity, the fairy tale appeals to the childish hope of living in a world in which evil and death have been defeated once and for all. The trouble with the story is that the reign of the wicked Witch resembles theocratic tyrannies even more than secular ones—the Taliban in Afghanistan or John Calvin's reign in Geneva. Like the latter, the

Witch has an aversion to human happiness in this world. The Witch outlaws Christmas, plum pudding, spring, and flowers. When the Taliban came to power in Afghanistan they outlawed music and kite-flying. When the Puritans came to power in England, they outlawed observations of Christmas by a Parliamentary edict in 1643. They would have outlawed flowers and spring if they could. In his autobiography, Augustine begged God's forgiveness for taking pleasure in the beauty of a spring day. In the story, when Aslan comes, winter is destroyed. But in reality, the advent of Christianity brought not peace, but the sword. And worst of all, it filled the world with zealots who hate Christmas, flowers, and spring because these things represent feasting, self-indulgence, and earthly happiness.

Another reason that the Witch is not believable is the same reason that the Christian conception of evil is not believable—namely, the evil of the witch is totally gratuitous; it has no point other than her own power and self-aggrandizement, which would be more easily secured if she were to behave like a benevolent queen. Evil regimes generally seek territory, empire, or conversion of the world to their own beliefs. I am not suggesting that gratuitous evil does not exist, but it is much rarer than Christians would lead us to believe. Human beings generally commit great evils in pursuit of some real or imaginary good. And it must be added that a great many evils have been committed in the impossible effort to make a world free of evil. It is the sort of dream that fuels the likes of George W. Bush and makes him a hero in the eyes of his people. The war on terrorism is a war intended to defeat evil once and for all. But since the war is endless, and cannot be won, those who embark on such a war turn themselves into the very ogres they are supposedly pursuing.

Two aspects of the story are of special theological interest—the character of Aslan and the nature of his sacrifice. Lewis acknowledges that Aslan, like the Christian God, is both good and terrible (pp. 126, 153, 164). He is gentle enough to allow the children to ride on his back and caress his wild mane; but his roar is terrifying, especially to his enemies. It is to Lewis's credit that he does not shrink from the harsh aspects of the Christian God in either his fictional or his theoretical works.

The story mimics the death of Christ as a ransom for sin. Aslan makes a bargain with the Witch to die in place of the Son of Adam—the proud and foolish Edmund, who is tempted by the Witch's Turkish delight and her promise of power and dominion. The Witch agrees, but is tricked. After the lion is jeered, taunted, tortured, and killed, he comes back to life in all his glory and triumphs over evil (i.e. the Witch and her allies) and over death itself. Lewis is providing a childish version of Christian theology as understood by those who think that God tricked the devil. What the devil did not know when he made the bargain, was that he could not hold on to the sinless soul of Christ. In my view, this interpretation of the Passion saves God from being a fiend who demands and relishes the torture and death of his own son. But it was not the interpretation accepted by the Church. See my discussion in Part I, "Ransom for Sin."

Lewis, C. S. *That Hideous Strength*. London: John Lane and Bodley Head Ltd., 1945.

Lewis tells us that this novel is about devilry, which is associated in the novel with scientific rationalism, which in turn is associated with human pride, which is the desire to replace God and control all of life, the whole planet, and even the universe. Science is represented not as an extension of human curiosity and the desire to know, but as a tool of wickedness and dominion. The "hideous strength" is an insatiable desire for mastery as an end in itself. This view of evil is typical of Christian writers—science is evil because it is about the pursuit of knowledge, and knowledge has always been evil because it has its source in human pride—in the human desire to be God. Similar themes are echoed in other Christian writers. See Part II, "Augustinian Chic," for a critique of this view of the world. It seems to me that reducing science to human wickedness is naïve and simplistic. I think that science and knowledge are often ends in themselves; but they are also means. As a means, science often leads us to embark on hazardous paths on the grounds that there are some goods to be attained that are worth the risks involved.

Lewis. C. S. *Preface to Paradise Lost*. London: Oxford University Press, 1942.

Lewis thinks that the admiration for Milton's Satan on the part of Blake, Shelly, and Dryden, is perverse. Satan is only admirable in the sense that he is brilliantly portrayed by Milton, but he is a dreadful creature to have around. Following good Christian dogma, Lewis adds that Milton does such a good job of Satan because Satan is just beneath the surface of every human personality, whereas goodness is foreign (p. 94). But he does not stop to consider that there could be a flaw in the biblical conception of morality. See my discussion in Part IV, "A Promethean Revolt" and "Romanticizing Evil."

Luther, Martin. "Preface to the Complete Edition of Luther's Latin Writings." John Dillenberger, ed., *Martin Luther: Selections from His Writings*. New York: Doubleday & Co., 1961.

This is a superb example of what makes Luther absolutely lovable—his honesty and his courage. Luther does not shrink from the darkest aspects of Christianity. See my discussion in Part III, "Inner State of Siege."

Luther, Martin. "Bondage of the Will." John Dillenberger, ed., *Martin Luther: Selections from His Writings*. New York: Doubleday & Co., 1961.

This is a response to Erasmus on the freedom of the will. The basic thesis is that there is no free will. We are either in bondage to God or Satan. And if we are in bondage to Satan, that is because God let it happen. God's Providence is supreme and freedom of the will is nothing. God alone has free will. He is omnipotent, omniscient, and free. There is nothing we can do to merit salvation; it is a gift from Christ. The disturbing thing about this work, besides the thesis itself, is that Luther confuses dissention from his own point of view with sin. Throughout the essay he asks Erasmus to repent, and ask for God's forgiveness, because falsehood in matters that concern salvation cannot be tolerated. Here Luther shows himself to be as authoritarian and as intolerant as the Catholic Church whose authority he was rebelling against.

His revolt is not the liberation of believers that it is often believed to be; he merely replaces his own authority for the authority of the Church as the measure of truth and goodness. Those who disagree are wicked, and must repent or be punished. See my discussion in Part II, "Christian Arrogance."

Luther, Martin. "Preface to the Epistle of Saint Paul to the Romans." John Dillenberger, ed., *Martin Luther: Selections from His Writings*. New York: Doubleday & Co., 1961.

Luther contrasts the requirements of the Law of God with the requirements of other laws. Unlike other laws, the Law of God is not fulfilled simply through outward compliance with its demands: "God judges according to your inmost convictions; His law must be fulfilled in your heart, and cannot be obeyed if you merely perform certain acts" (p. 20). But in the depths of our heart, we all hate the Law. No man does good work "without a certain reluctance and unwillingness in his heart" (p. 21).

Luther, Martin. "Preface to the New Testament." (1522). John Dillenberger, ed., *Martin Luther: Selections from His Writings*. New York: Doubleday & Co., 1961.

Even though he is eager for people to read the Gospels for themselves, Luther nevertheless tells readers what parts are important, and should be read first and most often: Saint Paul's Epistles, especially to the Romans, Galatians, and Ephesians, and Saint Peter's First Epistle. These are the books that "show Christ to you," and they are "everything you need to know for your salvation," he says. Then he proceeds to tell us what is new and important in these books. Luther contrasts the Old Testament with the New Testament. The former contains God's Laws and commandments, whereas the latter contains God's promised evangel. The former is a record of the men who kept God's Laws and those who didn't, whereas the latter is a record of those who believed and those who did not. The Old Testament emphasizes action, the New Testament emphasizes belief—faith not works is the Christian message. Luther goes so far as to claim that the New Testament condemns and despises works and demands only faith in Christ. Luther warns against turning Christ into another Moses. I argue in Part I, "Sin as Unbelief," that Luther was not inventing this emphasis on faith over works, and that his claims are grounded in what Jesus says in the Gospels.

Luther, Martin. "A Treatise on Christian Liberty." *Three Treatises*. Philadelphia, Pennsylvania: The Muhlenberg Press, 1943.

What Luther calls Christian liberty is liberty from damnation and from the onerous requirements of the Mosaic Law—circumcision, ceremonies, and the like. The thesis of this work can be expressed as follows. To be a Christian, you must first recognize your utter depravity, and your total inability to be righteous and to earn your salvation. Only then do you become aware of your desperate need for Christ. Once you recognize your own inadequacy, and your total reliance on Christ, then you are a Christian. This supposedly gives you freedom—freedom from the requirements of the law, and from the totally Sisyphean effort to achieve salvation through the works of the law. Now you realize that faith alone, through the "pure mercy of God" can save you (p. 272). The freedom of the Christian is freedom from the works and constraints of the law to justify him, make him righteous, or save him. Cognizant of your complete inability to save yourself by your own righteousness, you surrender to Christ and put your salvation in his hands. As long as your salvation depends on your own efforts, you are doomed. The key is utter self-contempt and total reliance on Christ. With the wedding ring of faith, the marriage of Christ and the soul is achieved (p. 260). But it must be admitted that they are a strange couple. She is sin, death, and damnation, while He is grace, life, and salvation. By her pledge of faith in Christ, the soul is free from sin, secure against hell and damnation, and endowed with righteousness. What Luther calls a "royal marriage" is in reality a very unusual romance. This rich and godly Bridegroom, Christ, marries this poor, wicked harlot, redeems her from all her evil, and adorns her with all His good (p. 261). The bride is totally worthless, and the bridegroom is a royal prince. Why is he willing to accept all the ignominy that his association with her involves? Why is he willing to endure so much pain and suffering on her account? What does he see in her? The bride has no idea. It is a great mystery to her. But maybe we can clear up the mystery just a little. After all, the fact that she is totally undeserving of this royal husband makes the soul eternally grateful, subservient, and submissive. She is also silent and uncomprehending. Is that precisely what He was looking for? Is that the source of her appeal? Certainly, the relationship between man and God in Christianity is more subservient and more uncomprehending than we find in Judaism. Granted that in Judaism we find the likes of Abraham, who is subservient and uncomprehending, but we also find the likes of Moses and Job who challenge and question God.

McKinnon, Christine. *Character, Virtue Theories, and the Vices*. Toronto: Broadview Press, 1999.

This is one of the contemporary Anglo-Saxon moral philosophers who are understandably turning to the Greeks to revitalize our conception of human virtue. McKinnon finds in the Greeks a sunnier understanding of morality. She argues that it is the responsibility of the individual to develop her character, and that having character is not a morally neutral phenomenon. Having character means cultivating virtues such as integrity, truthfulness, generosity, and courage, as opposed to vices such as hypocrisy, envy, cruelty, and selfishness. She believes that the cultivation of these virtues is integral to a functionally good human life—which is to say, human flourishing, wellbeing, and satisfaction in a life that is going well. McKinnon thinks that only a virtue-based ethic can provide human beings with a meaningful account of morality, because only this sort of ethic can give human beings a motivation to be moral. She thinks that other conceptions of morality fail to provide human beings with any motive to be moral that is related to their humanity—their natural desires, needs, and aspirations. For example, the deontological view of ethics conceives of moral virtue in terms of obedience either to God (in its religious version) or to the moral law (in its secular or Kantian incarnation). McKinnon argues that the desire to obey God or to respect the moral law is a second-order desire (i.e. a desire about what to desire), which is entirely different from natural desires. But McKinnon wishes to defend a naturalistic ethic that regards morality not as an adherence to rules, but as the cultivation of habits, dispositions, and virtues that contribute to a meaningful and satisfying human life.

McKinnon's approach to morality is refreshing. She invokes the ideas of Plato and Aristotle, but she is not as critical of them as she could be; she seems oblivious to the difficulties involved in returning to the Greeks after so many centuries of relying on biblical morality as our only source of guidance. She focuses so narrowly on individual life that she never considers the social implications of adopting pagan morality. Are we to follow Aristotle in extending instrumental reasoning to public policy? Are we to follow Aristotle in defending slavery and condoning infanticide?

Meynell, Hugo A. *Is Christianity True?* London: Geoffrey Chapman, 1994.

A sprightly written and forcefully argued book that is as informative as it is delightful to read. In the final analysis, Meynell claims that Christianity is true because it is a necessary remedy to the evil of human nature, which inclines individuals to prefer their own selfish interests or the interests of their group. But if there were a community that is impressive enough to inspire loyalty above all other communities, a loyalty that transcends loyalty to family, clan, or nation, and if that community had a leader whose goodness is heroic, then such a community would have only "evil as such" as its enemy. That community is what Christianity provides, and in so doing it offers a remedy for sin. In Part V, I argue that far from being a solution, this is precisely the problem. Far from dampening aggressive enthusiasm, this "solution" invites aggression on a global scale, unrestrained by recognition of our partiality and parochialism. It breeds individuals who confuse the triumph of their creed or clan with "the good as such."

Nietzsche, Friedrich. *Genealogy of Morals*. Francis Golffing, trans. New York: Doubleday Anchor, 1957.

In the First Essay, Nietzsche argues that concepts of justice are not natural, eternal, and unchanging. They have an origin in history. Their origin is in power, because they were originally constructed by the powerful, the well born, and favored by the gods. But unfortunately, there has been an effeminization of culture. Western civilization has gone from valuing, cherishing, commending, and admiring the masculine virtues of strength, power, courage, and action, to setting a higher premium on the feminine virtues of meekness, innocence, and purity of heart. The first set of valuations is from the point of view of the fortunate and well endowed—those who were blessed by nature with strength, power, courage, and beauty. Homer affirms this master-morality in his society of heroes and demigods. In that world, nature and justice are one. The inequalities of society are but the reflection of the inequalities of nature. But later, the unfortunate, downtrodden, envious, and misbegotten, gain control and declare nature to be unjust, and set out to compensate for her injustices. Thanks to Socrates and Jesus, the values of the downtrodden have triumphed and have usurped the values of the strong. The master-morality has been replaced by a slave-morality. Nietzsche is nostalgic for the Homeric (i.e. masculine) values of physical prowess, beauty, and display. But he need not worry that these values have been lost. Our world of sport heroes, celebrities, and supermodels, is a clear indication that these values are as robust as ever.

The question is: why does the introduction of the feminine values constitute a decline? The answer lies in their inward character. Their very invisibility makes them difficult to discern and allows hypocrisy and sham sentiments to pass for inner purity of heart. And it must be admitted by the staunchest defenders of the feminine virtues, that they lend themselves to abuse. And there is no doubt that Nietzsche's assault on the hypocrisy of Christianity's priestly cast rings true.

All his protestations to the contrary notwithstanding, Nietzsche thinks of nature as the true standard of morality. In the final analysis, the real reason that the transition from the pagan or master-morality to the Christian or slave-morality is a retrogression is that the new morality is contrary to nature as Nietzsche understands it. He valorizes nature understood as the dominance of the strong (no matter how brutal) and the subordination of the weak (no matter how noble). But this leaves the question: why is such a brutish model of nature a standard for human conduct? In nature, big fish eat little fish but it does not follow that big boys should eat little boys. What is appropriate for fish may not be fitting conduct for boys, even if they are deluded by Nietzsche into thinking that they are demigods.

In the Second Essay, Nietzsche examines the origin of justice, punishment, and conscience. He argues that there is no such thing as an eternal and unchanging justice. He believes that in its original and real sense, justice was the invention of the strong. It was an imposition of order, a manifestation of the will to power. No act of violence, rape, or exploitation is intrinsically wrong because life itself is violent, rapacious, and exploitative. The community provides protection from violence in exchange for obedience of the law of the strong. To disobey is to dare to lay hands on your benefactor. By repressing the aggressive instincts, society forces them inward against the self, where they manifest themselves in the form of guilt and bad conscience. This view of conscience is the source of Freud's fundamental inspiration.

Origen of Alexandria. *On First Principles*. New York: Harper & Row, 1966.

Origen is perhaps the most profound interpreter of the Scriptures. He argued that it is impossible to take everything in the Scriptures literally. For example, all the talk about being uncircumcised in I Corinthians 7:18, cannot be understood literally because it is impossible for the circumcised to become uncircumcised—we must look for a deeper meaning (bk. IV, ch. III, p. 293). The Scriptures contain many mysteries. This led him to some ingenious, but charitable interpretations, which were free of the mean-spiritedness of Augustine and of the Gospels themselves. Origen is also famous for his asceticism: he castrated himself out of ascetic zeal—apparently he feared that his chastity may be compromised by his many female students. This act disqualified him for the priesthood. I venture to suggest that the logic behind this decision is that once castrated, he did not suffer the constant agonies of sexual deprivation, and in my view, it is these agonies that make virginity a virtue in the Christian tradition. As a result of his preaching, and his brilliant commentaries, he was later ordained by the bishops of Jerusalem and

Caesarea, but his own bishop, Demetrius, banished him from Alexandria. See my discussion in Part I, "Hell and Damnation."

Penelhum, Terence. *God and Skepticism: A Study in Skepticism and Fidiesm.* Boston, Mass.: D. Reidel Publishing Co., 1983.

This is a penetrating analysis of the relation between faith and reason. Penelhum's discussion of fidiests such as Pascal and Kierkegaard is particularly illuminating. Simply stated, fideism is the view that faith is more fundamental than reason; knowledge depends on faith, which reason may not be able to give an account of. In its more radical form, fideism affirms the possibility of a faith that is unreasonable, impossible, or absurd. Penelhum shows how the fidiesm of Pascal and Kierkegaard differs from that of Erasmus and Montaigne.

Ranke-Heinemann, Uta. *Eunuchs for Heaven: The Catholic Church and Sexuality* (1988). John Brownjohn, trans. London: André Deutsch Ltd., 1990.

This Catholic scholar provides an unsurpassed documentary of the sexual phobias of the Church and its extravagant inhumanity. The work is historically exhaustive, and truly impressive. She puts to rest the long-standing myth that Christianity has been liberating to women. While I admire her work immensely, I think that her argument is not persuasive. She claims that the sources of these noxious doctrines are errors, mistranslation, and sheer inventions introduced to lend support to the Church's perverse insistence on celibacy, and have no connection to Jesus. See my discussion in Part III, "More than a Hint of Asceticism."

Russell, Bertrand. *Why I Am Not a Christian and Other Essays.* Paul Edwards, ed. New York: Simon and Schuster, 1957.

This is a superb collection of essays. Russell shares the view of Lucretius that religion is born out of fear and that it has been the source of untold misery for the human race. Russell does not think that Jesus has had much influence on Christian ethics: "Judge not that ye be not judged." What influence has that had on the Inquisition, he asks? Russell rightly respects those who believe that their religion is true, and argue for it, as Aquinas did, but not those who believe that religious dogmas must be accepted without question because they are useful or necessary to the survival of society (Leo Strauss and his cronies come to mind). The latter are led to stifle inquiry, falsify history, and make unorthodox opinions criminal.

Stone, Lawrence. *The Family, Sex and Marriage in England 1500–1800.* London: Penguin Books, 1977.

This book is a delightful history of family life in England, containing a breathtaking wealth of material, beautifully written, and displaying a philosophical sophistication that is rarely encountered among historians. Stone identifies three stages or models: the medieval, the Puritan, and the Enlightenment. Stone is generally opposed to the view that there has been progress from the medieval to the modern conceptions of the family. He does not believe that there are ever unmitigated triumphs, improvements, or gains; there are always losses as well as gains. Where sexual morality is concerned, he thinks that there are cycles of repression and permissiveness. I agree with Stone, but I would add that these cycles are integral to a Christian civilization in which the repression of sexuality is paramount. Excessive repression invariably gives way to heroic revolt, which in turn leads to excessive licentiousness, which is met by a reaffirmation of the need for repression, and so on. I consider Freud's philosophy as part of the Victorian backlash against eighteenth-century permissiveness. See my discussion of heroic revolt in Part IV, "A Promethean Revolt" and "Romanticizing Evil."

Taylor, Rattray, G. *Sex in History*. New York: The Vanguard Press, 1954.

This is a great Freudian book on the history of attitudes to sex during the Christian period. It reveals the sexual and psychological perversity of priests and the influence of the most disturbed among them on the Church. But despite his criticism of the Church, he has not transcended the Christian attitudes to sex any more than Freud. For example, he echoes the Christian belief in the intimate connection between sex and sin, sex and violence—a connection that Freud has blessed with scientific respectability. And like Freud and the Christians, Taylor assumes that there is a profound conflict between the dangerous and powerful forces of sexuality on one hand, and civilization and its inhibitions and restraints on the other. He regards civilization as an endless struggle with the forces of evil that lie just beneath the surface and that are represented by the id in Freudian psychology.

Torjesen, Karen Jo. *When Women Were Priests: Women's Leadership in the Early Church*. San Francisco: HarperSanFrancisco, 1993.

Torjesen is eager to absolve Christianity from its historical record of hatred and cruelty toward women. She acknowledges that women have been systematically demonized and excluded by the Church; she acknowledges that they have been prevented from teaching and preaching as Mary Magdalene and other female apostles did in the time of Christ. She acknowledges that the Gospel of Mary Magdalene has been excluded from the Bible; instead, she has been discredited by rumors that she was a whore. But Torjesen argues that all the Christian hatred and hostility toward women has its source in historically contingent practices that are not integral to Christianity. Supposedly, the free spirit of Christianity was quickly eclipsed by these historically contingent practices that robbed women of the freedom that was integral to their original Christian heritage. Torjesen believes that Christianity inherited its troubled relationship to sexuality from the Greco-Roman world in which it first took shape. It seems to me that if it is indeed the case that there is an original Christianity that is not reflected in the historical manifestations of that religion, then we must conclude that Christianity has been an abysmal failure. It has failed altogether to change the world. It has come into the world with new ideals and norms that contradict the existing practices, but instead of changing these practices, it has been subverted by these practices. This means that it leaves the world as it found it. But surely, this is false. Christianity has not left the world as it found it. It has made it much worse. There is little doubt that the hatred of women has its source in fear of their sexual power. And that fear is intensified by ascetic ideals and practices— monasticism, celibacy, asceticism, self-mutilation, and self-flagellation are not pagan inventions. In short, this apologetic argument flies in the face of all the evidence.

Voegelin, Eric. "The Turn of the Screw," *Southern Review*, Vol. VII (1971), pp. 9–48.

This essay provides an interesting interpretation of this enigmatic short story (by Henry James) of a governess and the two children left to her care by their busy father. The children die under mysterious circumstances. Voegelin maintains that it is the governess's refusal to allow the children to communicate directly with their father that kills them. Voegelin interprets the father as God—the children die because they are cut off from the source of all life. The children represent the condition of humanity cut off from God. I think that this is a very interesting interpretation of the story, but it is not an interpretation that Voegelin is in any position to make. If the father is God, then the governess is the Church and its priesthood. Like the governess, the Church does not allow the children of God to communicate directly with their father. She insists on intercepting their letters. In other words, the Catholicity of the governess is the source of the trouble. It seems to me that this interpretation is too Protestant for someone who is nostalgic for the medieval Church as the representation of the divine in the world—the "flash of eternity in time." See my discussion of Voegelin in Part II, "Augustinian Chic."

Westermarck, Edward. *Christianity and Morals*. New York: The Macmillan Co., 1939.

I am indebted to Westermarck's incisive criticisms of Christianity. However, I dissent from him on a most fundamental point that he shares with many critics as well as with defenders of Christianity. He thinks that there is a gulf between the teaching of Jesus and that of Saint Paul. He thinks that Saint Paul is not a reliable source for telling us what Jesus said and thought. Westermarck thinks that the doctrine of salvation by faith was a late imposition on the doctrine of Jesus, and that belief in his Messiahship is not essential for salvation. In the Part I, I tried to show that the doctrines that are often attributed to Paul, Augustine, or Luther, have their source in what Jesus said. Besides, much of what Jesus says in the Gospel of John also appears in Matthew, Mark, and Luke.

Westermarck, Edward. *The Origin and Development of Moral Ideas*, Vol. II. London: Macmillan and Co., 1917.

Westermark denies that incest is a strong natural instinct. See Freud's refutation of Westermarck in *Totem and Taboo*, pp. 158 ff. See my discussion of the debate in Part IV, "The Moses of Freud: A Criticism."

Wilkinson, Bruce. *The Prayer of Jabez*. Sisters, Oregon: Multnomah Publishers, 2000.

This little book sold millions of copies. It is particularly appealing to those who want to be happy and want to thrive without abandoning their Christianity. The book softens the God of the Old and New Testaments. Gone is the arbitrary, capricious, and vengeful God of the Old Testament. Gone is the Jesus Christ who threatens everyone who does not believe in him with eternal damnation. What we get is a sunny picture in which faith and goodness are inexorably linked to success and happiness in this world. We get a loving God who is eager to help us succeed and give us riches of a material as well as a spiritual nature, if only we would ask. The key is to use that success for His glory and His kingdom. Wilkinson is dead against pride, so he insists that we accept our success as God's doing and not get puffed up. The book is like a breath of fresh air for anyone suffocating from their Christianity. It abandons Christian gloom without escaping Christian dualism. The world remains for Wilkinson a struggle between God and Satan. God aims to enlarge his kingdom at Satan's expense. We are God's troops and we must be successful if He is to triumph. But once we succeed, then we are vulnerable to Satan's machinations and the temptations to sin. We must pray to God as did Jabez (an insignificant biblical figure). The prayer of Jabez is fourfold: (1) bless me, (2) enlarge my territory, (3) let your spirit work through me, and (4) keep me from evil (especially when I succeed and Satan is at my heels). Many readers claimed that the book changed their lives. And I can see why. If you work hard, are good to others, and use your success for the benefit of others and not for self-aggrandizement, then you are likely to be happy and successful. It has nothing to do with God blessing you in particular. Wilkinson was denounced by other Christians as a "prosperity theologian." The criticism highlights the incongruity of being Christian while being happy, successful, and thriving. Wilkinson certainly looks happy and prosperous. He was one of the leaders of the Promise Keepers—a movement that championed the Christian ideal of marriage, which is to say, the subordination of the wife to a Christ-like husband. Of course, if the husband is abusive and tyrannical, the wife still owes him obedience because a tyrannical husband must be understood as a deserved punishment from God. Needless to say, that aspect of the ideal was ignored. The uplifting message was directed at men to take charge of their families, to love their wives in selfless devotion and service—and watch how the wives respond. Wilkinson has written the sort of book to which I credit the resilience and rejuvenation of Christianity throughout the ages. Every so often, someone like Wilkinson comes along and helps us forget the dark side of Christianity and makes us believe that it stands merely for the eternal truths of love.

Wills, Gary. *Papal Sin*. New York: Doubleday, 2000.

In this book, Wills documents the moral depravity and intellectual bankruptcy of the papacy. Wills is particularly critical of the current pope. But after denouncing the pope, the Church, and the whole Catholic hierarchy, Wills remains a faithful Catholic. He thinks that the wickedness of the popes has no connection with the true faith. He champions Augustine as a defender of the true faith. Wills is a model of the Christian apologists that I argue against throughout Part I.

Wolf, Arthur P. *Sexual Attraction and Childhood Association: A Chinese Brief for Edward Westermarck*. Stanford, California: Stanford University Press, 1995.

This book provides recent anthropological support for Westermarck's thesis.

Yacowar, Maurice. *The Bold Testament*. Calgary, Alberta: Bayeux Arts Inc., 1999.

This delightful novel is a postmodern retelling of the story of Moses as well as the story of Samson and Delila. The narrators are Moses and Delila. They are in heaven, but have seen neither God nor Satan. They tell their stories from the inside in the style of novels—not just words and actions, as we see in the Bible but the thoughts and feelings of the narrators, and their interpretation of events.

In telling his story, Moses sticks close to the biblical facts. But as the story proceeds, it becomes clear that his God, Jehovah, is brutal. The Promised Land is densely populated, and Jehovah wants his people to conquer, slaughter, and destroy the original inhabitants. Moses makes no effort to humanize his God. And as the tale unfolds, one wonders if God or Moses is in charge. Moses has long talks with God and even gives Him advice, and then the decision is made, and the course of action is determined. When Delila takes over the narration, she clarifies the devastating results of these decisions. She is a Philistine, and her people were invaded and wiped out by the Hebrews. Why did they do it? Supposedly because the Philistines were unclean (i.e. uncircumcised). And here is where Delila makes a few caustic remarks about the Hebrew preoccupation with their "dicks." In fact, as she saw it, the whole covenant was about dicks. And with the end of the "Bold Testament," we get "The New Testicles." What Yacowar reveals is that the authors of the Bible are the PR guys of the Hebs. And this is all the more admirable since Yacowar is a Heb himself.

Index

Printed in the United States
79850LV00002B/128